Air Fryer Cookbook

500+ Delicious & Healthy Air Fryer Recipes For Home Cooking

Gloria Lee

Disclaimer:

This book is intended for entertainment and information purposes only. The author and any other contributors of this book are in no way liable or hold any responsibility for the adverse effects that you may take from directly or indirectly reading this book. It's advised that you seek a medical professional if you plan on altering your diet or take up any health related practice.

Table of Contents

Appetizer Recipes 220

Dinner Recipes..280

Introduction

Thank you for taking the time to pick up my cookbook "Air Fryer Cookbook – 500+ Delicious & Healthy Air Fryer Recipes for Home Cooking." In this cookbook I have created over 500 breakfast, snack, lunch, appetizer, dinner and dessert recipes that can be made in your Air Fryer. Whether you are an experienced cook, or just a first timer, I made each recipe's set of instructions as simple as possible so that all levels of cooks will have no trouble following along! The only major requirement you will need, is of course a suitable Air Fryer to cook each dish in. Below I will share some quick but important information about Air Fryers, which will be very handy to know if you are yet to buy an Air Fryer, or if you are wondering whether your Air Fryer is suitable for all 500+ of these yummy Air Fryer recipes!

Benefits of the Air Fryer:

My 3 favorite benefits of using an Air Fryer for cooking.

#1 Quick & Easy Cooking (Great for the lazy home chefs out there!)

It doesn't get much simpler than the Air Fryer. As the washing machine revolutionized the "clothes washing world" and the dishwashing took over our sink washing methods. The Air Fryer is doing the same in our cooking lives! It's so simple to use. With some meals I'll just throw in the food I want cooked, turn on the Air Fryer, and bam! – 20 minutes later one beautiful tasting meal is ready to be served.

#2 Less Oil

Yes! Since it relies on an air fryer system, you don't need to use unhealthy oils like vegetable oil. If you love making your own chips/fries like me, then this is a huge plus! And for any readers wondering, air fried chips taste better!

#3 Clean up time is ridiculously easy!

Most Air Fryers come with components that are all dishwashing safe. However, it is so easy to clean the Air Fryer components under a running tap that I hardly ever use the dishwasher for cleaning my Air Fryer.

Air Fryer Accessories (add on attachments)

Alright, let's talk about the massive 500+ delicious Air Fryer recipes I've created in this cookbook for you.

To create a cookbook that really puts the Air Fryer to good use, I've utilized some of the Air Fryer's add on attachments in a number of these recipes. These attachments include; the Air Fryer Basket (Standard with all Air Fryer models), Baking Pan, Double Layer Rack, Grill Pan and Food Separator. These are all accessories that can be attached to the Air Fryer to cook various recipes.

All Air Fryer's will come with the standard Air Fryer Basket attachment, and therefore most of the recipes in this cookbook only require the use of the Air Fryer Basket. However, if you have gone a step further and purchased an Air Fryer Baking Pan for your Air Fryer, then there are a bunch of extra recipes in this cookbook that will cater for you! On the odd occasion, some recipes will utilize the use of the Air Fryer Double Layer Rack, Grill Pan and Food Separator. If you are completely lost when it comes to Air Fryer accessories, don't worry! The most important Air Fryer accessory is your Air Fryer Basket that already comes with your Air Fryer.

Below I will include some information about the attachments for the Air Fryer. As stated before, the Air Fryer Basket and the Air Fryer Baking Pan will be the handiest attachment that you can own for your Air Fryer. The other Air Fryer attachments are useful too! But will not be used as frequently as the Air Fryer Basket and Baking Pan. Here are the Air Fryer attachments/accessories:

Air Fryer Basket

The Air Fryer Basket is an essential piece for all Air Fryers. This is simply the basket in which you place the food to cook in. It has tiny holes which allows the heat to travel through and cook the food. All Air Fryers come with their own Air Fryer Basket.

Air Fryer Baking Pan

The Air Fryer Baking Pan is used when dealing with foods that might fall through the holes of the Air Fryer Basket. Such foods include: Curries, soups, creamy/sauce-based foods etc. Not all Air Fryers are equipped with an Air Fryer Baking Pan. If you own an Air Fryer, I would recommend buying an Air Fryer Baking Pan as an added accessory if you do not already own one. This accessory will allow you to cook a much larger range of dishes.

Note: *If you are trying to get by without the Air Fryer Baking Pan, you may use ramekin dishes or similar style baking pans that will fit in your Air Fryer. However, please be 100% sure that whatever you're using is both safe for you and your Air Fryer.*

Air Fryer Double Layer Rack

The Air Fryer Double Layer Rack allows you to create another level within your Air Fryer Basket. This is not an essential accessory but does have some great benefits. The Air Fryer Double Layer Rack allows you to load up two racks of food to be cooked simultaneously, instead of just tossing everything at the bottom of the Air Fryer. This process of cooking will result towards the food being cooked through more evenly and quickly.

Air Fryer Grill Pan

In order to use this attachment you must remove the Air Fryer Basket attachment and secure in the Air Fryer Grill Pan attachment in its place. It allows you to grill the food you love the way you're used to, except this time you will be using your Air Fryer!

Air Fryer Food Separator

The Air Fryer Food Separator allows you to cook two dishes simultaneously in the Air Fryer. The Food Separator simply acts as a wall separating the Air Fryer into two parts, allowing you to cook one dish to the left of the Food Separator and another dish to the right of the Food Separator simultaneously! This is a great way to save extra time while cooking.

Note: *I only use the Air Fryer Food Separator for 5 recipes in this cookbook, as I generally prefer not to use it. However, if you are someone that regularly cooks two dishes at once, then the Air Fryer Food Separator can be very helpful!*

The more you use your Air Fryer, the quicker you will realize that it is a fantastic piece of kitchenware equipment that can greatly reduce the time it takes to cook a meal, as well as making your meal healthier too! I hope this cookbook allows you to fall in love with a bunch of new delicious dishes. With over 500 Air Fryer recipes, make sure to keep this cookbook at your fingertips, as it's a great cookbook to come back to when you need a completely new recipe!

Once again, thank you for downloading this cookbook. It has taken me a great deal of time to finally create over 500 yummy Air Fryer recipes! If you do find this cookbook to be helpful throughout your cooking endeavors, I would be most thankful if you would leave a review to share your positive experience(s)!

Read before attempting recipes

Some important information to understand while following the recipes in this cookbook.

- Preheating Air Fryer – Time needed to pre heat your Air Fryer is determined by your model of Air Fryer, therefore the preheating of your Air Fryer is not calculated towards the recipes preparation time or cooking time. Generally preheating will take between 2-3 minutes depending on your Air Fryer.
- If an instruction indicates "Set timer to 10 minutes". This simply means set the Air Fryer timer to 10 minutes and allow to Air Fry for 10 minutes (until the timer goes off). Once the 10 minute timer goes off, it's ready to begin the next step (unless instructed otherwise).
- Don't be afraid to improvise and add a few extra ingredients to the recipes or take some ingredients out. This is how the best Chefs are made!

Measurement Conversion Chart

This cookbook will be using the measurements "teaspoon, tablespoon, cup, ounce and pounds" – If you aren't familiar with all these measurements, I've included a conversion chart below.

Milliliters	Liters	Teaspoon	Tablespoon	Cup	Ounce
15	.015	3	1	1/16	1/2
30	.03	6	2	1/8	1
60	.06	12	4	¼	2
120	.12	24	8	½	4
235	.235	48	16	1	8
475	.475	96	32	2	16

Pounds	Kilograms
1	0.45
2	0.90
3	1.35
4	1.80
5	2.25

Breakfast Recipes

1 - One-Pan Molten Sweet Potato Hash

Servings: 2
Preparation Time: 5 minutes
Cooking Time: 15 minutes

Ingredients:
- 2 eggs
- 1 teaspoon garlic salt
- 2 cups sweet potatoes, grated
- 2 tablespoons spring onions, chopped
- ½ cup cheddar cheese, grated
- pepper, to taste
- 1 cup mozzarella cheese, grated

Directions:
1. Preheat the Air Fryer to 350°F/180°C.
2. Whisk the eggs with the garlic salt and pour into the Air Fryer Baking Pan.
3. Add the grated sweet potatoes and spring onions and mix well to combine.
4. Top with the grated cheddar cheese and season with the pepper.
5. Press the mixture lightly to the Air Fryer Baking Pan to remove any air bubbles.
6. Place the Air Fryer Baking Pan in the Air Fryer Basket and set the timer for 13 minutes.
7. Top with the grated mozzarella and set the timer for 2 more minutes.
8. Serve when mozzarella has melted.

2 - Aloha Eggs

Servings: 2
Preparation Time: 5 minutes
Cooking Time: 6 minutes

Ingredients:
- 3 eggs
- 1 tablespoon heavy cream
- salt and pepper, to taste
- 1 tablespoon chives, chopped
- ½ teaspoon paprika
- 4 slices deli ham, chopped
- ½ cup pineapple bits

Directions:
1. Preheat the Air Fryer to 350°F/180°C.
2. Whisk the eggs with the cream and season with salt and pepper.
3. Mix in the chives, paprika, chopped ham and pineapple bits.
4. Pour the egg mixture into the Air Fryer Baking Pan and place the Air Fryer Baking Pan in the Air Fryer Basket.
5. Set the timer for 6 minutes or until the eggs are cooked to your desired doneness.
6. Serve and enjoy!

3 - Coriander and Mushroom Omelet

Servings: 4
Preparation Time: 5 minutes
Cooking Time: 12 minutes

Ingredients:
- 4 eggs
- ¼ cup parmesan cheese, grated
- salt and pepper, to taste
- ¼ cup button mushrooms, sliced
- ¼ cup fresh coriander, chopped
- ¼ cup chives, chopped
- 1 avocado, skin and seed removed, and cut into cubes

Directions:
1. Preheat the Air Fryer to 350°F/180°C.
2. Whisk the eggs with the parmesan cheese and season with salt and pepper.
3. Place the mushrooms in the Air Fryer Baking Pan and spray with a little cooking spray.
4. Place the Air Fryer Baking Pan in the Air Fryer Basket and set the timer for 4 minutes.
5. Pour in the eggs and top with the fresh coriander and chives.
6. Return to the Air Fryer and set the timer for 8 more minutes are until the eggs are cooked to your desired doneness.
7. Top with the chopped avocados and it's ready to eat.

4 - Almond and Banana Breakfast Cake

Servings: 2
Preparation Time: 15 minutes
Cooking Time: 25 minutes

Ingredients:

- 1½ cups almond flour
- ¾ tablespoon baking powder
- ¼ teaspoon salt
- ⅛ cup sugar
- ¾ cup water
- 2 small bananas, mashed

- ½ tablespoon canola oil
- 1 small egg
- ½ teaspoon vanilla extract
- ¼ teaspoon ground nutmeg
- ½ teaspoon ground cinnamon
- 2 tablespoons macadamia nuts, chopped

Directions:

1. Preheat the Air Fryer to 350°F/180°C.
2. Spray the Air Fryer Baking Pan with cooking spray and line it with parchment paper.
3. Mix together the almond flour, baking powder, salt and sugar in a bowl and set aside.
4. Mix together the water, mashed bananas and canola oil and set aside.
5. Whisk the egg with the vanilla extract, ground nutmeg and ground cinnamon in a stand mixer.
6. Add alternate portions of the flour mixture and the banana mixture to the whisked egg and mix until well combined.
7. Fold in the chopped macadamia nuts and transfer the batter into the Air Fryer Baking Pan.
8. Set the timer for 25 minutes or until the cake is baked through.
9. Remove from the Air Fryer and allow the cake to cool in the Air Fryer Baking Pan.
10. Once cooled down, it's ready to serve up.

5 - One-Pan Potato Hash

Servings: 2
Preparation Time: 10 minutes
Cooking Time: 15 minutes

Ingredients:
- 2 eggs
- 1 teaspoon garlic salt
- 2 cups potatoes, grated
- 2 tablespoons spring onions, chopped
- ½ cup cheddar cheese, grated
- pepper, to taste

Directions:
1. Preheat the Air Fryer to 350°F/180°C.
2. Whisk the eggs with the garlic salt and pour into the Air Fryer Baking Pan.
3. Add the grated potatoes and spring onions and press down lightly to release any air bubbles.
4. Sprinkle with the grated cheddar cheese and season with pepper.
5. Place the Air Fryer Baking Pan in the Air Fryer Basket and set the timer for 15 minutes.
6. After the timer has timed out, serve up!

6 - Air Fried Tofu Omelet

Servings: 2
Preparation Time: 10 minutes
Cooking Time: 15 minutes

Ingredients:
- 8 ounces firm tofu, cubed
- 1 teaspoon soy sauce
- ½ teaspoon sesame oil
- 2 large eggs
- ½ teaspoon ground cumin
- ½ teaspoon turmeric
- ½ teaspoon paprika
- salt and pepper, to taste
- ¼ cup fresh coriander, chopped
- 1 tablespoon spring onions, chopped

Directions:
1. Preheat the Air Fryer to 400°F/200°C.
2. Place the tofu cubes in the Air Fryer Baking Pan and marinate them with the soy sauce and sesame oil.
3. Whisk the eggs with the ground cumin, turmeric, paprika, salt, and pepper.
4. Mix in the fresh coriander and spring onions and pour the eggs into the Air Fryer Baking Pan with the tofu cubes.
5. Place the Air Fryer Baking Pan in the Air Fryer Basket and set the timer for 15 minutes.
6. Serve and enjoy!

7 - One-Pan Zucchini Hash

Servings: 2
Preparation Time: 5 minutes
Cooking Time: 15 minutes

Ingredients:
- 1 egg
- ½ teaspoon garlic salt
- 1 large zucchini, grated
- 1 tablespoon spring onions, chopped
- ¼ cup cheddar cheese, grated
- pepper, to taste

Directions:
1. Preheat the Air Fryer to 350°F/180°C.
2. Whisk the egg with the garlic salt and pour into the Air Fryer Baking Pan.
3. Add the grated zucchinis and spring onions to the Air Fryer Baking Pan and press lightly to the Air Fryer Baking Pan to release any air bubbles.
4. Top with the grated cheese and season with pepper.
5. Place the Air Fryer Baking Pan in the Air Fryer Basket and set the timer for 15 minutes.
6. Serve and enjoy!

8 - Ternera Cubano

Servings: 2
Preparation time: 5 minutes
Cooking Time: 13 minutes

Ingredients:
- 4 ounces ground veal
- ½ teaspoon cumin
- ½ teaspoon paprika
- 1 tablespoon garlic, minced
- ¼ cup onions, finely chopped
- 1 tablespoon olive oil
- salt and pepper, to taste
- 1 banana, sliced
- 2 eggs
- ½ cup tomato sauce

Directions:
1. Preheat the Air Fryer to 400°F/200°C.
2. Mix together the ground veal, cumin, paprika, garlic, onions and olive oil in the Air Fryer Baking Pan.
3. Season with salt and pepper.
4. Place the Air Fryer Baking Pan in the Air Fryer Basket and set the timer for 5 minutes.
5. Add the banana slices and set the timer for 4 more minutes.
6. Make 2 hollows in the meat and crack an egg into each hole.
7. Season the egg with salt and pepper and cook for another 4 minutes or until desired doneness of the eggs.
8. Ready to serve.

9 - Oatmeal with Sultanas and Kiwi

Servings: 2
Preparation time: 5 minutes
Cooking Time: 8 minutes

Ingredients:
- 2 cups instant oatmeal
- 3 cups milk
- 2 tablespoons honey
- 2 tablespoons sultanas
- ½ cup fresh kiwis, sliced
- ¼ cup almond flakes

Directions:
1. Preheat the Air Fryer to 350°F/180°C.
2. Mix together the oatmeal and milk in the Air Fryer Baking Pan.
3. Stir in the honey and sultanas and place the Air Fryer Baking Pan in the Air Fryer Basket.
4. Set the timer for 8 minutes.
5. Top with the sliced kiwis and almond flakes.
6. Serve and enjoy!

10 - Oatmeal and Strawberries

Servings: 2
Preparation time: 5 minutes
Cooking Time: 8 minutes

Ingredients:
- 2 cups instant oatmeal
- 3 cups milk
- 2 tablespoons honey
- ½ cup fresh strawberries, stems removed and sliced
- ¼ cup almond flakes

Directions:
1. Preheat the Air Fryer to 350°F/180°C.
2. Place the oatmeal and milk in the Air Fryer Baking Pan.
3. Stir in a tablespoon of honey and set the timer for 8 minutes.
4. Top with the strawberries and almond flakes and drizzle over the remaining honey.
5. Serve in a round bowl.

11 - Stuffed Breakfast Peppers

Servings: 2
Preparation time: 10 minutes
Cooking Time: 15 minutes

Ingredients:

- 4 medium bell peppers
- 2 cups cooked rice
- 1 can SPAM®, cut into small cubes
- ¼ cup onions, chopped
- 4 eggs
- ½ cup feta cheese
- 2 tablespoons fresh cilantro, finely chopped

Directions:

1. Preheat the Air Fryer to 400°F/200°C.
2. Cut the tops off the bell peppers and remove the seeds. Trim a little off their bottoms if needed so that they can stand.
3. Fill the peppers with cooked rice until they are half full.
4. Top with the SPAM® until they are three-quarters full.
5. Top with onions and crack an egg into each pepper.
6. Top with the feta cheese and fresh cilantro.
7. Arrange the bell peppers in the Air Fryer Basket.
8. Set the timer for 15 minutes.
9. Allow the peppers to breathe for a few minutes and serve.

12 - Breakfast Cups

Servings: 2
Preparation Time: 10 minutes
Cooking Time: 4 minutes

Ingredients:
- 2 slices bread
- 6 rashers bacon
- 2 tablespoons tomatoes, diced
- ½ cup spring onions, sliced
- 3 tablespoons low-fat mayonnaise, optional
- 4 eggs
- salt and pepper, to taste

Directions:
1. Preheat the Air Fryer to 350°F/180°C.
2. Lightly spray 4 muffin cups with cooking spray.
3. Cut 4 bread circles to fit the base of the muffin cups.
4. Line the sides of the muffin cups with bacon.
5. Fill the cups with tomatoes and spring onions.
6. Add a dollop of mayonnaise in each cup, if desired.
7. Crack an egg into each cup and season with salt and pepper.
8. Place the muffin cups in the Air Fryer Basket and set the timer for 4 minutes, or until the bacon is crisp and the eggs are of your desired doneness. Ready to eat!

13 - Big Breakfast!

Servings: 1
Preparation Time: 5 minutes
Cooking Time: 9 minutes

Ingredients:
- 3 slices deli honey ham, chopped
- 4 button mushrooms, quartered
- 4 cherry tomatoes, halved
- ¼ cup fresh mozzarella, grated
- 2 tablespoons fresh rosemary, chopped
- 1 egg
- 1 croissant

Directions:
1. Preheat the Air Fryer to 325°F/170°C.
2. Lightly spray the Air Fryer Baking Pan with cooking spray.
3. Add the ham, mushrooms, cherry tomatoes, mozzarella cheese and fresh rosemary to the Air Fryer Baking Pan.
4. Crack in the egg.
5. Place the Air Fryer Baking Pan in the Air Fryer Basket and set the timer for 7 minutes.
6. Make some room to the side of the Air Fryer Baking Pan and add the croissant to bottom of the Air Fryer Baking Pan.
7. Set the timer for 2 more minutes.
8. Ready to eat!

14 - Mushroom and Onion Omelet

Servings: 2
Preparation Time: 5 minutes
Cooking Time: 20 minutes

Ingredients:
- 1 clove garlic, minced
- ½ cup onions, sliced
- 1 cup button mushrooms, sliced
- 3 eggs
- salt and pepper, to taste

Directions:
1. Preheat the Air Fryer to 350°F/180°C.
2. Lightly spray the Air Fryer Baking Pan with cooking spray.
3. Add the garlic, onions and mushrooms to the Air Fryer Baking Pan.
4. Place the Air Fryer Baking Pan in the Air Fryer Basket and set the timer for 5 minutes.
5. Whisk the eggs with salt and pepper and pour into the Air Fryer Baking Pan.
6. Set the timer for 15 more minutes or until desired doneness of eggs.
7. Serve and enjoy!

15 - Herbed French Bread Sticks

Servings: 2
Preparation Time: 10 minutes
Cooking Time: 6 minutes

Ingredients:
- 2 eggs
- ½ teaspoon ground nutmeg
- 1 teaspoon garlic powder
- 1 teaspoon dried basil
- salt and pepper, to taste
- 4 slices bread
- 2 tablespoons butter
- 1 tablespoon maple syrup or powdered sugar, optional

Directions:
1. Preheat the Air Fryer to 350°F/180°C.
2. Whisk the eggs with the ground nutmeg, garlic powder, dried basil, salt and pepper and set aside.
3. Spread both sides of the bread with butter and slice them into sticks.
4. Dip the bread sticks in the egg mixture.
5. Drip off excess egg and arrange the bread sticks in the Air Fryer Baking Pan.
6. Place the Air Fryer Baking Pan in the Air Fryer Basket and set the timer for 2 minutes.
7. Flip the bread sticks over and spray with cooking spray if desired.
8. Set the timer for 4 more minutes or until the bread sticks are golden brown.
9. Serve it up and top with maple syrup or powdered sugar as desired.

16 - Wrapped Pigs in a Blanket

Servings: 4
Preparation time: 15 minutes plus 30 minutes freezing time
Cooking Time: 8 minutes

Ingredients:
- 1 packet store-bought dough
- 20 cocktail hot dogs
- 10 rashers bacon, halved
- 2 egg yolks, lightly beaten

Directions:
1. Cut the dough into 1 x 1½-inch rectangle strips.
2. To prepare the pigs in a blanket: Pat the cocktail hot dogs dry with paper towels and wrap each hot dog with a bacon slice. Roll the dough strips around the bacon hot dogs with the ends of the hotdogs visible. Freeze until they are firm, about 30 minutes.
3. Preheat the Air Fryer to 350°F/180°C.
4. Remove the pigs in the blankets from the freezer and brush the dough with the whisked egg yolk.
5. Arrange them in the Air Fryer Basket and use the Air Fryer Double Layer Rack if needed.
6. Set the timer for 8 minutes or until the hot dogs are cooked through and the dough turns lightly golden brown.
7. Once cooked through, it's ready to eat!

17 - Roasted Herbed Potatoes

Servings: 2
Preparation time: 5 minutes
Cooking Time: 25 minutes

Ingredients:
- 2 large potatoes, diced
- 1 teaspoon olive oil
- ½ teaspoon garlic powder
- ½ teaspoon paprika
- ½ teaspoon dried oregano
- ½ teaspoon dried sage
- ½ tablespoon fresh parsley, chopped

Directions:
1. Preheat the Air Fryer to 350°F/180°C.
2. Place the diced potatoes in the Air Fryer Baking Pan.
3. Toss the potatoes with the olive oil, garlic powder, paprika, dried oregano and dried sage until well combined.
4. Place the Air Fryer Baking Pan in the Air Fryer Basket and set the timer for 20 minutes.
5. Mix in the fresh parsley and set the timer for 5 more minutes or until desired crispness of potatoes.
6. Serve on a warm plate.

18 - Cajun Hash

Servings: 2
Preparation time: 5 minutes
Cooking Time: 33 minutes

Ingredients:

- 1 teaspoon bacon fat
- ½ medium onion, sliced
- 1 tablespoon red bell peppers, diced
- 2 medium potatoes, peeled and diced
- ¼ teaspoon dried thyme
- ½ teaspoon Cajun seasoning
- ½ teaspoon garlic powder
- salt and pepper, to taste
- 1 egg

Directions:

1. Preheat the Air Fryer to 350°F/180°C.
2. Place the bacon fat, onions and bell peppers in the Air Fryer Baking Pan.
3. Set the timer for 5 minutes.
4. Add the diced potatoes, dried thyme, Cajun seasoning, garlic powder, salt and pepper to the Air Fryer Baking Pan.
5. Set the timer for 15 minutes.
6. Stir in the potatoes so that they can be cooked evenly and set the timer for another 5 minutes.
7. Remove Air Fryer Baking Pan from the Air Fryer.
8. Place ramekin dish inside the Air Fryer Basket and crack an egg into the ramekin dish.
9. Set the timer for 5 minutes or until the egg is cooked to your desired doneness.
10. Remove the egg from the ramekin and mix it with the potatoes in the Air Fryer Baking Pan.
11. Place the Air Fryer Baking Pan back in the Air Fryer and set the timer for 3 more minutes.
12. Ready to serve once the timer starts ticking!

19 - Blueberry Oatmeal Loaf

Servings: 2
Preparation time: 5 minutes plus 15 minutes resting time
Cooking Time: 10 minutes

Ingredients:

- ¼ cup unsalted butter
- ¼ cup powdered sugar
- ½ cup fresh blueberries
- ¼ cup uncooked instant oatmeal
- ¼ cup flour
- ½ teaspoon baking powder
- 1 tablespoon milk

Directions:

1. Preheat the Air Fryer to 325°F/170°C.
2. Lightly grease the Air Fryer Baking Pan with cooking spray and set aside.
3. Cream the butter and sugar in a mixing bowl.
4. Gently fold in blueberries.
5. Mix in the oatmeal, flour and baking powder to the creamed butter mixture.
6. Gradually stir in the milk to make a batter.
7. Pour the batter into the prepared Air Fryer Baking Pan and place the Air Fryer Baking Pan in the Air Fryer Basket.
8. Set the timer for 10 minutes or until the loaf is cooked through.
9. Leave the loaf in the Air Fryer on standby mode for another 10 minutes.
10. Remove from the Air Fryer and allow to cool before removing from the Air Fryer Baking Pan.
11. Once cooled, begin to serve your meal.

20 - Cinnamon Egg Tarts

Servings: Makes 8 egg tarts
Preparation time: 20 minutes
Cooking Time: 10 minutes

Ingredients:

- 1 pack pre-made puff pastry, about 12 ounces
- ¾ cup whole milk
- 1 tablespoon all-purpose flour
- ¼ teaspoon vanilla extract

- 3 egg yolks
- 1 cup granulated sugar
- ⅓ cup water
- 1 teaspoon ground cinnamon

Directions:

1. Preheat the Air Fryer to 450°F/230°C.
2. Grease 8 small tart molds with cooking spray.
3. To make the tart crust: Cut the pastry roll into ½-inch wide squares. Flatten each pastry piece and press them into the greased tart molds using your thumb and index fingers. Set aside.
4. Whisk ¼-cup of milk, flour, vanilla extract and egg yolks together in a bowl.
5. Warm the remaining ½-cup of the milk in a saucepan.
6. In a separate saucepan, bring the sugar, water and ground cinnamon to a boil.
7. Whisk the warm milk into the egg mixture and then add the sugar mixture (syrup).
8. Whisk the mixture until it is very smooth and pour into the prepared molds until each mold is three-quarters full.
9. Arrange the tarts in the Air Fryer Basket and use the Air Fryer Double Layer Rack if needed.
10. Set the timer for 10 minutes or until the pastry is golden brown and the egg custard is set.
11. Remove the tarts from the Air Fryer and allow to cool before serving.

21 - No Crust Quiche Lorraine

Servings: 2
Preparation time: 15 minutes
Cooking Time: 10 minutes

Ingredients:
- 4 large eggs
- ¼ cup heavy cream
- salt and pepper, to taste
- ¼ cup mushrooms, sliced
- ¼ cup onions, sliced
- ¼ cup red bell peppers, diced
- ¼ cup deli ham, diced
- ⅓ cup cheddar cheese, grated
- 2 tablespoons chives, chopped

Directions:
1. Preheat the Air Fryer to 400°F/200°C.
2. Lightly spray the Air Fryer Baking Pan with cooking spray.
3. Whisk the eggs with the cream and season with salt and pepper.
4. Pour the eggs into the Air Fryer Baking Pan and add the mushrooms, onions, bell peppers and ham.
5. Fold in the cheese.
6. Place the Air Fryer Baking Pan in the Air Fryer Basket and set the timer for 10 minutes or until desired doneness of eggs.
7. Remove from the Air Fryer and top with chives before serving.

22 - Tomatoes and Ham Omelet

Servings: 2
Preparation time: 5 minutes
Cooking Time: 10 minutes

Ingredients:
- 4 large eggs
- 2 tablespoons heavy cream
- salt and pepper, to taste
- ½ cup cherry tomatoes, halved
- 2 slices deli ham, chopped
- ¼ cup onions, sliced
- 3 tablespoons parmesan cheese, grated
- 2 tablespoons chives, chopped

Directions:
1. Preheat the Air Fryer to 400°F/200°C.
2. Lightly grease the Air Fryer Baking Pan with cooking spray.
3. Whisk the eggs with the heavy cream and season with salt and pepper.
4. Pour the eggs into the Air Fryer Baking Pan and add the cherry tomatoes, ham and onions.
5. Fold in the parmesan cheese and top with the chives.
6. Set the timer for 10 minutes or until desired doneness of eggs.
7. Serve when ready.

23 - Sunny-Side Up Bacon Cups

Servings: Makes 6 cups
Preparation time: 10 minutes
Cooking Time: 5 minutes

Ingredients:
- 6 rashers bacon
- 6 eggs
- ¼ cup green bell peppers, finely diced
- 1 teaspoon paprika
- 2 tablespoons chives, chopped

Directions:
1. Preheat the Air Fryer to 350°F/180°C.
2. Lightly grease six muffin cups with cooking spray.
3. Line the sides of each muffin cup with a bacon strip.
4. Crack an egg into each cup.
5. Top with the green bell peppers, paprika and chives.
6. Arrange the cups in the Air Fryer Basket and use the Air Fryer Double Layer Rack if needed.
7. Set the timer for 5 minutes or until desired doneness of eggs.
8. Serve and enjoy!

24 - One Pan Omelet

Servings: 2
Preparation time: 5 minutes
Cooking Time: 8 minutes

Ingredients:
- 4 eggs
- salt and pepper, to taste
- ¼ cup cheddar cheese, grated
- ¼ cup pineapple bits
- 4 slices deli ham, chopped
- ¼ cup onions, sliced
- ¼ cup mushrooms, sliced

Directions:
1. Preheat the Air Fryer to 325°F/170°C.
2. Lightly grease the Air Fryer Baking Pan with cooking spray.
3. Whisk the eggs with some salt and pepper and pour it into the Air Fryer Baking Pan.
4. Mix in the cheddar cheese, pineapple bits and ham.
5. Top with the onions and mushrooms.
6. Place the Air Fryer Baking Pan in the Air Fryer Basket and set the timer for 8 minutes or until desired doneness of eggs.
7. Serve when ready.

25 - Ham and Pineapple Skewers

Servings: 2
Preparation time: 15 minutes
Cooking Time: 10 minutes

Ingredients:
- ¼ cup sour cream
- 1 cup Greek yogurt
- 1 teaspoon garlic, minced
- 2 tablespoons fresh parsley, chopped
- salt and pepper, to taste
- ½ cup pineapple chunks
- 8 slices of ham
- 1 teaspoon paprika

Directions:
1. To make the yogurt dip: Mix together the sour cream, Greek yogurt, minced garlic and fresh parsley. Season with salt and pepper and set aside.
2. Preheat the Air Fryer to 400°F/200°C.
3. Use the skewers from the Air Fryer Double Layer Rack and skewer the pineapples and ham slices alternately.
4. Season with the paprika, salt and pepper.
5. Place the rack in the Air Fryer Basket and set the timer for 10 minutes.
6. Remove the skewers from the rack and drizzle over with the yogurt dip before serving.

26 - Multigrain Bread

Servings: 2
Preparation time: 15 minutes
Cooking Time: 30 minutes

Ingredients:

- ¾ cup all-purpose flour, plus more for dusting the pan
- 4 tablespoons butter, softened
- ¼ cup brown sugar
- ¼ cup sugar
- 2 large eggs
- ¾ teaspoon vanilla extract
- ¼ teaspoon salt
- ¼ teaspoon baking soda
- 1 tablespoon rolled oats
- 1 tablespoon barley
- 1 tablespoon millet

Directions:

1. Preheat the Air Fryer to 350°F/180°C.
2. Grease the Air Fryer Baking Pan with cooking spray and lightly dust the Air Fryer Baking Pan with flour. Tap out the excess flour and set aside.
3. Cream the butter, brown sugar and sugar in a stand mixer.
4. Add the eggs one at a time, mixing well between each addition.
5. Mix in the vanilla extract.
6. Combine the flour, salt and baking soda and gradually add them to the mixer.
7. Pour the batter into the prepared Air Fryer Baking Pan and top with the oats, barley and millet.
8. Place the Air Fryer Baking Pan in the Air Fryer Basket and set the timer for 30 minutes.
9. Remove from the Air Fryer and allow the bread to cool in the Air Fryer Baking Pan.
10. Serve and enjoy!

27 - Bacon, Spinach and Tomato Omelet

Servings: 2
Preparation Time: 5 minutes
Cooking Time: 8 minutes

Ingredients:
- 4 eggs
- Salt and pepper, to taste
- ½ cup spinach, chopped
- 1 tomato, diced
- 4 slices lightly pre-cooked bacon, chopped

Directions:
1. Preheat the Air Fryer to 325°F/170°C.
2. Lightly grease the Air Fryer Baking Pan with cooking spray.
3. Whisk the eggs with some salt and pepper and pour it into the Air Fryer Baking Pan.
4. Mix in the spinach, tomatoes and bacon.
5. Place the Air Fryer Baking Pan in the Air Fryer Basket and set the timer for 8 minutes or until desired doneness of eggs.
6. Serve and enjoy!

28 - Stuffed Breakfast Shroom

Servings: 2
Preparation time: 15 minutes
Cooking Time: 15 minutes

Ingredients:

- 1 onion, thinly sliced
- ¼ cup bell peppers, chopped
- 5 eggs
- 1 cup feta cheese, crumbled
- salt and pepper, to taste
- 1 tablespoon olive oil
- 4 shiitake mushrooms, stems remove

Directions:

1. Preheat the Air Fryer to 350°F/180°C.
2. Lightly grease the Air Fryer Baking Pan and add the onions and bell peppers.
3. Place the Air Fryer Baking Pan in the Air Fryer Basket and set the timer for 5 minutes or until the onions are translucent.
4. Remove from the Air Fryer and whisk in the eggs.
5. Mix in the cheese with the egg and season with salt and pepper.
6. Drizzle some olive oil into each inverted shiitake mushroom cup and fill with the egg mixture.
7. Carefully arrange the mushrooms into the Air Fryer and use the Air Fryer Double Layer Rack if needed. If the mushroom heads are not able to stand in the Air Fryer Basket, place the mushrooms on a small baking tray that will fit snugly into the Air Fryer.
8. Set the timer for 10 minutes or until the eggs are cooked through.
9. Serve once cooked.

Snack Recipes

29 - Squash Chips

Servings: 2
Preparation time: 5 minutes
Cooking Time: 15 minutes

Ingredients:
- ½ cup all-purpose flour
- 1 teaspoon garlic powder
- ½ cup parmesan cheese, finely grated
- 1 teaspoon paprika
- 1 medium squash, thinly sliced
- olive oil spray
- salt and pepper, to taste

Directions:
1. Preheat the Air Fryer to 350°F/180°C.
2. Mix the flour, garlic powder, parmesan cheese and paprika together in a bowl.
3. Coat the squash slices in the flour mixture.
4. Place the squash slices (chips) in the Air Fryer Basket and spray lightly with cooking spray.
5. Set the timer for 15 minutes or until the chips become golden brown. Halfway through the cooking time, give the Air Fryer Basket a shake to allow even cooking.
6. Serve and season with salt and pepper to taste.

30 - Roasted Peanuts with Garlic Chips

Servings: 2
Preparation time: 5 minutes
Cooking Time: 15 minutes

Ingredients:
- 1 cup garlic cloves, sliced thinly
- 2 cups runner peanuts, shells removed
- salt, to taste

Directions:
1. Preheat the Air Fryer to 350°F/180°C.
2. Place the garlic slices in the Air Fryer Baking Pan.
3. Add the runner peanuts and season with salt.
4. Spray lightly with cooking spray and toss to coat evenly.
5. Place the Air Fryer Baking Pan in the Air Fryer Basket and set the timer for 15 minutes. Halfway through the cooking time, give the Air Fryer Baking Pan a stir to allow even cooking.
6. Serve and enjoy!

31 - Crispy Chicken Skins

Servings: 2
Preparation time: 10 minutes
Cooking Time: 15 minutes

Ingredients:
- 9 ounces chicken skins
- 2 teaspoons garlic powder
- 2 teaspoons onion powder
- 1 teaspoon paprika
- salt and pepper, to taste

Directions:
1. Preheat the Air Fryer to 400°F/200°C.
2. Wash the chicken skins and pat dry with paper towels.
3. Mix together the garlic powder, onion powder and paprika, and rub into the chicken skins.
4. Place the skins, fat sides down, into the Air Fryer Basket.
5. Set the timer for 15 minutes and flip the skins over halfway through the cooking time.
6. Serve and season with salt and pepper to taste.

32 - Corn on the Cob with Salted Butter

Servings: 4
Preparation time: 5 minutes
Cooking Time: 10 minutes

Ingredients:
- 4 large corn on the cob, halved
- ½ cup butter
- salt and pepper, to taste

Directions:
1. Preheat the Air Fryer to 350°F/180°C.
2. Rub the corn with a little butter and season with salt and pepper.
3. Arrange the corn in the Air Fryer Basket and set the timer for 10 minutes.
4. Slather with the remaining butter.
5. Serve and enjoy!

33 - Lime-Peppered Fish Bites

Servings: 4
Preparation Time: 10 minutes
Cooking Time: 5 minutes

Ingredients:
- 4 trout fillets, cut into 3-inch sticks
- salt and pepper, to taste
- ½ cup panko
- 1 teaspoon lime juice
- ¼ cup parsley, chopped
- 2 tablespoons lime rinds, grated

Directions:
1. Preheat the Air Fryer to 350°F/180°C.
2. Season the fish sticks with salt and pepper and spray with cooking spray.
3. Coat the fish sticks evenly with the panko and arrange them in the Air Fryer Basket. Use the Air Fryer Double Layer Rack if needed.
4. Drizzle over with the lime juice.
5. Set the timer for 5 minutes or until just tender.
6. Serve and garnish with the parsley and lime rinds.

34 - Carrot Chips

Servings: 2
Preparation Time: 5 minutes
Cooking Time: 8 minutes

Ingredients:
- 1 cup flour
- 1 teaspoon paprika
- 1 teaspoon ground cumin
- salt and pepper, to taste
- ½ teaspoon garlic powder
- 2 large carrots, cut thinly
- 1 tablespoon olive oil

Directions:
1. Preheat the Air Fryer to 400°F/200°C.
2. Mix together the flour, paprika, ground cumin, salt, pepper and garlic powder in a bowl.
3. Toss the carrots in the olive oil and coat evenly with the flour mixture.
4. Set the timer for 8 minutes or until the carrots are crisp.
5. Serve and enjoy!

35 - Bacon Wrapped Avocado Fritters

Servings: 4
Preparation time: 5 minutes
Cooking Time: 12 minutes

Ingredients:
- 12 rashers bacon
- 2 avocados, peels and seeds removed, each cut into 6 slices per avocado

Directions:
1. Preheat the Air Fryer to 400°F/200°C.
2. Wrap a rasher of bacon around each slice of avocado.
3. Arrange them in the Air Fryer Basket and use the Air Fryer Double Layer Rack if needed.
4. Set the timer for 12 minutes.
5. Serve once 12 minutes is up!

36 - Cinnamon Caramel Apple Crisps

Servings: 2
Preparation time: 10 minutes
Cooking Time: 15 minutes

Ingredients:
- 4 apples, peeled, cored and sliced thinly
- ¼ cup caster sugar
- 2 teaspoons ground cinnamon
- ¼ cup caramel discs, melted

Directions:
1. Preheat the Air Fryer to 350°F/180°C.
2. Place the apples in the Air Fryer Basket and spray lightly with cooking spray.
3. Set the timer for 15 minutes or until the apples are crisp. Shake the Air Fryer Basket halfway through the cooking time to allow the apples to cook evenly.
4. Mix together the sugar and cinnamon in a bowl.
5. Remove the apples from the Air Fryer and coat evenly with the cinnamon and sugar mixture.
6. Serve on a plate and drizzle over the melted caramel.

37 - Sour Cream Arugula Crisps

Servings: 2
Preparation time: 10 minutes
Cooking Time: 3 minutes

Ingredients:
- 1 tablespoon olive oil
- 1 teaspoon soy sauce
- 2 cups baby arugula leaves, coarsely chopped
- 2 tablespoons sour cream powder
- salt and pepper, to taste

Directions:
1. Preheat the Air Fryer to 400°F/200°C.
2. Mix together the olive oil and soy sauce in a bowl.
3. Toss the arugula leaves in the olive oil mixture.
4. Place the arugula leaves in the Air Fryer Basket and set the timer for 3 minutes. Shake the Air Fryer Basket halfway through the cooking time to allow the leaves to cook evenly.
5. Toss the arugula crisps with the sour cream powder, salt and pepper.
6. Serve and enjoy!

38 - Skin-On Spicy Potato Discs

Servings: 2
Preparation time: 10 minutes
Cooking Time: 15 minutes

Ingredients:
- 5 small potatoes, cut into ¼-inch slices
- 1 tablespoon canola oil
- 1 teaspoon paprika
- 1 teaspoon taco seasoning
- 1 teaspoon garlic powder
- salt and pepper, to taste

Directions:
1. Boil the potato slices in salted water until they are softened.
2. Drain from the water, pat dry and allow to cool completely.
3. Preheat the Air Fryer to 400°F/200°C.
4. Toss the potatoes with the oil, paprika, taco seasoning, garlic powder, salt and pepper until they are well coated.
5. Place the potato slices in the Air Fryer Basket in a single layer. Use the Air Fryer Double Layer Rack if needed or cook the potatoes in 2 batches.
6. Set the time for 15 minutes or until the potatoes turn golden brown. Halfway through the cooking time, flip the potato slices over with a pair of kitchen tongs.
7. Serve hot on a plate or in a bowl.

39 - Italian Seasoned Chips

Servings: 2
Preparation time: 5 minutes plus 30 minutes soaking time
Cooking Time: 30 minutes

Ingredients:

- 2 large russet potatoes, sliced thinly
- 1 teaspoon Italian seasoning
- 1 teaspoon paprika
- 1 tablespoon fresh parsley, chopped
- salt and pepper, to taste

Directions:

1. Soak the sliced potatoes in water for 30 minutes to remove the starch.
2. Preheat the Air Fryer to 350°F/180°C.
3. Spray the potatoes with cooking spray and place them in the Air Fryer Basket.
4. Set the timer for 30 minutes. Shake the Air Fryer Basket halfway through the cooking time to ensure the chips are cooked evenly.
5. Remove the chips from the Air Fryer and toss well with the Italian seasoning, paprika and fresh parsley.
6. Before serving, season with salt and pepper to taste.

40 - Garlic Fries

Servings: 2
Preparation time: 5 minutes plus 30 minutes soaking time
Cooking Time: 20 minutes

Ingredients:

- 3 large potatoes, peeled and cut into thin fries
- 1 teaspoon garlic powder
- 1 teaspoon onion powder
- 1 tablespoon chives, chopped
- 1 tablespoon olive oil
- salt and pepper, to taste

Directions:

1. Soak the fries in water for 30 minutes to remove the starch.
2. Drain the potatoes and pat dry thoroughly with paper towels.
3. Preheat the Air Fryer to 350°F/180°C.
4. Toss the fries together with the garlic powder, onion powder, chives and olive oil until well combined.
5. Place the fries in the Air Fryer Basket and set the timer for 20 minutes. Shake the Air Fryer Basket halfway through the cooking time to ensure the fries are cooked evenly.
6. Remove from the Air Fryer and season with salt and pepper to taste.
7. Serve and enjoy!

41 - Air Fried Cheese Balls

Servings: 4
Preparation time: 10 minutes plus 40 minutes chilling time
Cooking Time: 10 minutes

Ingredients:
- ¼ cup feta cheese
- ¼ cup cream cheese
- ¼ cup sharp cheddar cheese, grated
- ¼ cup mozzarella cheese, grated
- 2 tablespoons fresh basil, chopped
- 1 teaspoon garlic powder
- ½ cup breadcrumbs
- 1 teaspoon paprika
- 1 egg
- salt and pepper, to taste

Directions:
1. Mix together the feta cheese, cream cheese, cheddar cheese, mozzarella cheese, fresh basil and garlic powder until well combined.
2. Make cheese balls from the mixture and chill in the fridge for 30 minutes.
3. Combine the breadcrumbs and paprika in a bowl and set aside.
4. Whisk the egg with salt and pepper and set aside.
5. Dip the cheese balls into the whisked egg and coat them evenly with the breadcrumbs.
6. Chill for another 10 minutes until the crumb coating has set and does not fall off the cheese balls.
7. Preheat the Air Fryer to 450°F/230°C.
8. Spray the balls with cooking spray and arrange them in the Air Fryer Basket. Use the Air Fryer Double Layer Rack if needed.
9. Set the timer for 10 minutes or until they turn golden brown. Use a pair of kitchen tongs to rotate the balls so that they cook evenly.
10. Serve while hot!

42 - Duck Fat Truffle Chips

Servings: 2
Preparation time: 10 minutes plus 10 minutes soaking time
Cooking Time: 20 minutes

Ingredients:
- 2 medium potatoes, thinly sliced into chips
- 1 tablespoon duck fat
- 1 tablespoon truffle oil
- ¼ cup parmesan cheese, shavings
- 1 teaspoon garlic salt

Directions:
1. Soak the chips in water for 10 minutes.
2. Drain the chips and thoroughly pat them dry with paper towels.
3. Preheat the Air Fryer to 350°F/180°C.
4. Place the duck fat in a microwave-safe bowl and microwave for 15 seconds.
5. Drizzle the duck fat onto the chips and toss well to ensure they are evenly coated.
6. Place the chips in the Air Fryer Basket and set the timer for 20 minutes or until the chips are crisp.
7. Remove from the Air Fryer and drizzle over with the truffle oil.
8. Serve and top with the parmesan shavings and garlic salt.

43 - BBQ Banana Chips

Servings: 2
Preparation time: 5 minutes
Cooking Time: 15 minutes

Ingredients:
- 4 bananas, cut into thin slices
- ½ teaspoon barbeque powder
- 1 teaspoon salt

Directions:
1. Preheat the Air Fryer to 350°F/180°C.
2. Mix together the banana chips, barbeque powder and salt.
3. Spray the banana chips with some cooking spray and place them in the Air Fryer Basket.
4. Set the timer for 15 minutes and shake the Air Fryer Basket halfway through the cooking time so that the chips can cook evenly.
5. Serve after the timer goes off!

44 - Cajun Baby Corns

Servings: 2
Preparation time: 15 minutes
Cooking Time: 10 minutes

Ingredients:
- 1 cup all-purpose flour
- ⅛ teaspoon baking soda
- ¼ cup water
- 2 teaspoons ginger, minced
- 1 teaspoon Cajun seasoning
- chili flakes, to taste
- 1 teaspoon olive oil
- 9 ounces baby corns, boiled
- salt and pepper, to taste

Directions:
1. Preheat the Air Fryer to 350°F/180°C.
2. Mix together the flour, baking soda and water to make a thin batter.
3. Mix in the minced ginger, Cajun seasoning, chili flakes and olive oil.
4. Coat the baby corns with the batter and arrange them in Air Fryer Basket.
5. Set the timer for 10 minutes.
6. Allow the baby corns to cool in the Air Fryer.
7. Season with salt and pepper to taste.
8. Serve and enjoy!

45 - Crispy Sweet Potato Chips

Servings: 4
Preparation time: 10 minutes
Cooking Time: 30 minutes

Ingredients:
- 2 large sweet potatoes, peeled and thinly sliced
- 1 tablespoon ground cumin
- 1½ teaspoons salt
- 2 teaspoons paprika
- 2 teaspoons turmeric

Directions:
1. Preheat the Air Fryer to 350°F/180°C.
2. Spray the sweet potatoes with cooking spray.
3. Mix together the ground cumin, salt, paprika and turmeric.
4. Evenly coat the sweet potatoes with the cumin mixture.
5. Place them in the Air Fryer Basket and use the Air Fryer Double Layer Rack if needed.
6. Set the timer for 30 minutes or until the chips are crisp. Shake the Air Fryer Basket halfway through the cooking time or use a pair of kitchen tongs to flip the chips over if using the rack, to ensure that the chips are evenly cooked.
7. Serve and enjoy!

46 - Tortilla Chips and Garlic Yogurt Dip

Servings: 2
Preparation time: 5 minutes
Cooking Time: 3 minutes

Ingredients:
- 8 corn tortillas
- 1 tablespoon olive oil
- salt and pepper, to taste
- ½ cup yogurt
- 1 tablespoon minced garlic
- 2 teaspoons chives, chopped

Directions:
1. Preheat the Air Fryer to 400°F/200°C.
2. Cut the tortillas into small triangles and brush them with olive oil.
3. Arrange them in the Air Fryer Basket and use the Air Fryer Double Layer Rack if needed.
4. Set the timer for 3 minutes.
5. Allow to cool and season with salt and pepper.
6. To make the garlic yogurt dip: Mix together the yogurt, garlic and chives in a bowl, and season with a dash of pepper.
7. Serve and enjoy!

47 - Cajun Crispy Fried Pickles

Servings: 4
Preparation time: 15 minutes
Cooking Time: 8 minutes

Ingredients:
- 4 large dill pickles, cut diagonally into ¼-inch thick slices
- 1 egg
- ¼ cup milk
- pepper, to taste
- 1 teaspoon Cajun seasoning
- ½ cup breadcrumbs
- ½ teaspoon garlic powder
- ½ teaspoon paprika
- 2 tablespoons fresh parsley, chopped

Directions:
1. Preheat the Air Fryer to 350°F/180°C.
2. Pat the sliced pickles dry with a paper towel and set aside.
3. Whisk the egg with the milk and season with pepper. Set aside.
4. Combine the Cajun seasoning, breadcrumbs, garlic powder, paprika, parsley, and pepper.
5. Dust the pickles lightly with the crumb mix. Dip into the egg mixture and coat evenly again with the crumb mix.
6. Spray the pickles with cooking spray and arrange them in the Air Fryer Basket. Use the Air Fryer Double Layer Rack if needed.
7. Set the timer for 5 to 8 minutes or until the crumb coat turns golden brown.
8. Serve once the timer goes off.

48 - BBQ Kale Crisps

Servings: 2
Preparation time: 5 minutes
Cooking Time: 3 minutes

Ingredients:
- 2 cups kale leaves, cleaned and cut into bite sizes
- 1 tablespoon olive oil
- 1 teaspoon soy sauce
- 2 tablespoons barbeque powder
- salt and pepper, to taste

Directions:
1. Preheat the Air Fryer to 400°F/200°C.
2. Toss the kale leaves with the olive oil and soy sauce.
3. Place the leaves in the Air Fryer Basket and set the timer for 3 minutes.
4. Shake the Air Fryer Basket halfway through the cooking time to allow the leaves to cook evenly.
5. Remove from the oven and transfer onto a serving plate.
6. Season with the barbeque powder, salt and pepper.

49 - Jalapeño Bombs

Servings: Makes 12 jalapeño bombs
Preparation time: 10 minutes
Cooking Time: 8 minutes

Ingredients:
- 12 jalapeño peppers, seeds and piths removed
- 12 cheddar cheese sticks
- 12 spring roll wrappers
- salt and pepper to taste

Directions:
1. Preheat the Air Fryer to 350°F/180°C.
2. Place a jalapeño pepper and a cheese stick onto each spring roll wrapper.
3. Season with salt and pepper and roll the spring roll tightly. Wet the edges with water to seal.
4. Repeat to make the remaining spring rolls.
5. Arrange them in the Air Fryer Basket and use the Air Fryer Double Layer Rack if needed.
6. Set the timer for 8 minutes.
7. After 8 minutes is up, serve it while it's hot!

50 - Zucchini Crisps

Servings: 4
Preparation time: 10 minutes
Cooking Time: 10 minutes

Ingredients:

- 2 large zucchinis, thinly sliced
- 1 cup breadcrumbs
- 1 teaspoon garlic powder
- 1 teaspoon onion powder
- 1 teaspoon ground nutmeg
- 1 teaspoon paprika
- 1 egg
- salt and pepper, to taste

Directions:

1. Preheat the Air Fryer to 350°F/180°C.
2. Dry the zucchini slices thoroughly with paper towel and set aside.
3. Mix together the breadcrumbs, garlic powder, onion powder, ground nutmeg and paprika.
4. Whisk the egg and season with salt and pepper.
5. Dip the zucchini slices in the egg mixture and then coat them evenly with the crumb mixture.
6. Spray the slices with cooking spray and arrange them in the Air Fryer Basket. Use the Air Fryer Double Layer Rack if needed.
7. Set the timer for 10 minutes or until they are crisp. Flip the vegetables using a pair of kitchen tongs halfway through the cooking time to allow the vegetables to cook evenly.
8. Serve and enjoy!

51 - Seafood Tostadas

Servings: 4
Preparation time: 10 minutes
Cooking Time: 10 minutes

Ingredients:
- 18 shrimps, peeled and deveined
- 1 teaspoon garlic powder
- 1 teaspoon paprika
- salt and pepper, to taste
- 12 ounces nacho chips
- ½ cup tomatoes, diced
- 2 tablespoons olives, sliced
- ¼ cup sour cream
- ¼ cup cheese sauce

Directions:
1. Preheat the Air Fryer to 350°F/180°C.
2. Season the shrimps with the garlic powder, paprika, salt and pepper.
3. Place the shrimps in the Air Fryer Basket and set the timer for 3 to 5 minutes or until the shrimps are cooked through.
4. Remove from the Air Fryer and set aside.
5. Place the nachos into the Air Fryer Basket and set the timer for 3 to 5 minutes or until they are well toasted.
6. Remove the chips from the Air Fryer and arrange them on a serving plate.
7. Top the nachos with the shrimps, tomatoes, olives, sour cream and cheese sauce.

52 - Easy Chicken Fingers

Servings: 4
Preparation time: 15 minutes
Cooking Time: 8 minutes

Ingredients:

- 2 large chicken breasts, cut into strips
- salt and pepper, to taste
- 1 cup breadcrumbs
- ½ cup parmesan cheese, grated
- 1 teaspoon garlic powder
- 1 teaspoon Italian seasoning
- 1 teaspoon paprika
- 1 egg

Directions:

1. Season the chicken strips with salt and pepper and set aside.
2. Mix together the breadcrumbs, parmesan cheese, garlic powder, Italian seasoning and paprika and set aside.
3. Whisk the eggs with the salt and pepper.
4. Dip the chicken strips into whisked egg and coat evenly with the breadcrumbs.
5. Set aside for 5 minutes for the breadcrumbs to set. Meantime, preheat the Air Fryer to 400°F/200°C.
6. Spray the chicken strips with cooking spray and arrange them in the Air Fryer Basket. Use the Air Fryer Double Layer Rack if needed.
7. Set the timer for 8 minutes or until the chicken is cooked through.
8. Once properly cooked through, your meal is ready to be served.

53 - Crispy Onion Rings

Servings: 2
Preparation time: 10 minutes
Cooking Time: 10 minutes

Ingredients:
- 2 eggs
- salt and pepper, to taste
- ½ cup flour
- 1 teaspoon paprika
- 2 cups breadcrumbs
- ½ cup parmesan cheese, grated
- 1 teaspoon garlic powder
- 1 teaspoon ground allspice
- 2 large onions, cut into rings

Directions:
1. Preheat the Air Fryer to 350°F/180°C.
2. Whisk the eggs with the salt and pepper and set aside.
3. Combine the flour and paprika in a bowl and set aside.
4. Mix the breadcrumbs, parmesan cheese, garlic powder and ground allspice in another bowl and set aside.
5. Coat the onion rings with the flour mixture first.
6. Then dip them into the whisked egg and coat evenly with breadcrumbs.
7. Spray the onion rings with cooking spray and arrange them in the Air Fryer Basket. Use the Air Fryer Double Layer Rack if needed.
8. Set the timer for 10 minutes or until the onion rings turn golden brown. Flip the onion rings over with a pair of kitchen tongs halfway through the cooking time to allow them to cook evenly.
9. Serve while still hot.

54 - Sweet Potato Fritters

Servings: 2
Preparation time: 10 minutes
Cooking Time: 10 minutes

Ingredients:
- 2 eggs
- salt and pepper, to taste
- ½ cup flour
- 1 teaspoon paprika
- 1 cup breadcrumbs
- ½ cup parmesan cheese, grated
- 1 teaspoon garlic powder
- 1 large sweet potato, peeled, boiled and cut into thin wedges
- ¼ cup sour cream
- 2 tablespoons chives, chopped

Directions:
1. Preheat the Air Fryer to 350°F/180°C.
2. Whisk the eggs with the salt and pepper.
3. Combine the flour and paprika in a bowl and set aside.
4. Mix the breadcrumbs, parmesan cheese and garlic powder in another bowl and set aside.
5. Dry the sweet potato wedges thoroughly with paper towels.
6. Dust the wedges with the flour.
7. Dip them in the whisked egg and coat evenly with the breadcrumbs.
8. Place the wedges into the Air Fryer Basket and use the Air Fryer Double Layer Rack if needed.
9. Set the timer for 10 minutes or until they turn golden brown. Shake the Air Fryer Basket halfway through the cooking time or flip them over using kitchen tongs to allow even cooking.
10. Remove from the Air Fryer and transfer to a serving plate.
11. Dollop over with the sour cream and top with the chives.

55 - Crispy Okra Rolls

Servings: 2
Preparation time: 10 minutes
Cooking Time: 20 minutes

Ingredients:
- 10 pieces okra
- salt and pepper, to taste
- 10 spring roll wrappers

Directions:
1. Preheat the Air Fryer to 350°F/180°C.
2. Season the okras with salt and pepper.
3. Wrap each okra tightly with a spring roll wrapper and wet the edges to seal.
4. Spray the rolls with cooking spray and arrange them in the Air Fryer Basket. Use the Air Fryer Double Layer Rack if needed.
5. Set the timer for 20 minutes or until the rolls become golden brown.
6. Serve once the timer goes off!

56 - Zucchini Fries

Servings: 2
Preparation time: 10 minutes
Cooking Time: 15 minutes

Ingredients:
- 2 large zucchinis, cut into sticks resembling fries
- salt and pepper, to taste
- 2 eggs
- 1 cup breadcrumbs
- 1 teaspoon paprika
- 1 teaspoon onion powder
- 1 teaspoon garlic powder

Directions:
1. Preheat the Air Fryer to 350°F/180°C.
2. Season the zucchini fries with salt and pepper.
3. Whisk the eggs and set aside.
4. Combine the breadcrumbs, paprika, onion powder, garlic powder, salt and pepper in a bowl and set aside.
5. Dip the zucchini fries in the egg mixture and coat them evenly with the breadcrumbs.
6. Spray the fries with cooking spray and arrange them in the Air Fryer Basket. Use the Air Fryer Double Layer Rack if needed.
7. Set the timer for 15 minutes or until the fries become golden brown. Shake the Air Fryer Basket or use a pair of kitchen tongs to flip the fries, halfway through the cooking time to allow the fries to cook evenly.
8. Serve fries in a bowl of your liking.

57 - Allspice Eggplant Crisps

Servings: 2
Preparation time: 10 minutes
Cooking Time: 12 minutes

Ingredients:

- 1 cup breadcrumbs
- 1 teaspoon paprika
- 1 teaspoon ground allspice
- 1 teaspoon chili powder
- ½ teaspoon garlic powder
- 2 eggs
- salt and pepper to taste
- 1 large eggplant, sliced thinly to resemble chips
- ½ teaspoon garlic salt

Directions:

1. Preheat the Air Fryer to 400°F/200°C.
2. Mix the breadcrumbs, paprika, ground allspice, chili powder and garlic powder in a bowl and set aside.
3. Whisk the eggs with the salt and pepper and set aside.
4. Dip the eggplant chips into the egg mixture and coat evenly with the breadcrumbs.
5. Set aside for a few minutes to let the breadcrumbs set.
6. Spray the eggplant chips with cooking spray and arrange them in a single layer in the Air Fryer Basket. Use the Air Fryer Double Layer Rack if needed.
7. Set the timer for 12 minutes and use a pair of kitchen tongs to flip the eggplant chips over halfway through the cooking time to allow the chips to cook evenly.
8. Remove from the Air Fryer and sprinkle with garlic salt.
9. Serve in a bowl.

58 - Honey Crispy Sweet Potato Fries

Servings: 2
Preparation time: 5 minutes
Cooking Time: 12 minutes

Ingredients:

- 1 tablespoon olive oil
- 2 tablespoons honey
- 1 teaspoon paprika
- 1 teaspoon sesame seeds
- 1 large sweet potato, cut into thin sticks to resemble fries
- salt and pepper, to taste

Directions:

1. Preheat the Air Fryer to 400°F/200°C.
2. Mix together the olive oil, honey, paprika and sesame seeds in a bowl.
3. Coat the sweet potato fries in the honey mixture evenly.
4. Arrange the sweet potato fries in the Air Fryer Basket.
5. Set the timer for 12 minutes and use a pair of kitchen tongs to flip the sweet potato fries over halfway through the cooking time to allow them to cook evenly.
6. Remove the sweet potato fries from the Air Fryer and season with salt and pepper.

59 - Crispy Curry Pickles

Servings: 2
Preparation time: 10 minutes
Cooking Time: 8 minutes

Ingredients:

- ½ cup flour
- ½ teaspoon garlic powder
- 1 teaspoon curry powder
- ½ teaspoon ground allspice
- salt and pepper, to taste
- 1 egg
- 2 large pickles, sliced thinly
- ½ cup breadcrumbs

Directions:

1. Mix together the flour, garlic powder, curry powder, ground allspice, salt and pepper in a bowl and set aside.
2. Whisk the egg in a bowl and set aside.
3. Dust the pickle slices in the flour mixture.
4. Dip them into the egg mixture and coat evenly with the breadcrumbs.
5. Set aside for a few minutes to set the breadcrumbs so they do not fall off the pickles.
6. Preheat the Air Fryer to 400°F/200°C.
7. Spray the pickle slices with cooking spray and arrange them in a single layer in the Air Fryer Basket. Use the Air Fryer Double Layer Rack if needed.
8. Set the timer for 8 minutes or until they turn golden brown.
9. Once they turn golden brown, they are ready to be served.

60 - Crispy Watercress Chips

Servings: 2
Preparation time: 10 minutes
Cooking Time: 8 minutes

Ingredients:
- 2 cups Chinese watercress leaves
- 1 tablespoon olive oil
- 1 cup flour
- 1 teaspoon onion powder
- 1 teaspoon garlic powder
- salt and pepper, to taste

Directions:
1. Spray the Air Fryer Basket with cooking spray to prevent the watercress leaves from sticking to the Air Fryer Basket.
2. Preheat the Air Fryer to 400°F/200°C.
3. Toss the watercress leaves in a bowl with the olive oil until well combined and set aside.
4. Mix together the flour, onion powder, garlic powder, salt and pepper in a bowl.
5. Coat the watercress leaves evenly with the flour mixture.
6. Shake off any excess flour and transfer the leaves to the Air Fryer Basket.
7. Set the timer for 8 minutes and shake the Air Fryer Basket halfway through the cooking time to allow the leaves to cook evenly.
8. Serve up in a bowl.

61 - Cinnamon Apple Chips

Servings: 2
Preparation time: 5 minutes
Cooking Time: 8 minutes

Ingredients:
- 1 teaspoon ground cinnamon
- 1 teaspoon ground nutmeg
- 3 granny smith apples, peeled, cored and sliced thinly

Directions:
1. Preheat the Air Fryer to 400°F/200°C.
2. Combine the ground cinnamon and ground nutmeg in a bowl.
3. Spray the apple slices with cooking spray and coat them with the spice mix.
4. Arrange the apple slices in a single layer in the Air Fryer Basket and use the Double Layer Rack if needed.
5. Set the timer for 8 minutes and use a pair of kitchen tongs to flip the apples over halfway through the cooking time to allow the apples to cook evenly.
6. Serve in a bowl.

62 - Cajun Asparagus Spears

Servings: Makes 20 asparagus crisps
Preparation time: 10 minutes
Cooking Time: 8 minutes

Ingredients:

- 1 cup breadcrumbs
- ¼ cup parmesan cheese, grated
- 2 tablespoons Cajun seasoning
- 1 tablespoon garlic powder
- 2 eggs
- salt and pepper, to taste
- 20 spears asparagus

Dircctions:

1. Preheat the Air Fryer to 400°F/200°C.
2. Mix together the breadcrumbs, parmesan cheese, Cajun seasoning and garlic powder and set aside.
3. Whisk the eggs with salt and pepper and set aside.
4. Dip the asparagus spears into the egg mixture and coat evenly with the breadcrumbs.
5. Spray with cooking spray and arrange them in the Air Fryer Basket. Use the Air Fryer Double Layer Rack if needed.
6. Set the timer for 8 minutes or until the spears turn golden brown. Flip the spears using a pair of kitchen tongs halfway through the cooking time to allow the asparagus to cook evenly.
7. Serve and enjoy!

63 - Crispy Beets Chips with Spicy Dip

Servings: 2
Preparation time: 10 minutes
Cooking Time: 15 minutes

Ingredients:
- 1 cup sour cream
- ¼ cup horseradish
- 1 teaspoon garlic, minced
- 1 cup flour
- 2 teaspoons paprika
- 2 teaspoons onion powder
- 2 teaspoons garlic powder
- 4 medium beets, sliced thinly to resemble chips
- salt and pepper, to taste

Directions:
1. To make the spicy dip: Combine the sour cream, horseradish and minced garlic in a bowl and set aside to chill.
2. Preheat the Air Fryer to 400°F/200°C.
3. Mix the flour, paprika, onion powder and garlic powder in a bowl.
4. Lightly dust the beet slices with the flour mixture and spray them with cooking spray.
5. Arrange the beets in the Air Fryer Basket and use the Air Fryer Double Layer Rack if needed.
6. Set the timer for 15 minutes or until the beets are crisp.
7. Remove the beets chips from the Air Fryer and season with salt and pepper.
8. Serve with the spicy dip and enjoy!

64 - Purple Yam Crisps

Servings: 2
Preparation Time: 10 minutes
Cooking Time: 8 minutes

Ingredients:

- 1 medium purple yam, sliced thinly to resemble chips
- ¼ cup breadcrumbs
- ¼ cup parmesan cheese, grated
- ½ teaspoon garlic powder
- 1 tablespoon olive oil

Directions:

1. Wash the yam chips twice to remove as much starch as possible.
2. Pat dry thoroughly with kitchen towels.
3. Combine the breadcrumbs, parmesan cheese and garlic powder in a bowl.
4. Toss the yam chips in the olive oil and coat evenly with the breadcrumbs. Set aside for a few minutes to let the breadcrumbs set so that they do not fall off during cooking.
5. Preheat the Air Fryer to 400°F/200°C.
6. Arrange the yam chips in the Air Fryer Basket in a single layer and use the Air Fryer Double Layer Rack if needed.
7. Set the timer for 8 minutes or until the chips are crisp.
8. Once crisp, serve and enjoy!

65 - Tangy Onion Flowers

Servings: 2
Preparation Time: 20 minutes
Cooking Time: 8 minutes

Ingredients:

- 2 tablespoons mayonnaise
- 2 tablespoons sour cream
- 1½ teaspoons ketchup
- ½ teaspoon Worcestershire sauce
- ¼ teaspoon paprika
- salt and pepper, to taste
- 2 large sweet onions
- 2½ cups breadcrumbs
- 1 teaspoon cayenne pepper
- 2 tablespoons paprika
- ½ teaspoon dried thyme
- ½ teaspoon dried oregano
- ½ teaspoon ground cumin
- 2 large eggs
- 1 cup whole milk
- cornstarch, for dusting

Directions:

1. To make the tangy tip: Mix together the mayonnaise, sour cream, ketchup, Worcestershire sauce and paprika in a bowl. Season with salt and pepper and chill until the onion flowers are cooked.
2. To make the onion flowers: Cut the root ends off each sweet onion and remove the onion skins. Slice each onion into 16 even wedges to resemble the flower petals, taking care to end about ½-inch from the bottom of the onion so that the wedges are still all intact. Gently separate the segments so that the onion now resembles a water lily.
3. Preheat the Air Fryer to 400°F/200°C.
4. Mix together the breadcrumbs, cayenne pepper, paprika, dried thyme, dried oregano, ground cumin, salt, and pepper in a bowl and set aside.
5. Whisk eggs with the milk and set aside.
6. Dust the onion flowers with cornstarch and dip them in the whisked egg.
7. Allow any excess egg to drip off and coat the onion flowers evenly with the breadcrumbs. Ensure that the parts near the stem of the flowers are also well coated.
8. Arrange the onion flowers in the Air Fryer Basket.
9. Spray the onion flowers with cooking spray and set the timer for 8 minutes or until they become golden and crisp.
10. Once crisp, serve and enjoy!

66 - Caramel Banana Crisps

Servings: 2
Preparation Time: 5 minutes
Cooking Time: 8 minutes

Ingredients:
- 2 bananas, peeled and sliced to resemble chips
- salt, to taste
- ¼ cup brown sugar

Directions:
1. Preheat Air Fryer to 350°F/180°C.
2. Season the bananas with some salt and coat them evenly with the brown sugar.
3. Arrange the bananas in the Air Fryer Basket and use the Air Fryer Double Layer Rack if needed.
4. Set the timer for 10 minutes or until the bananas are crisp. Give the Air Fryer Basket a shake or flip the banana chips using a pair of kitchen tongs if using the Air Fryer Double Layer Rack, halfway through the cooking time to allow the bananas to cook evenly.
5. Serve and enjoy!

67 - Salmon Sushi Crisp

Servings: 1
Preparation Time: 10 minutes
Cooking Time: 13 minutes

Ingredients:
- 1 cup of cooked sushi rice
- 1 tablespoon rice vinegar
- ½ teaspoon of sugar
- 2 ounces sashimi grade salmon, sliced
- ½ cucumber, diced into small pieces

Directions:
1. Preheat the Air Fryer to 400°F/200°C.
2. Combine the sushi rice, vinegar and sugar and set aside.
3. Place rice on a flat surface. Mold and roll into a long strip. Cut into bite size.
4. Carefully place rice bites into the Air Fryer and set the timer for 13 minutes.
5. Mix together the salmon and cucumber.
6. Top each rice bite with some salmon and cucumber.
7. Serve and enjoy!

68 - Cucumber Fries

Servings: 2
Preparation Time: 10 minutes
Cooking Time: 15 minutes

Ingredients:

- 2 large cucumbers, cut into sticks resembling fries
- Salt and pepper, to taste
- 2 eggs
- 1 cup breadcrumbs
- 1 teaspoon paprika
- 1 teaspoon onion powder
- 1 teaspoon garlic powder

Directions:

1. Preheat the Air Fryer to 350°F/180°C.
2. Season the cucumber fries with salt and pepper.
3. Whisk the eggs and set aside.
4. Combine the breadcrumbs, paprika, onion powder, garlic powder, salt and pepper in a bowl and set aside.
5. Dip the cucumber fries in the egg mixture and coat them evenly with the breadcrumbs.
6. Spray the fries with cooking spray and arrange them in the Air Fryer Basket. Use the Air Fryer Double Layer Rack if needed.
7. Set the timer for 15 minutes or until the fries become golden brown. Shake the Air Fryer Basket or use a pair of kitchen tongs to flip the fries, halfway through the cooking time to allow the fries to cook evenly.
8. Once golden brown, serve and enjoy!

69 - Pumpkin Strips

Servings: 4
Preparation Time: 10 minutes
Cooking Time: 30 minutes

Ingredients:
- 1 large pumpkin, peeled and thinly sliced into strips
- 1 tablespoon ground cumin
- 1½ teaspoons salt
- 2 teaspoons paprika
- 2 teaspoons turmeric

Directions:
1. Preheat the Air Fryer to 350°F/180°C.
2. Spray the pumpkin strips with cooking spray.
3. Mix together the ground cumin, salt, paprika and turmeric.
4. Evenly coat the pumpkin strips with the cumin mixture.
5. Place them in the Air Fryer Basket and use the Air Fryer Double Layer Rack if needed.
6. Set the timer for 30 minutes or until the strips are crisp. Shake the Air Fryer Basket halfway through the cooking time or use a pair of kitchen tongs to flip the strips over if using the rack, to ensure that the strips are evenly cooked.
7. Once crisp, serve and enjoy!

70 - Apple Crisps

Servings: 2
Preparation Time: 5 minutes
Cooking Time: 8 minutes

Ingredients:
- 1 cup flour
- 1 teaspoon paprika
- 1 teaspoon ground cumin
- Salt and pepper, to taste
- ½ teaspoon garlic powder
- 2 apples, sliced thinly
- 1 tablespoon olive oil

Directions:
1. Preheat the Air Fryer to 400°F/200°C.
2. Mix together the flour, paprika, ground cumin, salt, pepper and garlic powder in a bowl.
3. Toss the apples in the olive oil and coat evenly with the flour mixture.
4. Set the timer for 8 minutes or until the apples are crisp.
5. Once crisp, serve and enjoy!

71 - Roasted Spicy Pumpkin

Servings: 2
Preparation Time: 5 minutes
Cooking Time: 25 minutes

Ingredients:
- 1 pumpkin, diced
- 1 teaspoon olive oil
- 1 teaspoon garlic powder
- 1 teaspoon paprika
- 1 teaspoon dried oregano
- 1 teaspoon chili flakes
- 1 tablespoon fresh parsley, chopped

Directions:
1. Preheat the Air Fryer to 350°F/180°C.
2. Place the diced pumpkin in the Air Fryer Baking Pan.
3. Toss the potatoes with the olive oil, garlic powder, paprika, dried oregano and chili flakes until well combined.
4. Place the Air Fryer Baking Pan in the Air Fryer Basket and set the timer for 20 minutes.
5. Mix in the fresh parsley and set the timer for 5 more minutes or until desired crispness of pumpkin.
6. Once crispy enough for your liking, serve and enjoy!

72 - Crispy Vegan Nibbles

Servings: 4
Preparation Time: 10 minutes
Cooking Time: 20 minutes

Ingredients:
- ½ cup panko
- 2 teaspoons garlic powder
- 2 teaspoons onion powder
- 1 teaspoon cayenne pepper
- 1 tablespoon dried basil
- 2 teaspoons dried parsley flakes
- 1 tablespoon dried oregano
- 16 ounces firm tofu, cut into strips to resemble fries
- ½ cup soy milk

Directions:
1. Preheat the Air Fryer to 350°F/180°C.
2. Mix together the panko, garlic powder, onion powder, cayenne pepper, dried basil, dried parsley and dried oregano in a bowl and set aside.
3. Dip the tofu fries in the soy milk and coat them evenly with the panko mixture.
4. Spray the tofu fries with cooking spray and arrange them in a single layer in the Air Fryer Basket. Use the Air Fryer Double Layer Rack if needed.
5. Set the timer for 20 minutes or until the tofu fries are crisp.
6. Once crisp, serve and enjoy!

Lunch Recipes

73 - Ginger Lime Dory Fillets

Servings: 2
Preparation Time: 5 minutes
Cooking Time: 10 minutes

Ingredients:
- 1 pound dory fillets
- 5 cloves garlic, sliced
- ¼ cup ginger, sliced
- 1 teaspoon olive oil
- 2 teaspoons lime juice
- 1 cup seafood stock
- ¼ cup fresh cilantro, chopped

Directions:
1. Preheat the Air Fryer to 350°F/180°C.
2. Place the dory fillets with the garlic and ginger slices in the Air Fryer Baking Pan.
3. Drizzle over the olive oil.
4. Pour in the lime juice and seafood stock.
5. Add the fresh cilantro.
6. Place the Air Fryer Baking Pan in the Air Fryer Basket and set the timer for 10 minutes.
7. After 10 minutes, serve on a plate.

74 - Spicy Beef Rice

Servings: 2
Preparation Time: 5 minutes
Cooking Time: 15 minutes

Ingredients:
- 500 grams beef, sliced thinly into strips
- 2 tablespoons olive oil
- Salt and pepper, to taste
- ½ cup shallots, sliced
- 1 teaspoon ginger, minced
- ¼ cup beef stock
- 2 tablespoons hot chili paste
- 2 cups cooked rice

Directions:
1. Preheat the Air Fryer to 350°F/180°C.
2. Place the beef strips in the Air Fryer Baking Pan and season with olive oil and salt and pepper.
3. Add the shallots and ginger to the Air Fryer Baking Pan.
4. Place the Air Fryer Baking Pan in the Air Fryer Basket and set the timer for 10 minutes.
5. Stir in the beef stock and hot chili paste and set the timer for 5 more minutes.
6. Pour contents from the Air Fryer Baking Pan over the cooked rice.
7. Eat up!

75 - Stuffed Peppers with Bacon and Cheese

Servings: 2
Preparation Time: 10 minutes
Cooking Time: 8 minutes

Ingredients:
- 2 large bell peppers
- ¼ cup bacon, chopped
- ½ cup mozzarella cheese, grated
- 2 cloves garlic, minced
- ½ cup tomatoes, diced
- 1 teaspoon paprika
- Salt and pepper, to taste

Directions:
1. Preheat the Air Fryer to 350°F/180°C.
2. Cut the tops off the bell peppers. Remove the seeds and the rest of the insides of the bell peppers, so they are completely hollow.
3. Mix together the bacon, mozzarella cheese, garlic, tomatoes, paprika, salt and pepper in a medium size bowl.
4. Fill both bell peppers with the bowl mixture.
5. Place the bell peppers in the Air Fryer Basket and set the timer for 8 minutes.
6. Serve and enjoy!

76 - Bacon and Brussels Sprouts

Servings: 4
Preparation Time: 5 minutes
Cooking Time: 20 minutes

Ingredients:

- 6 rashers bacon, chopped
- 2 cups of brussels sprouts, halved
- ½ cup white onions, chopped
- 4 cloves garlic, sliced
- 1 teaspoon garlic powder
- 1 teaspoon cayenne pepper
- ¼ cup chives, chopped
- 2 tablespoons parmesan cheese, shavings

Directions:

1. Preheat the Air Fryer to 350°F/180°C.
2. Place the bacon in the Air Fryer Baking Pan and set the timer for 10 minutes or until the bacon is crisp.
3. Remove the bacon from the Air Fryer Baking Pan and set aside.
4. Add the brussels sprouts and white onions to the Air Fryer Baking Pan.
5. Add the sliced garlic, garlic powder and cayenne pepper and mix well to combine.
6. Return to the Air Fryer and set the timer for 10 minutes.
7. Remove from the Air Fryer and mix in the chives.
8. Top with the parmesan shavings and bacon bits.
9. Serve and enjoy!

77 - Red Cabbage and Sweet Potatoes

Servings: 2
Preparation Time: 5 minutes
Cooking Time: 18 minutes

Ingredients:
- 4 rashers bacon, chopped
- ¼ cup onions, finely chopped
- ¼ head red cabbage, chopped
- 1 cup sweet potatoes, diced
- 1 tablespoon garlic, minced
- ⅛ cup carrots, diced
- ¼ cup celery, chopped
- 1 tablespoon button mushrooms, minced
- ½ teaspoon garlic powder
- ½ teaspoon ground allspice
- 1 tablespoon fresh parsley, finely chopped

Directions:
1. Preheat the Air Fryer to 350°F/180°C.
2. Place the bacon in the Air Fryer Baking Pan and place the Air Fryer Baking Pan in the Air Fryer Basket.
3. Set the timer for 10 minutes or until the bacon is crispy.
4. Add the onions, red cabbage, sweet potatoes, minced garlic, carrots, celery and mushrooms.
5. Mix well with the garlic powder and ground allspice.
6. Set the timer for another 8 minutes.
7. Remove from the Air Fryer and top with the fresh parsley.

78 - Hearty Frittata

Servings: 4
Preparation Time: 5 minutes
Cooking Time: 15 minutes

Ingredients:
- 5 eggs
- 2 tablespoons cream
- ½ cup onions, sliced
- 1 cup cherry tomatoes, halved
- ¼ cup red bell peppers, seeds removed and chopped
- salt and pepper, to taste
- 1 cup boiled potatoes, diced
- ½ cup fresh coriander, finely chopped

Directions:
1. Preheat the Air Fryer to 350°F/180°C.
2. Whisk together the eggs and cream.
3. Add the onions, cherry tomatoes and bell peppers.
4. Season with salt and pepper.
5. Add the diced potatoes.
6. Pour into the Air Fryer Baking Pan and place the Air Fryer Baking Pan in the Air Fryer Basket.
7. Set the timer for 15 minutes.
8. Remove from the Air Fryer Basket and top with the fresh coriander.

79 - Lean Meatballs

Servings: 4
Preparation Time: 5 minutes plus 25 minutes chilling time
Cooking Time: 15 minutes

Ingredients:
- 1 pound lean ground beef
- ¼ cup onions, finely chopped
- 1 tablespoon garlic, minced
- 1 tablespoon low sodium soy sauce
- 2 teaspoons paprika
- 1 teaspoon garlic salt
- pepper, to taste
- ¼ cup fresh cilantro, chopped

Directions:
1. Mix together the ground beef, onions and garlic.
2. Season with the soy sauce, paprika, garlic salt and pepper.
3. Add the fresh cilantro and mix until well combined.
4. Form meatballs and chill for 25 minutes.
5. Preheat the Air Fryer to 400°F/200°C.
6. Arrange the meatballs in the Air Fryer Basket. Use the Air Fryer Double Layer Rack if needed.
7. Set the timer for 15 minutes.
8. Serve up once the timer goes off.

80 - Linguine with Lemon Chicken and Capers

Servings: 2
Preparation Time: 5 minutes
Cooking Time: 20 minutes

Ingredients:
- 2 chicken breast fillets, cut into strips
- salt and pepper, to taste
- 1 tablespoon garlic, minced
- ½ tablespoon lemon juice
- ¼ cup butter
- ½ cup cream
- ⅛ cup capers
- 1 tablespoon fresh parsley, chopped
- 6 ounces linguine, cooked

Directions:
1. Preheat the Air Fryer to 400°F/200°C.
2. Season the chicken strips with salt and pepper and place them in the Air Fryer Baking Pan.
3. Add the minced garlic, lemon juice and butter.
4. Place the Air Fryer Baking Pan in the Air Fryer Basket and set the timer for 12 minutes.
5. Remove the Air Fryer Baking Pan from the Air Fryer Basket and turn over the chicken strips.
6. Add the cream and set the timer for another 8 minutes or until the chicken is cooked through.
7. Pour the chicken and sauce over the pasta and mix with the capers and fresh parsley.
8. Serve and enjoy!

81 - Easy Veggie Soup

Servings: 2
Preparation Time: 5 minutes
Cooking Time: 19 minutes

Ingredients:
- ¼ cup onions, sliced
- ½ cup carrots, diced
- 1 cup squash, cubed
- 1 cup potatoes, diced
- 2 tablespoons garlic, minced
- 1 teaspoon garlic salt
- 3 cups vegetable stock
- ¼ cup fresh flat-leaf parsley leaves, chopped

Directions:
1. Preheat the Air Fryer to 350°F/180°C.
2. Place the onions and carrots in the Air Fryer Baking Pan and set the timer for 4 minutes.
3. Add the squash and potatoes and set the timer for 5 minutes.
4. Add the minced garlic and garlic salt and set the timer for 5 minutes.
5. Pour in the vegetable stock and set the timer for 5 more minutes
6. Add the parsley and stir well to combine.
7. Serve in a bowl.

82 - Air Fryer Chicken Fajitas

Servings: 2
Preparation Time: 5 minutes
Cooking Time: 16 minutes

Ingredients:

- 2 chicken breast fillets, sliced
- 2 teaspoons lime juice
- salt and pepper, to taste
- ¼ cup onions, sliced
- 2 tablespoons garlic, minced
- ½ cup red bell peppers, seeds removed and sliced lengthwise
- ½ cup yellow bell peppers, seeds removed and sliced lengthwise
- 1 teaspoon paprika
- 1 teaspoon garlic salt
- ¼ cup fresh cilantro, chopped
- ¼ cup flat-leaf parsley leaves, chopped
- 4 lime slices

Directions:

1. Preheat the Air Fryer to 350°F/180°C.
2. Place the chicken slices in the Air Fryer Baking Pan and season with the lime juice, salt and pepper.
3. Place the Air Fryer Baking Pan in the Air Fryer Basket and set the timer for 8 minutes.
4. Add the onions, garlic, red and yellow bell peppers.
5. Mix in the paprika and garlic salt and stir well to combine.
6. Set the timer for 2 minutes.
7. Stir the ingredients again and set the timer for 6 more minutes.
8. Mix in the fresh cilantro and fresh parsley leaves.
9. Top with the lime slices.
10. Serve and enjoy!

83 - Tzatziki Chicken

Servings: 2
Preparation Time: 5 minutes
Cooking Time: 12 minutes

Ingredients:
- 2 chicken breast fillets, cubed
- salt and pepper, to taste
- 1 cup yogurt
- 2 tablespoons garlic, minced
- ¼ cup onions, finely chopped
- ¼ cup cucumbers, finely diced
- ¼ cup fresh dill, chopped
- 1 teaspoon garlic salt

Directions:
1. Preheat the Air Fryer to 350°F/180°C.
2. Season the chicken with salt and pepper and place them in the Air Fryer Basket.
3. Set the timer for 12 minutes or until the chicken is cooked through.
4. Mix together the yogurt, garlic, onions, cucumbers, dill, garlic salt and pepper in a bowl and set aside.
5. Remove the chicken from the Air Fryer and serve with the yogurt dip.

84 - Caprese Scallops

Servings: 2
Preparation Time: 10 minutes
Cooking Time: 6 minutes

Ingredients:
- 1 tablespoon garlic, minced
- 1 tablespoon olive oil
- ½ teaspoon balsamic vinegar
- 6 scallops
- salt and pepper, to taste
- 1 tablespoon pesto
- 6 slices fresh mozzarella
- 6 slices tomatoes
- ¼ cup fresh basil, finely chopped

Directions:
1. Preheat the Air Fryer to 350°F/180°C.
2. To make the balsamic vinaigrette: Mix together the minced garlic, olive oil and balsamic vinegar in a bowl.
3. Season the scallops with salt and pepper and place them in the Air Fryer Baking Pan.
4. Place the Air Fryer Baking Pan in the Air Fryer Basket and set the timer for 5 minutes.
5. Remove the Air Fryer Baking Pan from the Air Fryer and spread the pesto on the scallops.
6. Drizzle over with the balsamic vinaigrette.
7. Place the mozzarella and tomato slices on the scallops and return the Air Fryer Baking Pan to the Air Fryer.
8. Set the timer for another minute.
9. Remove from the Air Fryer and top with the fresh basil.
10. Serve and enjoy!

85 - Chicken Aioli Fusilli

Servings: 2
Preparation Time: 10 minutes
Cooking Time: 13 minutes

Ingredients:

- 2 egg yolks
- 1 tablespoon lemon juice
- 2 tablespoons garlic, sliced
- ¼ cup olive oil
- salt and pepper, to taste
- 1 large chicken breast, sliced
- ½ teaspoon garlic salt
- 6 oz fusilli, cooked
- ¼ cup fresh parsley, finely chopped

Directions:

1. Preheat the Air Fryer to 350°F/180°C.
2. To make the aioli sauce: Blend the egg yolks, lemon juice and garlic until the mixture becomes light and creamy. Slowly add in the olive oil and continue blending until the sauce becomes thick, creamy and smooth. Season with salt and pepper and set aside.
3. Season the chicken slices with garlic salt and pepper and place them in the Air Fryer Baking Pan.
4. Place the Air Fryer Baking Pan in the Air Fryer Basket and set the timer for 8 minutes.
5. Remove the Air Fryer Baking Pan from the Air Fryer and add the sauce to the Air Fryer Baking Pan.
6. Return to the Air Fryer and set the timer for 5 more minutes or until the chicken is cooked through.
7. Mix the fusilli with the chicken and top with the fresh parsley.
8. Serve and enjoy

86 - Coriander Curry Shrimps

Servings: 2
Preparation Time: 5 minutes
Cooking Time: 10 minutes

Ingredients:
- 1 pound shrimps, peeled and deveined
- ½ cup breadcrumbs
- ½ cup coconut shavings
- ⅓ cup parmesan cheese, grated
- ½ cup buttermilk
- 1 teaspoon curry powder
- ¼ cup fresh coriander, finely chopped

Directions:
1. Preheat the Air Fryer to 350°F/180°C.
2. Mix the breadcrumbs, coconut shavings and parmesan cheese and set aside.
3. Whisk together the buttermilk, curry powder and fresh coriander.
4. Dip the shrimps with the buttermilk and coat evenly with the breadcrumbs mixture.
5. Arrange the shrimps in the Air Fryer Basket and set the timer for 10 minutes.
6. Transfer to a bowl or plate to serve.

87 - Curried Meatballs

Servings: 2
Preparation Time: 10 minutes
Cooking Time: 12 minutes

Ingredients:
- 1 pound ground beef
- 1 tablespoon garlic, minced
- 1 teaspoon chili flakes
- 1 tablespoon fresh cilantro, chopped
- 2 tablespoons celery, minced
- 1 teaspoon garlic powder
- 1 teaspoon curry powder
- 2 tablespoons breadcrumbs
- 1 egg

Directions:
1. Preheat the Air Fryer to 350°F/180°C.
2. Mix the ground beef, minced garlic, chili flakes, fresh cilantro, celery, garlic powder and curry powder in a bowl.
3. Add the breadcrumbs and egg and mix until well combined.
4. Form meatballs the size of ping pong balls and arrange them in the Air Fryer Basket. Use the Air Fryer Double Layer Rack if needed.
5. Set the timer for 12 minutes.
6. Once cooked, serve and enjoy!

88 - Herbed Mushroom Prata Roti

Servings: 2
Preparation Time: 5 minutes
Cooking Time: 5 minutes

Ingredients:
- ½ cup button mushrooms, chopped
- 1 teaspoon Italian seasoning
- 1 teaspoon garlic powder
- 2 pieces prata roti, thawed

Directions:
1. Preheat the Air Fryer to 350°F/180°C.
2. Mix together the mushrooms, Italian seasoning and garlic powder in a bowl.
3. Stretch the prata roti a little.
4. Add the herbed mushrooms in the center of the prata roti.
5. Place the prata roti in the Air Fryer Basket and use the Air Fryer Double Layer Rack if needed.
6. Spray the prata roti with cooking spray and set the timer to 5 minutes.
7. Once cooked, serve and enjoy!

89 - Roasted Bell Pepper Soup

Servings: 2
Preparation Time: 10 minutes
Cooking Time: 30 minutes

Ingredients:

- 2 red bell peppers, seeds removed and diced
- 1 medium tomatoes, diced
- 1 small sweet onion, finely chopped
- 3 cloves garlic, minced
- 1 teaspoon extra virgin olive oil
- 1½ cup chicken stock
- ¼ teaspoon ground cumin
- ¼ teaspoon smoked sweet paprika
- salt & pepper to taste
- ½ avocado, diced
- ¼ cup fresh cilantro, chopped
- 2 tablespoons sour cream

Directions:

1. Preheat the Air Fryer to 350°F/180°C.
2. Add the red bell peppers, tomatoes, onions, garlic and extra virgin olive oil in the Air Fryer Baking Pan.
3. Place the Air Fryer Baking Pan in the Air Fryer Basket.
4. Set the timer for 20 minutes or until peppers are cooked and caramelized.
5. Remove the Air Fryer Baking Pan from the Air Fryer.
6. Mix in the chicken stock, ground cumin, smoked sweet paprika and season with salt and pepper.
7. Return to the Air Fryer for 6 to 10 more minutes.
8. Remove the Air Fryer Baking Pan from the Air Fryer and allow to cool a little.
9. Pour into the blender and blend until smooth.
10. Top with the avocados, fresh cilantro and sour cream.
11. Serve in a bowl.

90 - Mango Fish Tacos

Servings: 4
Preparation Time: 10 minutes
Cooking Time: 8 minutes

Ingredients:
- 1½ cups flour
- 1 teaspoon salt
- 1 teaspoon baking powder
- 1 can beer
- 4 halibut fillets, sliced in strips
- 1 cup mangoes, diced
- 4 corn taco shells
- ¾ cup guacamole
- 2 tablespoons fresh cilantro, finely chopped
- Cholula sauce, optional

Directions:
1. Preheat the Air Fryer to 400°F/200°C.
2. Mix together the flour, salt, baking powder and beer until it forms a batter consistency.
3. Dust the halibuts lightly with flour and coat with the beer batter.
4. Place the halibuts in the Air Fryer Basket and use the Air Fryer Double Layer Rack if needed.
5. Set the timer for 8 minutes or until they turn golden brown.
6. Place some mangoes on each tortilla.
7. Remove the halibuts from the Air Fryer and place on the mangoes.
8. Top with the guacamole and fresh cilantro and fold. Serve with Cholula hot sauce if desired.

91 - Summer Squash Dal

Servings: 2
Preparation Time: 5 minutes
Cooking Time: 25 minutes

Ingredients:

- 4 cloves garlic, minced
- 1 fresh red chili
- ½ tablespoon olive oil
- 1½ teaspoons black mustard seeds
- ¾ teaspoon cumin seeds
- ½ handful of curry leaves
- 1 onion, sliced
- ½ tablespoon ginger, minced
- 1 tablespoon fresh coriander, finely chopped
- ½ cup butternut squash
- 1 cup split red lentils
- 1½ tablespoons natural yogurt
- 1 tablespoon lime juice
- 4 poppadoms, cooked

Directions:

1. Preheat the Air Fryer to 275°F/140°C.
2. Mix together the garlic, red chilis, olive oil, mustard seeds, cumin seeds, curry leaves, onions, ginger, fresh coriander butternut squash, red lentils, yogurt and lime juice in the Air Fryer Baking Pan.
3. Place the Air Fryer Baking Pan in the Air Fryer Basket and set the timer for 25 minutes.
4. Remove from the Air Fryer and serve with the poppadoms.

92 - Cauliflower Pesto Delight

Servings: 2
Preparation Time: 10 minutes
Cooking Time: 32 minutes

Ingredients:
- 2 tablespoons walnuts
- 1 sprig rosemary, stem removed
- 1 sprig fresh thyme, stem removed
- 1 teaspoon lemon juice
- 1 tablespoon olive oil
- salt and pepper, to taste
- 1 cup cannellini beans, cooked and mashed
- ½ teaspoon ground dried chili
- 1 cup cauliflower, cut in florets and blanched

Directions:
1. Preheat the Air Fryer to 275°F/140°C.
2. Place the walnuts in the Air Fryer Basket and set the timer for 2 minutes or until the walnuts are toasted.
3. Blend the walnuts, rosemary, thyme, lemon juice, olive oil, salt and pepper until it becomes a thin consistency. Add more olive oil if needed.
4. Mix the cannellini beans with the dried chili.
5. Spread the mashed beans in the Air Fryer Baking Pan and top with the cauliflower florets. Drizzle in the walnut dressing and top with the onion rings.
6. Place the Air Fryer Baking Pan in the Air Fryer Basket and set the timer for 30 minutes.
7. Serve up once timer goes off.

93 - Easy Kebabs

Servings: 4
Preparation Time: 10 minutes
Cooking Time: 13 minutes

Ingredients:
- ¼ cup yellow bell peppers, diced
- 1 zucchini, diced
- ½ cup cherry tomatoes
- 2 tablespoons lemon juice
- salt and pepper, to taste
- ½ cup halloumi cheese, diced

Directions:
1. Preheat the Air Fryer to 275°F/140°C.
2. Mix the vegetables with the lemon juice, salt and pepper.
3. Insert the vegetables and cheese in the skewers of the Air Fryer Double Layer Rack according to your desired order.
4. Place in the Air Fryer and set the timer for 13 minutes.
5. Serve up once timer goes off.

94 - Mango Kheer

Servings: 2
Preparation Time: 5 minutes
Cooking Time: 20 minutes

Ingredients:
- 2 cups coconut milk
- 2 cups milk
- 3 tablespoons white sugar
- ½ cup basmati rice
- ¼ cup mangoes, diced
- ½ teaspoon ground cardamom
- ¼ cup sliced almonds, toasted
- ¼ cup pistachios, chopped

Directions:
1. Preheat the Air Fryer to 275°F/140°C.
2. Mix together the coconut milk, milk, sugar and basmati rice in the Air Fryer Baking Pan.
3. Place the Air Fryer Baking Pan in the Air Fryer Basket and set the timer for 20 minutes.
4. Remove from the Air Fryer and stir in the mangoes, ground cardamom, almonds and pistachios.
5. Serve and enjoy!

95 - One Pot Bacon Pasta

Servings: 2
Preparation Time: 5 minutes
Cooking Time: 20 minutes

Ingredients:
- 2 egg yolks
- 2 tablespoons butter, melted
- 2 cups pasta, cooked
- 1 cup sour cream
- ½ cup bacon, chopped
- ½ cup cheese, grated

Directions:
1. Preheat the Air Fryer to 275°F/140°C.
2. Whisk the egg yolks with the butter and pour into the Air Fryer Baking Pan.
3. Stir in the pasta, sour cream and bacon.
4. Place the Air Fryer Baking Pan into the Air Fryer Basket and set the timer for 10 minutes.
5. Top with the grated cheese and set the timer for 10 more minutes.
6. Serve up once the timer goes off.

96 - King Prawns with Honey Roasted Sweet Potatoes

Servings: 4
Preparation Time: 10 minutes plus 1 hour marinating time
Cooking Time: 21 minutes

Ingredients:
- 8 king prawns, peeled and deveined
- 5 cloves garlic, minced
- 1 red chili, finely sliced
- 1 medium onion, chopped
- 2 tablespoons olive oil
- ¼ teaspoon cayenne powder
- 5 sweet potatoes, sliced
- 2 tablespoons fresh cilantro, chopped
- 1 tablespoon honey
- 8 stalks lemongrass

Directions:
1. Marinate the prawns with the minced garlic, chili, onions, olive oil and cayenne powder at least 1 hour
2. Preheat the Air Fryer to 350°F/180°C.
3. Season the sweet potatoes with the fresh cilantro and honey and place them in the Air Fryer Basket.
4. Set the timer for 15 minutes.
5. While the sweet potatoes are cooking, skewer the marinated prawns with the lemongrass stalks.
6. Place the Air Fryer Double Layer Rack into the Air Fryer Basket and arrange the prawns on the rack.
7. Increase the Air Fryer temperature to 400°F/200°C and set the timer for 6 minutes or until the prawns are cooked through. Serve and enjoy!

97 - Bacon wrapped stuffed Chicken

Servings: 4
Preparation Time: 15 minutes
Cooking Time: 15 minutes

Ingredients:
- 4 chicken breast fillets
- 4 slices sharp cheese slices
- ¼ cup cream cheese
- 12 rashers bacon

Directions:
1. Preheat the Air Fryer to 350°F/180°C.
2. Slice the chicken fillets almost all the way to the end but leave half an inch uncut.
3. Pound the breasts lightly until flattened and season with salt and pepper.
4. Place a slice of cheese and a dollop of cream cheese on each chicken.
5. Roll the chicken and wrap each chicken breast with 3 rashers of bacon.
6. Use a toothpick to secure the bacon and chicken in place.
7. Arrange them in the Air Fryer Basket and use the Air Fryer Double Layer Rack if needed.
8. Set the timer for 15 minutes or until the bacon is golden brown and the chicken is cooked through. Check chicken is properly cooked through and serve in a bowl/plate.

98 - Spicy Pork Cubes

Servings: 4
Preparation Time: 5 minutes plus 15 minutes marinating time
Cooking Time: 12 minutes

Ingredients:
- 1 pound lean pork loin, cubed
- 2 cloves garlic, minced
- 1 tablespoon fresh ginger root, grated
- 1 teaspoon chili flakes
- 1 tablespoon curry powder
- 1 tablespoon soy sauce
- 1 teaspoon fresh cilantro, finely chopped

Directions:
1. Preheat the Air Fryer to 400°F/200°C.
2. Marinate the pork with the garlic, ginger, chili flakes, curry powder and soy sauce for at least 15 minutes.
3. Remove the meat from the marinade and drip off any excess sauce.
4. Arrange the pork cubes in the Air Fryer and set the timer for 12 minutes or until the meat is cooked through. Shake the meat once halfway through cooking to help evenly cook the meat.
5. Remove from the fryer and top with the fresh cilantro.
6. Serve and enjoy.

99 - Garlicky Chicken Stuffed Bread Bowl

Servings: 2
Preparation Time: 10 minutes plus 1 hour marinating time
Cooking Time: 15 minutes

Ingredients:

- 2 chicken thigh fillets, cubed
- 2 tablespoons olive oil
- ½ teaspoon chili flakes
- 1 teaspoon paprika
- 1 teaspoon garlic salt
- pepper, to taste
- 1 cup yogurt
- 2 tablespoons garlic, minced
- 1 tablespoon fresh parsley, chopped
- 2 bread bowls
- 1 cup tomatoes, diced
- ¼ cup red onions, cut into rings

Directions:

1. Marinate the chicken with the olive oil, chili flakes, paprika, garlic salt and pepper for at least 1 hour.
2. Mix together the yogurt, minced garlic and parsley. Cover with a plastic wrap and set aside to chill.
3. Preheat the Air Fryer to 400°F/200°C.
4. Arrange the chicken cubes in the Air Fryer Basket and set the timer for 15 minutes or until the chicken is cooked through.
5. Cut the top of the bread bowls and remove the bread from the bowl leaving just the crusts.
6. Fill the bread bowls with the cooked chicken and top with the tomatoes and onions.
7. Serve up and drizzle over with the garlic yogurt sauce.

100 - Tuna and Sweet Potato Chips

Servings: 2
Preparation Time: 15 minutes plus 30 minutes soaking time
Cooking Time: 30 minutes

Ingredients:

- 4 large sweet potatoes, peeled and sliced
- salt and pepper, to taste
- 1 cup canned tuna, in water
- 2 tablespoons yogurt
- ¼ teaspoon cayenne pepper
- ¼ cup onions, chopped
- ¼ cup celery, chopped
- pepper, to taste

Directions:

1. Preheat the Air Fryer to 350°F/180°C.
2. Soak the sweet potatoes in water for 30 minutes. Drain and pat dry.
3. Season the sweet potatoes with salt and pepper and spray with some cooking spray.
4. Place the sweet potatoes in the Air Fryer Basket and set the timer for 30 minutes or until the sweet potatoes are fried and crispy.
5. Mix together the tuna, yogurt, cayenne powder, onions and celery and season with pepper.
6. Serve the tuna with the sweet potato chips.
7. Serve and enjoy!

101 - Cilantro & Feta Beef Meatballs

Servings: Makes 10 meatballs
Preparation time: 10 minutes
Cooking Time: 10 minutes

Ingredients:

- 1 pound ground beef
- 1 tablespoon garlic, minced
- ½ cup fresh cilantro, chopped
- 1 teaspoon paprika
- ¼ cup feta cheese, crumbled
- salt and pepper, to taste
- ½ cup breadcrumbs

Directions:

1. Preheat the Air Fryer to 400°F/200°C.
2. Mix together the ground beef, minced garlic, fresh cilantro, paprika and feta cheese.
3. Season with salt and pepper.
4. Add the breadcrumbs.
5. Divide the beef mixture into 10 balls and smoothen them wet palms.
6. Arrange the meatballs into the Air Fryer Basket and use the Air Fryer Double Layer Rack if needed.
7. Set the timer to 10 minutes or until the meatballs are cooked through.
8. Once cooked through, serve up!

102 - Garlic Peppered Mushroom Caps

Servings: 2
Preparation time: 10 minutes
Cooking Time: 10 minutes

Ingredients:
- 4 large shiitake mushrooms, stems removed
- salt and pepper, to taste
- 1 cup breadcrumbs
- 1 tablespoon garlic, minced
- 1 teaspoon garlic powder
- 1 teaspoon paprika
- 1 tablespoon fresh parsley, finely chopped

Directions:
1. Preheat the Air Fryer to 400°F/200°C.
2. Season the mushrooms with salt and pepper and spray with a little cooking spray.
3. Mix together the breadcrumbs, garlic, garlic powder, paprika and parsley.
4. Fill the mushrooms with the breadcrumbs mixture.
5. Arrange the mushrooms in the Air Fryer Basket and set the timer for 10 minutes.
6. Once timer goes off, serve up!

103 - Chicken and Mushroom Rolls

Servings: 4
Preparation time: 15 minutes
Cooking Time: 5 minutes

Ingredients:
- 2 cooked chicken breasts, shredded
- ½ cup button mushrooms, sliced
- 1 medium carrot, grated
- 1 celery stalk, finely chopped
- ½ teaspoon ginger, minced
- ½ teaspoon sugar
- 1 teaspoon taco seasoning
- 1 tablespoon chicken stock
- 1 egg
- 1 teaspoon cornstarch
- salt and pepper, to taste
- 8 spring roll wrappers

Directions:
1. Preheat the Air Fryer to 400°F/200°C.
2. Mix the shredded chicken with the sliced mushrooms, carrots and celery in a bowl.
3. Add the ginger, sugar, taco seasoning and chicken stock and stir well to combine.
4. In another bowl, whisk the egg with the cornstarch to make a thick paste and season with salt and pepper.
5. To assemble: Spoon some chicken filling on a spring roll wrapper. Roll and brush the ends with the egg paste to seal well. Repeat for the remaining spring roll wrappers.
6. Arrange the spring rolls in the Air Fryer Basket and spray with a little cooking spray.
7. Set the timer for 5 minutes or until the spring rolls become golden brown.
8. Once golden brown is achieved, serve and enjoy!

104 - Bacon & Ham Burger Patties

Servings: 4
Preparation Time: 10 minutes
Cooking Time: 8 minutes

Ingredients:
- 1 pound ground beef
- ¼ cup bacon, chopped
- ¼ cup deli ham, chopped
- 3 tablespoons breadcrumbs
- 1 teaspoon ground nutmeg
- 1 teaspoon Italian seasoning
- ¼ green onions, chopped
- salt and pepper, to taste

Directions:
1. Preheat the Air Fryer to 400°F/200°C.
2. Mix together the ground beef, chopped bacon and ham.
3. In another bowl, mix together the breadcrumbs, ground nutmeg, Italian seasoning, green onions, salt and pepper.
4. Add the meat mixture to the breadcrumbs mixture and knead well to combine.
5. Divide into 4 equal portions and flatten them slightly to form patties.
6. Place the patties into the Air Fryer Basket and use the Air Fryer Double Layer Rack if needed.
7. Set the timer to 8 minutes or until the meat is cooked through and browned.
8. Once properly cooked through, serve and enjoy!

105 - Curried Chicken Skewers

Serves: 2
Preparation time: 15 minutes plus 2 hours marinating time
Cooking Time: 6 minutes

Ingredients:
- 1 teaspoon curry powder
- 2 tablespoons garlic, minced
- 1 stalk green onion, chopped
- 1 tablespoon ginger, minced
- ¼ cup olive oil
- 2 chicken breast fillets, cut in cubes
- 2 teaspoons sesame seeds

Directions:
1. To make the curry marinade: Mix together the curry powder, minced garlic, green onion, ginger and olive oil.
2. Marinate the chicken cubes with the curry marinade and chill for 2 hours.
3. Preheat the Air Fryer to 350°F/180°C.
4. Skewer the chicken cubes with the skewers in the Air Fryer Double Rack.
5. Sprinkle over the sesame seeds and place the rack into the Air Fryer Basket.
6. Set the timer for 6 minutes or until the chicken is cooked through.
7. Serve up on a plate.

106 - Garlic Lemon Prawns Wrapped in Bacon

Servings: 2
Preparation time: 10 minutes plus 15 minutes chilling time
Cooking Time: 6 minutes

Ingredients:
- 1 tablespoon ghee, melted
- 1 teaspoon garlic, minced
- ¼ teaspoon lemon juice
- 1 tablespoon flat-leaf parsley leaves, chopped
- 6 large tiger prawns, peeled and deveined but leave on the tails
- 6 rashers bacon

Directions:
1. Preheat the Air Fryer to 350°F/180°C.
2. Mix together the melted ghee, minced garlic, lemon juice and chopped parsley.
3. Brush the ghee mixture on the prawns and season with some pepper.
4. Wrap the prawns with the slices of bacon and chill for 15 minutes.
5. Arrange the prawns in the Air Fryer Basket and use the Air Fryer Double Layer Rack if needed.
6. Set the timer for 6 minutes or until the prawns are cooked through.
7. Once cooked, serve and enjoy.

107 - Mushroom Head Pizza

Servings: 2
Preparation time: 10 minutes
Cooking Time: 6 minutes

Ingredients:
- 4 large portobello mushrooms, stems removed
- salt and pepper, to taste
- 1 teaspoon Italian seasoning
- 4 tomato slices
- 2 tablespoons canned tomatoes, crushed
- 1 cup mozzarella cheese, grated
- 8 slices pepperoni sausage

Directions:
1. Preheat the Air Fryer to 350°F/180°C.
2. Spray the mushroom caps with cooking spray.
3. Season the insides of the mushroom caps with salt, pepper and Italian seasoning.
4. Place the tomato slices, crushed tomatoes and mozzarella cheese in each cap and arrange in the Air Fryer Basket. Use the Air Fryer Double Layer Rack if needed.
5. Set the timer for 6 minutes or until the cheese is melted.
6. Remove from the Air Fryer and finish with topping the pepperoni slices.

108 - Lemon Garlic Cod Fillet

Servings: 4
Preparation time: 10 minutes plus 30 minutes marinating time
Cooking Time: 10 minutes

Ingredients:
- ¼ cup low sodium soy sauce
- 2 tablespoons lemon juice
- 5 cloves garlic, sliced
- ¼ teaspoon ground red pepper
- ¼ teaspoon ground ginger
- 4 cod fillets
- 8 lemon slices

Directions:
1. Place the soy sauce, lemon juice, garlic, ground red pepper and ground ginger in a large ziplock bag.
2. Place the cod fillets in the ziplock bag and marinate well with the seasonings. Chill for at least 30 minutes.
3. Preheat the Air Fryer to 350°F/180°C.
4. Drip off the excess seasoning from the fillets and arrange the fillets in the Air Fryer Basket. Use the Air Fryer Double Layer Rack if needed.
5. Top each fillet with lemon slices and set the timer for 8 minutes or until the fish is cooked through.
6. Once cooked through, serve up!

109 - Crispy Chicken Drumsticks

Servings: 2
Preparation time: 10 minutes
Cooking Time: 20 minutes

Ingredients:
- 1 cup breadcrumbs
- 1 teaspoon chili powder
- 1 clove garlic, minced
- 4 chicken drumsticks
- 2 tablespoons mustard

Directions:
1. Preheat the Air Fryer to 400°F/200°C.
2. Mix the breadcrumbs, chili powder and minced garlic and set aside.
3. Score the chicken and rub well with the mustard.
4. Coat the drumsticks with the breadcrumbs and spray with cooking spray.
5. Arrange the drumsticks in the Air Fryer Basket.
6. Set the timer to 10 minutes or until they turn golden brown.
7. Reduce the temperature to 300°F/150°C and set the timer for 10 more minutes.
8. After 10 minutes, serve and enjoy!

110 - Halibut and Sweet Potato Wedges

Servings: 2
Preparation Time: 15 minutes plus 30 minutes soaking time
Cooking Time: 12 minutes

Ingredients:
- 2 cups sweet potato, cut lengthwise into wedges
- 4 halibut fillets
- ½ tablespoon lemon juice
- salt and pepper, to taste
- 1 cup breadcrumbs
- 1 teaspoon paprika
- 1 egg

Directions:
1. Attach the Air Fryer Food Separator and preheat the Air Fryer to 350°F/180°C.
2. Soak the sweet potatoes in water for 30 minutes. Pat dry and spray with cooking spray.
3. While the sweet potatoes are soaking, season the halibut fillets with the lemon juice, salt and pepper and set aside for 5 minutes.
4. Mix the breadcrumbs with the paprika and set aside.
5. Whisk the egg in a bowl and season with salt and pepper.
6. Dip the halibut fillets in the seasoned egg and then coat evenly with the breadcrumbs.
7. Place the halibut fillets in one section of the Air Fryer Basket and sweet potato wedges in the other.
8. Set the timer to 12 minutes.
9. Serve and enjoy!

111 - Chicken and Turkey Meatballs

Servings: 2
Preparation time: 15 minutes plus 1 hour chilling time
Cooking Time: 10 minutes

Ingredients:
- 5 ounces ground turkey
- 5 ounces ground chicken
- ½ cup breadcrumbs
- ¼ cup feta cheese, crumbled
- 1 tablespoon fresh basil, finely chopped
- 1 teaspoon paprika
- 1 teaspoon onion powder
- salt and pepper, to taste

Directions:
1. Combine the ground turkey and ground chicken with the breadcrumbs.
2. Add the feta cheese, fresh basil, paprika and onion powder.
3. Season with salt and pepper.
4. Knead well and form the meatballs with wet palms.
5. Chill for 1 hour.
6. Preheat the Air Fryer to 450°F/230°C.
7. Place the meatballs in the Air Fryer Basket and set the timer for 10 minutes.
8. Once timer goes off, serve up your meatballs!

112 - Cheesy Bacon and Potato Gratin

Servings: 4
Preparation time: 20 minutes plus 30 minutes soaking time
Cooking Time: 20 minutes

Ingredients:

- 2 large potatoes, skins on and thinly sliced
- ½ cup cream
- 1 tablespoon garlic, minced
- ¼ cup onions, finely chopped
- salt and pepper, to taste
- ½ cup bacon bits
- ¼ cup cheddar cheese, grated

Directions:

1. Soak the potatoes in water for 30 minutes. Drain the potatoes and pat dry with kitchen paper.
2. Preheat the Air Fryer to 350°F/180°C.
3. Place the potatoes in the Air Fryer Basket and set the timer for 10 minutes or until the potatoes are crispy.
4. While the potatoes are cooking, mix together the cream, garlic and onions and season with salt and pepper.
5. Remove the potatoes from the Air Fryer and increase the temperature to 400°F/200°C.
6. To assemble: Line the four ramekins with some fried potatoes. Scoop a dollop of cream mixture into the ramekins and top with some bacon bits and cheddar cheese. Repeat the layers until the ramekins are filled.
7. Place the ramekins into the Air Fryer Basket and use the Air Fryer Double Layer Rack if needed.
8. Set the timer for 10 minutes.
9. After timer goes off, serve up!

113 - Allspice Turkey Burgers

Servings: 4
Preparation time: 10 minutes plus 30 minutes chilling time
Cooking Time: 15 minutes

Ingredients:
- 1 pound ground turkey
- 1 tablespoon Worcestershire sauce
- 1 teaspoon soy sauce
- ½ teaspoon garlic powder
- ½ teaspoon onion powder
- ½ teaspoon ground allspice
- 1 teaspoon paprika
- 2 tablespoons garlic, minced
- ¼ cup onions, minced

Directions:
1. Mix the ground turkey with the Worcestershire sauce, soy sauce, garlic powder, onion powder, ground allspice, paprika, minced garlic and onions.
2. Divide the mixture into 4 equal portions and flatten to form patties.
3. Chill the patties for 30 minutes.
4. Preheat the Air Fryer to 350°F/180°C.
5. Arrange the patties in the Air Fryer Basket and set the timer for 15 minutes or until the meat is cooked through.
6. Check meat is properly cooked through and proceed to serving up your meal.

114 - Roasted Herbed Tomatoes

Servings: 2
Preparation time: 10 minutes
Cooking Time: 20 minutes

Ingredients:
- 2 large tomatoes, halved
- ½ teaspoon dried parsley
- ½ teaspoon dried oregano
- ½ teaspoon dried basil
- ½ teaspoon dried thyme
- salt and pepper, to taste

Directions:
1. Preheat the Air Fryer to 300°F/150°C.
2. Spray the bottoms and the tops of the tomatoes lightly with cooking spray.
3. Mix together the dried parsley, dried oregano, dried basil and dried thyme and top over the tomatoes.
4. Season with salt and pepper.
5. Arrange the tomatoes in the Air Fryer Basket and set the timer for 20 minutes.
6. Once the timer sounds, it's ready to serve.

115 - Eggplant Parmigiana

Servings: 2
Preparation time: 10 minutes
Cooking Time: 10 minutes

Ingredients:
- 1 cup breadcrumbs
- ¼ cup parmesan cheese, grated
- 1 teaspoon paprika
- 1 teaspoon red pepper, freshly ground
- 2 eggs
- salt and pepper, to taste
- 2 medium eggplants, sliced into ½-inch thick slices diagonally

Directions:
1. Preheat the Air Fryer to 350°F/180°C.
2. Mix the breadcrumbs, parmesan cheese, paprika and fresh red pepper.
3. Whisk the eggs and season with salt and pepper.
4. Pat the eggplants to remove any excess water.
5. Coat the eggplants first with the egg mixture and then with the breadcrumbs.
6. Arrange the eggplants in the Air Fryer Basket and use the Air Fryer Double Layer Rack if needed.
7. Set the timer for 10 minutes and give the Air Fryer Basket a shake in between so that the eggplants will not stick to the racks.
8. Serve and enjoy!

116 - Cheesy Cream Stuffed Mushroom

Servings: 2
Preparation time: 10 minutes
Cooking Time: 15 minutes

Ingredients:

- 4 large Portobello mushrooms, stems removed (just mushroom head)
- 2 rashers bacon, chopped
- ½ onions, sliced
- ½ cup button mushrooms, sliced
- 3 cloves garlic, minced
- ½ cup cream
- 1 cup grated cheese
- pepper, to taste

Directions:

1. Preheat the Air Fryer to 350°F/180°C.
2. Place the bacon, onions, button mushrooms and garlic to the Air Fryer Baking Pan and place the Air Fryer Baking Pan in the Air Fryer Basket.
3. Set the timer for 6 minutes.
4. Add the cream and parmesan cheese and season with pepper.
5. Return to the Air Fryer and cook for another 2 minutes.
6. Remove the Air Fryer Baking Pan from the Air Fryer and allow to cool slightly.
7. Stuff as much cream mushroom mixture into the underside of the Portobello mushroom heads as possible (where the stems were removed) and then keep lathering the rest of the cream mushroom mixture all over the underside of the mushroom head (make sure the mixture doesn't fall off the mushroom!).
8. Arrange the mushrooms in the Air Fryer Basket. Mushroom heads should be resting on the bottom of the Air Fryer Basket to prevent cream mixture falling off.
9. Set the timer for 7 minutes.
10. After 7 minutes, serve up!

117 - Glass Noodle Spring Rolls

Servings: 4
Preparation time: 15 minutes
Cooking Time: 14 minutes

Ingredients:

- ½ cup vermicelli noodles, soaked in hot water
- ¼ cup onions, sliced
- 1 clove garlic, minced
- ¼ cup carrots, shredded
- ¼ cup zucchini, shredded
- 2 teaspoons sesame oil
- 2 teaspoons soy sauce
- 1 packet rice wrappers

Directions:

1. Preheat the Air Fryer to 350°F/180°C.
2. Drain the noodles and cut into shorter strands with a pair of scissors. Set aside.
3. Mix together the onions, garlic, carrots, zucchinis, sesame oil and soy sauce in the Air Fryer Baking Pan and place the Air Fryer Baking Pan in the Air Fryer Basket.
4. Set the timer to 6 minutes.
5. Mix in the noodles to the Air Fryer Baking Pan and set the timer for 8 more minutes.
6. Damp the rice paper on a chopping board and add a spoonful of filling.
7. Roll into a spring roll and repeat for the remaining rice wrappers.
8. Once they have been all rolled up, it's ready to eat!

118 - Crispy Cod with Mango Salsa

Servings: 4
Preparation time: 15 minutes
Cooking Time: 10 minutes

Ingredients:
- 1 egg
- salt and pepper, to taste
- ½ cup breadcrumbs
- 4 cod fillets

- ½ cup green mangoes, diced
- ¼ cup onions, sliced
- ¼ cup tomatoes, diced
- 2 tablespoons apple cider vinegar

Directions:
1. Preheat the Air Fryer to 350°F/180°C.
2. Whisk the egg with some salt and pepper and set aside.
3. Season the breadcrumbs with salt and pepper and set aside.
4. Dip the cod fillets in the egg and coat with the breadcrumbs.
5. Shake off excess breadcrumbs and spray the fillets with cooking spray.
6. Arrange the cod fillets in Air Fryer Basket and use the Air Fryer Double Layer Rack if needed.
7. Set the timer for 10 minutes or until the fish is cooked through and the breadcrumbs are golden.
8. To make the salsa: Mix together the mangoes, onions, tomatoes and apple cider vinegar.
9. Serve and top the salsa on the crispy cod fillets.

119 - Green Curry Tofu & Vegetables

Servings: 2
Preparation time: 5 minutes
Cooking Time: 12 minutes

Ingredients:
- ½ cup extra firm tofu, cubed
- 3 tablespoons soy sauce
- ¾ tablespoon fish sauce
- ½ teaspoon sesame oil
- ¼ cup button mushrooms, sliced
- 1 small carrot, shredded
- 2 stalks spring onions, chopped
- ½ cup shrimps, peeled and deveined
- 2 tablespoons Thai green curry paste
- 1 cup cabbage, shredded

Directions:
1. Preheat the Air Fryer to 350°F/180°C.
2. Marinate the tofu cubes with the soy sauce, fish sauce and sesame oil.
3. Place the tofu cubes in the Air Fryer and set the timer for 4 minutes. Shake the Air Fryer Basket halfway through to ensure the tofu cubes are evenly cooked and browned.
4. Remove the tofu cubes from the Air Fryer and allow to cool.
5. Pour in the remaining tofu marinade in the Air Fryer Baking Pan.
6. Add the mushrooms, carrots, spring onions, shrimps, curry paste and cabbage.
7. Place in the Air Fryer and set the timer for 8 minutes or until the vegetables are softened and shrimps are cooked through.
8. Remove from the Air Fryer and toss in the tofu cubes.

120 - White Wine Mussels

Servings: 2
Preparation time: 5 minutes
Cooking Time: 13 minutes

Ingredients:

- 1 pound mussels
- 1 cup white wine
- 1 tablespoon olive oil
- ¼ cup onions, sliced
- 2 teaspoons garlic, minced
- 1 teaspoon paprika
- 1 teaspoon garlic powder
- 1 tablespoon butter, melted
- salt and pepper, to taste
- 1 cup baby spinach leaves

Directions:

1. Preheat the Air Fryer to 350°F/180°C.
2. Place the mussels in the Air Fryer Baking Pan.
3. Mix in the white wine, olive oil, onions, garlic, paprika, garlic powder and butter.
4. Season with salt and pepper.
5. Place the Air Fryer Baking Pan in the Air Fryer Basket and set the timer for 8 minutes.
6. Remove from the Air Fryer and stir the mussels.
7. Return to the Air Fryer and set the timer for 5 more minutes.
8. Stir in the baby spinach leaves and serve on a plate.

121 - Baked Macaroni Cups

Servings: 4
Preparation time: 15 minutes
Cooking Time: 5 minutes

Ingredients:
- 2 cups macaroni, half cooked
- 1 tablespoon salted butter, melted
- 1 cup milk
- ¼ cup cream
- ½ cup cheddar cheese
- ½ cup mozzarella, grated
- 1 teaspoon dried basil
- salt and pepper, to taste

Directions:
1. Melt the butter in a non-stick frying pan on medium heat.
2. Add the flour and the milk and keep stirring to prevent lumps from forming.
3. Mix in the cheddar cheese and mozzarella cheese to make a smooth sauce.
4. Simmer for a few minutes and remove from the heat.
5. Allow to cool and season with the salt and pepper.
6. Add the cooked macaroni to the cheese sauce.
7. Preheat the Air Fryer to 350°F/180°C.
8. Divide the macaroni into 4 ramekins and place them inside the Air Fryer Basket. Use the Air Fryer Double Layer Rack if needed.
9. Set the timer for 5 minutes.
10. Mix in the fresh basil and serve up!

122 - Cheesy Baked Potatoes

Servings: 2
Preparation time: 5 minutes
Cooking Time: 8 minutes

Ingredients:
- 3 medium potatoes, diced
- 1 teaspoon paprika
- 1 teaspoon garlic powder
- ½ cup mozzarella, grated
- 2 tablespoons fresh parsley, chopped

Directions:
1. Preheat the Air Fryer to 350°F/180°C.
2. Place the diced potatoes in the Air Fryer Baking Pan and season with the paprika and garlic powder.
3. Spray with cooking spray and place the Air Fryer Baking Pan in the Air Fryer Basket.
4. Set the timer for 6 minutes or until the potatoes are cooked.
5. Top with the grated mozzarella cheese and add the parsley.
6. Return to the Air Fryer and set the timer for 2 more minutes.
7. Once timer sounds, serve up!

123 - Roasted Chicken with Tomato Salsa

Servings: 2
Preparation time: 10 minutes plus 30 minutes chilling time
Cooking Time: 22 minutes

Ingredients:
- 4 chicken thighs
- ¼ cup Dijon mustard
- 1 tablespoon onion powder
- 1 teaspoon garlic powder
- 2 tablespoons olive oil
- 1 cup tomatoes, diced
- ¼ cup onions, chopped
- 2 tablespoons fresh basil, chopped
- 1 teaspoon chili flakes
- 2 teaspoons apple cider vinegar

Directions:
1. Rub the chicken thighs with the Dijon mustard, onion powder, garlic powder and olive oil.
2. Chill the chicken in the fridge for 30 minutes.
3. Preheat the Air Fryer to 350°F/180°C.
4. Arrange the chicken in the Air Fryer Basket and use the Air Fryer Double Layer Rack if needed.
5. Set the timer for 12 minutes.
6. Rotate the chickens and bake for another 10 minutes for a crispier skin.
7. To make the tomato salsa: Mix the chopped tomatoes, onions, fresh basil, chili flakes and apple cider vinegar in a bowl.
8. Top the chicken thighs with the tomato salsa.

9. Serve on a plate.

---

124 - Easy Cheesy Pesto Lasagna

Servings: 2
Preparation time: 15 minutes
Cooking time 45 minutes

Ingredients:
- ½ cup mozzarella cheese, grated
- 1 cup parmesan cheese, grated
- 6 oz no-boil lasagna noodles
- ¼ cup pesto sauce, ready-made from the supermarket
- ½ cup onions, finely chopped
- 1 cup ricotta cheese, crumbled
- ½ cup tomato and basil pasta sauce, ready-made from the supermarket

Directions:
1. Preheat the Air Fryer to 325°F/170°C.
2. Grease the Air Fryer Baking Pan with cooking spray.
3. Mix together the mozzarella and parmesan cheese and set aside.
4. Line the base of the Air Fryer Baking Pan with the lasagna noodles and trim the noodles to fit the Air Fryer Baking Pan.
5. Spread a layer of the pesto sauce on the noodles.
6. Add some onions and ricotta cheese.
7. Add another layer of lasagna noodles.
8. Add some of the cheese mixture and tomato and basil sauce.
9. Repeat the layers of the lasagna and ending with the cheese mixture and tomato and basil sauce on the top.
10. Cover the Air Fryer Baking Pan with aluminum foil.
11. Place the Air Fryer Baking Pan in the Air Fryer and set the timer for 40 minutes.
12. Remove the foil and set the timer for 5 more minutes.
13. Serve on a plate.

---

125 - Broccoli and Sausage Mozzarella Melt

Servings: 2
Preparation time: 5 minutes
Cooking Time: 15 minutes

Ingredients:
- 1 cup portobello mushrooms, sliced
- 1 German sausage, diced
- 2 cup broccoli, cut into small florets
- ½ cup cream
- salt and pepper, to taste
- ½ cup mozzarella cheese

Directions:
1. Preheat the Air Fryer to 350°F/180°C.
2. Place the mushrooms and sausages in the Air Fryer Baking Pan.
3. Place the Air Fryer Baking Pan in the Air Fryer Basket and set the timer for 5 minutes.
4. Add the broccoli florets to the Air Fryer Baking Pan.
5. Pour in the cream and season with salt and pepper.
6. Top with the mozzarella cheese.
7. Set the timer for 10 minutes or until the cheese has melted.
8. Serve and enjoy!

126 - Salmon Horseradish and Asparagus

Servings: 2
Preparation time: 10 minutes
Cooking Time: 10 minutes

Ingredients:
- 6 asparagus stalks
- salt and pepper, to taste
- 2 salmon fillets
- 1 tablespoon lemon juice
- 4 lemon slices
- ¼ cup horseradish
- 2 tablespoons olives, sliced
- ¼ cup onions, sliced
- 2 tablespoons dill

Directions:
1. Preheat the Air Fryer to 350°F/180°C.
2. Season the asparagus with salt and pepper and place them in the Air Fryer Basket.
3. Attach the Air Fryer Grill Pan to the Air Fryer Basket and place the salmon fillets on the Air Fryer Grill Pan.
4. Season the salmon fillets with the salt, pepper and lemon juice.
5. Place the lemon slices on the salmon and set the timer for 10 minutes.
6. Remove the salmon and asparagus from the Air Fryer.
7. Top the salmon with the horseradish, olives and dill.
8. Serve and enjoy!

127 - Mexican Shrimps with Tofu

Servings: 2
Preparation time: 5 minutes
Cooking Time: 10 minutes

Ingredients:
- 2 cups firm tofu, cubed
- 1 teaspoon taco seasoning
- salt and pepper, to taste
- 1 cup shrimps, peeled and deveined
- 1 teaspoon garlic, minced

Directions:
1. Preheat the Air Fryer to 350°F/180°C.
2. Season the tofu with the taco seasoning, salt and pepper.
3. Place the Air Fryer Food Separator in the Air Fryer Basket and place the tofu cubes on one side.
4. Season the shrimps with the salt, pepper and garlic and place them on the other side of the Air Fryer Basket.
5. Set the timer for 10 minutes or until the prawns are cooked through.
6. Once properly cooked through, serve up!

128 - Spicy Chicken Coriander Curry

Servings: 2
Preparation time: 10 minutes
Cooking Time: 25 minutes

Ingredients:
- ½ teaspoon ginger garlic paste
- 2 teaspoons curry powder
- ¼ teaspoon coriander powder
- ½ cup fresh coriander, chopped
- 1 tablespoon lemon juice
- 4 chicken thighs, scored
- ½ cup coconut milk

Directions:
1. Preheat the Air Fryer to 400°F/200°C.
2. Mix the ginger garlic paste, curry powder, coriander powder, coriander and lemon juice.
3. Rub the paste on the chicken thighs and place them in the Air Fryer Baking Pan.
4. Pour in the coconut milk.
5. Place the Air Fryer Baking Pan in the Air Fryer Basket and set the timer for 15 minutes.
6. Flip over the chickens and set the timer for another 10 minutes.
7. Check that the chicken is cooked through and serve in a bowl.

129 - Baked Cauliflower and Bacon

Servings: 2
Preparation time: 10 minutes
Cooking Time: 15 minutes

Ingredients:
- 1 cup breadcrumbs
- ¼ cup parmesan cheese, grated
- ½ teaspoon paprika
- ¼ cup milk
- 1 tablespoon garlic, minced
- 2 cups cauliflower florets
- ¼ cup onions, sliced
- 5 rashers bacon, chopped

Directions:
1. Preheat the Air Fryer to 350°F/180°C.
2. Mix the breadcrumbs, parmesan cheese and paprika and set aside.
3. Whisk the milk with the minced garlic and set aside.
4. Place the cauliflower florets in the Air Fryer Baking Pan.
5. Add the onions and the garlic milk.
6. Top with the breadcrumbs and chopped bacon.
7. Place the Air Fryer Baking Pan in the Air Fryer Basket.
8. Set the timer for 15 minutes.
9. Serve up once timer goes off.

130 - Curried Chicken Cubes

Servings: 2
Preparation time: 5 minutes plus 4 hours marinating time
Cooking Time: 12 minutes

Ingredients:
- 2 chicken breast fillets, cut in cubes
- 1 teaspoon turmeric
- ¼ teaspoon masala powder
- 1 teaspoon chili powder
- 2 tablespoons garlic, minced
- 1 teaspoon apple cider vinegar
- salt and pepper, to taste

Directions:
1. Mix together the chicken cubes, turmeric powder, masala powder, chili powder, minced garlic, apple cider vinegar, salt and pepper.
2. Coat the chicken evenly and chill for 4 hours or overnight.
3. Preheat the Air Fryer to 350°F/180°C.
4. Place the chicken cubes into the Air Fryer Basket and set the timer for 8 minutes.
5. Remove the Air Fryer Basket, give it a shake and set the timer for 4 more minutes.
6. Once timer goes off, serve up.

131 - Chicken Alfredo

Servings: 2
Preparation time: 5 minutes
Cooking Time: 25 minutes

Ingredients:

- 8 rashers bacon, chopped
- 2 tablespoons garlic, minced
- ½ cup button mushrooms, sliced
- 2 chicken breasts, cubed
- 1 cup cream
- ½ cup parmesan cheese, grated
- 2 tablespoons fresh parsley, chopped
- salt and pepper, to taste

Directions:

1. Preheat the Air Fryer to 275°F/140°C.
2. Add the bacon and set the timer for 5 minutes or until the bacon is browned.
3. Add the minced garlic and mushrooms and set the timer for 5 minutes.
4. Add the chicken cubes, cream, parmesan cheese and fresh parsley.
5. Season with salt and pepper.
6. Return to the Air Fryer and set the timer for 15 more minutes.
7. Check chicken is properly cooked through and serve up.

132 - Pasta with Prawns and Mushrooms

Servings: 1
Preparation time: 5 minutes
Cooking Time: 15 minutes

Ingredients:

- 2 teaspoons olive oil
- ½ cup prawns, peeled and deveined
- ½ cup mushrooms, sliced
- 1 tablespoon garlic, minced
- 1 teaspoon chili flakes
- salt and pepper, to taste
- 3 oz spaghetti, cooked

Directions:

1. Preheat the Air Fryer to 350°F/180°C.
2. Place a teaspoon of olive oil, prawns and mushrooms in the Air Fryer Baking Pan.
3. Set the timer for 10 minutes.
4. Remove the Air Fryer Baking Pan from the Air Fryer and season with the minced garlic, chili flakes, salt, black pepper and the remaining teaspoon of olive oil.
5. Add the spaghetti and toss well to combine.
6. Return to the Air Fryer and set the timer for 5 more minutes.
7. After timer goes off it's ready to serve.

133 - Mac and Four Cheeses

Servings: 2
Preparation time: 5 minutes
Cooking Time: 20 minutes

Ingredients:
- ¼ cup butter
- ¼ cup onions
- 1 tablespoon garlic, minced
- ½ cup milk
- ½ cup cream
- 1 cup mozzarella cheese
- 1 cup cheddar cheese
- 1 cup cream cheese
- ½ cup parmesan cheese, grated
- 2 cups macaroni, cooked
- 2 tablespoons chives, chopped

Directions:
1. Preheat the Air Fryer to 325°F/170°C.
2. Place the butter, onions and garlic in the Air Fryer Baking Pan and set the timer for 5 minutes.
3. Add the milk, cream and cheeses and stir until smooth.
4. Add the macaroni and return the Air Fryer Baking Pan to the Air Fryer.
5. Set the timer for 15 minutes.
6. Remove from the Air Fryer and top with chives.
7. Serve and enjoy!

134 - Beef Meatballs

Servings: 4
Preparation time: 10 minutes plus 1 hour chilling time
Cooking Time: 15 minutes

Ingredients:
- 1 pound ground beef
- ½ cup onions, finely chopped
- ¼ cup carrots, finely chopped
- 2 tablespoons garlic, minced
- 1 teaspoon paprika
- 1 tablespoon soy sauce
- 2 tablespoons fresh parsley, chopped
- 2 tablespoons chives, chopped
- 1 egg
- ½ cup breadcrumbs

Directions:
1. In a large bowl, mix in the ground beef, onions, carrots and garlic.
2. Add in the paprika, soy sauce, parsley and chives.
3. Add the egg with the breadcrumbs and knead well to combine.
4. Form meatballs of your desired size and chill for an hour.
5. Preheat the Air Fryer to 350°F/180°C.
6. Arrange the meatballs in the Air Fryer Basket.
7. Set the timer for 15 minutes or until the meatballs are cooked through. Ready to serve!

135 - Bread Rolls with Potato Filling

Servings: 4
Preparation time: 20 minutes
Cooking Time: 17 minutes

Ingredients:
- 2 tablespoons onions
- ½ teaspoon ground turmeric
- 1 teaspoon curry powder
- 1 tablespoon chives, finely chopped
- 1 teaspoon chili flakes
- 5 potatoes, boiled and mashed
- salt, to taste
- 8 white bread slices, crusts removed

Directions:
1. Preheat the Air Fryer to 400°F/200°C.
2. Place the onions the Air Fryer Baking Pan and spray with some cooking spray.
3. Set the timer for 5 minutes or until the onions are translucent.
4. Add the ground turmeric, curry powder, chives and chili flakes.
5. Add the mashed potato and salt and mix well to combine.
6. Divide the potato filling into 8 equal portions.
7. Wet a slice of bread with water and press the bread to remove the excess water.
8. Roll the bread around a portion of the filling and seal the edges to encase the filling.
9. Repeat for the remaining bread and filling.
10. Arrange the bread rolls in the Air Fryer Basket and use the Air Fryer Double Layer Rack if needed.
11. Spray the bread rolls with cooking spray.
12. Set the timer for 12 minutes.
13. Once timer goes off, serve up!

136 - All Veggie Spring Rolls

Servings: 2
Preparation time: 15 minutes
Cooking times: 22 minutes

Ingredients:
- 1 tablespoon garlic, minced
- ¼ onions, sliced
- ¼ cup carrots, shredded
- 1½ cups cabbage, shredded
- ½ red bell pepper, seeds removed and sliced thinly
- 1 teaspoon soy sauce
- white pepper, to taste
- 10 sheets spring roll wrapper
- water, to seal the wrappers

Directions:
1. Preheat the Air Fryer to 350°F/180°C.
2. Place the minced garlic, onions, and carrots in the Air Fryer Baking Pan and set the timer for 5 minutes or until the onions are translucent.
3. Add the cabbage, red bell peppers, soy sauce and white pepper and set the timer for 5 more minutes or until the vegetables are softened. Set aside to cool.
4. Place a tablespoon of filling in a corner of a spring roll wrapper. Fold in the sides and roll tightly to encase the filling. Dab a little water at the edges to seal the spring roll.
5. Repeat for the remaining spring roll wrappers and filling.
6. Arrange the spring rolls in the Air Fryer Basket and use the Air Fryer Double Layer Rack if needed.
7. Spray the spring rolls with cooking spray and set the timer for 12 minutes or until they turn golden brown. Halfway through the cooking time, flip the spring rolls so that they can cook and brown evenly.
8. Once brown color is achieved, serve up!

137 - Spinach Macaroni and Cheese

Servings: 2
Preparation time: 5 minutes
Cooking Time: 15 minutes

Ingredients:

- 6 ounces elbow pasta, cooked
- ½ tablespoon unsalted butter, melted
- ¼ cup whole milk
- ¼ cup cream
- ¼ cup grated mozzarella cheese
- ¼ cup grated gruyere cheese
- ¼ cup grated cheddar cheese
- salt and pepper, to taste
- 1 cup baby spinach leaves

Directions:

1. Preheat the Air Fryer to 350°F/180°C.
2. Place the pasta in the Air Fryer Baking Pan or another casserole dish that can fit snugly in the Air Fryer Basket.
3. Add the butter, milk, cream, mozzarella cheese, gruyere cheese and cheddar cheese and season with salt and pepper.
4. Stir in the baby spinach leaves.
5. Place the Air Fryer Baking Pan in the Air Fryer Basket and set the timer for 15 minutes.
6. Once timer goes off, serve up.

138 - Zucchini Squash and Carrot Medley

Servings: 2
Preparation time: 5 minutes
Cooking Time: 25 minutes

Ingredients:
- ½ cup carrots, cubed
- ½ cup squash, cubed
- 1 large zucchini, cubed
- salt and pepper, to taste
- 2 cups broccoli, cut into small florets
- 1 tablespoon fresh cilantro, chopped

Directions:
1. Preheat the Air Fryer to 400°F/200°C.
2. Combine the carrots, squash and zucchinis in the Air Fryer Baking Pan and season with salt and pepper.
3. Place the Air Fryer Baking Pan in the Air Fryer Basket.
4. Set the timer for 5 minutes.
5. Mix in the broccoli florets, season with more salt and pepper if desired and set the timer for 20 more minutes. Toss the Air Fryer Baking Pan a few times during cooking so that the vegetables are evenly cooked and browned.
6. Serve and top with the fresh cilantro leaves.

139 - One Pan Broccoli, Bacon and Corn

Servings: 2
Preparation time: 10 minutes
Cooking Time: 40 minutes

Ingredients:
- 5 rashers bacon, chopped
- 1 cup corn kernels
- ¼ cup onions, sliced
- 1 teaspoon garlic, minced
- 1 cup broccoli florets
- ¾ cup whole milk
- ¼ cup cream
- 1 large egg
- salt and pepper, to taste
- ⅛ teaspoon cayenne pepper
- ½ cup pepper jack cheese, grated
- 1½ tablespoons parmesan cheese, grated

Directions:
1. Preheat the Air Fryer to 350°F/180°C.
2. Place the chopped bacon in the Air Fryer Baking Pan and place the Air Fryer Baking Pan in the Air Fryer Basket.
3. Set the timer for 5 minutes or until the bacon is crisp. Remove from the Air Fryer Baking Pan and set aside.
4. Add the corn, onions and broccoli florets to the bacon fat and set the timer for 5 minutes or until the vegetables have softened slightly.
5. While the vegetables are cooking, whisk together the milk, cream and egg and season with salt, pepper and cayenne pepper.
6. Stir in the pepper jack cheese and return the Air Fryer Baking Pan to the Air Fryer.
7. Set the timer for 20 minutes.
8. Top with parmesan cheese and set the timer for another 10 minutes.
9. Remove from the Air Fryer and allow to cool for at least 15 minutes before serving.
10. Serve and top with the bacon bits.

140 - Roasted Broccoli, Tomatoes and Olive Salad

Servings: 2
Preparation time: 5 minutes
Cooking Time: 10 minutes

Ingredients:

- 2 cups broccoli florets
- salt and pepper, to taste
- ¼ cup green olives, halved and pitted green olives
- 2 teaspoons grated lemon zest
- ¾ cup tomatoes, diced
- ¼ cup onions, sliced
- ⅓ cup parmesan cheese, grated
- 3 teaspoons balsamic vinegar
- ¼ cup olive oil

Directions:

1. Preheat the Air Fryer to 400°F/200°C.
2. Place the broccoli florets in the Air Fryer Baking Pan and season with salt and pepper.
3. Spray a little cooking spray and place the Air Fryer Baking Pan in the Air Fryer Basket.
4. Set the timer for 10 minutes and toss the broccolis halfway through cooking so that they can be evenly cooked and browned.
5. Remove the broccoli from the Air Fryer and pour into a serving bowl.
6. Toss in the olives, lemon zest, tomatoes, onions and parmesan cheese.
7. Mix together the balsamic vinegar and olive oil. Season with salt and pepper and drizzle over the salad.

141 - Twice Fried Potato Wedges

Servings: 2
Preparation time: 5 minutes
Cooking Time: 1 hour 10 minutes

Ingredients:

- 2 large potatoes, cut into wedges
- 2 rashers bacon, chopped
- ⅓ cups cheddar cheese
- 2 tablespoons cream
- 1 tablespoon unsalted butter
- 2 tablespoons chives, chopped
- salt and pepper, to taste

Directions:

1. Preheat the Air Fryer to 400°F/200°C.
2. Place the potato wedges in the Air Fryer Basket.
3. Set the timer for 30 minutes. Shake the Air Fryer Basket halfway through the cooking time.
4. Set the timer for another 30 minutes until the potatoes are fork-tender.
5. Remove the potatoes from the Air Fryer and allow to cool on a cooling rack for at least 20 minutes.
6. Reduce the temperature to 350°F/180°C.
7. Place the chopped bacon in the Air Fryer Baking Pan and set the timer for 5 minutes.
8. Whisk in the cheddar cheese, cream and butter and season with salt and pepper.
9. Set the timer for another 5 minutes or until the cheese has melted.
10. Serve and pour over the potatoes wedges as well as topping the wedges with chives.

142 - Spiced Ham and Pineapple Pie

Servings: 2
Preparation time: 10 minutes
Cooking Time: 1 hour

Note: You will need a Non-Stick Pie Pan that is small enough to fit inside the Air Fryer Basket.

Ingredients:
- 1 large potato, diced
- 9-inch pie dough
- ½ cup pineapple chunks
- 2 slices deli ham, chopped
- 2 eggs
- ¼ cup cream
- 2 tablespoons maple syrup
- 1 tablespoon sugar
- 1 tablespoon melted butter
- ½ teaspoon salt
- ½ teaspoon ground cinnamon

Directions:
1. Preheat the Air Fryer to 400°F/200°C.
2. Place the potatoes in the Air Fryer Basket and spray with some cooking spray.
3. Set the timer for 30 minutes or until the potatoes are tender.
4. Remove the potatoes from the Air Fryer and allow to cool for at least 20 minutes.
5. Grease the pie pan with cooking spray.
6. Roll out the pie dough until it is large enough to line the pie pan.
7. Crimp the edges of the dough to make a decorative edge.
8. Fill the pie pan with the potatoes, pineapple chunks and ham.
9. Whisk together the eggs, cream, maple syrup, sugar, butter, salt and ground cinnamon and pour into the pie pan.
10. Place the pie pan in the Air Fryer Basket and set the timer for 30 minutes.
11. Remove the pie pan from the Air Fryer and allow to cool completely.
12. Once cooled, serve up!

143 - Goat Cheese and Tapenade Ciabattas

Servings: 4
Prep Time: 10 minutes
Cook Time: 8 minutes

Ingredients:
- 1 cup green olives, without pits
- 1 tablespoon capers
- 1 clove garlic, minced
- 1 tablespoon freshly squeezed lemon juice
- 1 teaspoon sugar
- ¼ cup extra virgin olive oil
- 1 ciabatta bread, sliced
- 2-3 tablespoons softened butter
- 1½ cups goat cheese

Directions:
1. To make the tapenade: Pulse together the olives, capers, garlic, lemon juice, sugar and olive oil until the mixture becomes a paste.
2. Preheat the Air Fryer to 350°F/180°C.
3. Spread butter on one side of each ciabatta and arrange them in the Air Fryer Basket. Use the Air Fryer Double Layer Rack if needed.
4. Set the timer for 3 minutes.
5. Remove the ciabatta slices from the Air Fryer and on the unbuttered sides, spread some of the tapenade and top with the goat cheese.
6. Return the ciabattas to the Air Fryer and set the timer for 5 minutes or until the cheese melts.
7. Once cheese has melted, serve up!

144 - Beef and German Sausage Meatballs

Servings: 4
Preparation time: 5 minutes plus 30 minutes chilling time
Cooking Time: 15 minutes

Ingredients:
- 1 pound ground beef
- 2 German sausages, diced
- ½ cup onions, minced
- 1 teaspoon dried sage
- 3 tablespoons breadcrumbs
- 2 tablespoons red bell peppers, finely chopped
- 2 tablespoons chives, chopped
- salt and pepper, to taste

Directions:
1. Knead together the ground beef, sausages, onions, dried sage, breadcrumbs, bell peppers, chives, salt and pepper.
2. Form meatballs of your desired size and chill them for 30 minutes.
3. Preheat the Air Fryer to 350°F/180°C.
4. Arrange the meatballs in the Air Fryer Basket and use the Air Fryer Double Layer Rack if needed.
5. Set the timer for 15 minutes or until the meatballs are cooked through. Serve up!

145 - Spicy Mashed Potatoes

Servings: 2
Preparation time: 10 minutes
Cooking Time: 40 minutes

Ingredients:

- 3 large potatoes, peeled and diced
- 1 tablespoon garlic powder
- 2 tablespoons butter, melted
- ¼ cup cream
- 1 teaspoon paprika
- 1 tablespoon fresh parsley, chopped
- salt and pepper, to taste

Directions:

1. Preheat the Air Fryer to 400°F/200°C.
2. Place the potatoes in the Air Fryer Baking Pan and set the timer for 40 minutes or until the potatoes are fork-tender.
3. Mash the potatoes with a fork.
4. Mix together the garlic powder, butter, cream, paprika and fresh parsley and season with salt and pepper.
5. Pour into the mashed potatoes and whisk well until the potatoes are fluffy.
6. Serve and enjoy!

146 - Easy Fried Rice

Servings: 2
Preparation time: 5 minutes
Cooking Time: 8 minutes

Ingredients:
- ¼ cup onions, sliced
- 1 teaspoon garlic, minced
- 3 eggs
- salt and pepper, to taste
- 2 frankfurters, thinly sliced
- 3 slices deli ham, chopped
- 1 tablespoon oyster sauce
- 1½ cups cooked, day-old rice
- 2 tablespoons chicken stock

Directions:
1. Preheat the Air Fryer to 400°F/200°C.
2. Spray the Air Fryer Baking Pan with cooking spray.
3. Add the onions and garlic for 4 minutes or until the onions are translucent.
4. Whisk the eggs with the salt and pepper and pour into the Air Fryer Baking Pan.
5. Add the sliced frankfurters and ham.
6. Stir in the oyster sauce.
7. Mix in the rice.
8. Stir in the chicken stock until well combined.
9. Season with pepper.
10. Return the Air Fryer Baking Pan to the Air Fryer and set the timer for 4 minutes.
11. Remove from the Air Fryer and fluff the rice. Ready to serve.

147 - Mushroom Pockets

Servings: 2
Preparation time: 5 minutes
Cooking Time: 10 minutes

Ingredients:
- ½ cup button mushrooms, sliced
- ¼ cup onions, sliced
- ½ teaspoon garlic powder
- ½ teaspoon taco seasoning
- 2 pita breads, halved to make pockets
- ½ cup tomatoes, diced
- ½ cup mozzarella cheese, grated

Directions:
1. Preheat the Air Fryer to 300°F/150°C.
2. Spray the Air Fryer Baking Pan with cooking spray and add the mushrooms, onions, garlic powder and taco seasoning to the Air Fryer Baking Pan.
3. Set the timer for 5 minutes or until the onions are translucent.
4. Remove from the Air Fryer and allow to cool a little.
5. Fill each pita pocket with the mushroom filling and tomatoes and top with the grated mozzarella cheese.
6. Arrange the pita pockets in the Air Fryer Basket and set the timer for 5 minutes or until the pita pockets becomes lightly toasted and the cheese has melted.
7. Serve on a plate.

148 - Halibut Fillets with Lemon and Garlic Butter Sauce

Servings: 2
Preparation time: 5 minutes
Cooking Time: 10 minutes

Ingredients:
- 2 halibut fillets
- salt and pepper, to taste
- ¼ cup butter
- 2 teaspoons garlic, minced
- 2 teaspoons lemon juice
- 4 lemon slices
- 1 teaspoon olive oil
- 2 tablespoons fresh dill, chopped

Directions:
1. Preheat the Air Fryer to 350°F/180°C.
2. Season the halibut fillets with salt and pepper.
3. Add the butter, garlic and lemon juice in the Air Fryer Baking Pan and set the timer for 2 minutes or until the butter has melted.
4. Place the fish fillets in the Air Fryer Baking Pan and top with the lemon slices.
5. Drizzle over with the olive oil and top with the fresh dill.
6. Set the timer for 8 minutes. After it's cooked, ready to serve!

149 - Lemongrass Roast Chicken

Servings: 2
Preparation time: 10 minutes plus 4 hours marinating time
Cooking Time: 40 minutes

Ingredients:

- 6 chicken thighs
- salt and pepper, to taste
- 4 tablespoons soy sauce
- ¼ cup garlic, sliced
- 1 stalk of lemongrass, smashed
- 2 tablespoons butter
- ¼ cup spring onions, finely chopped

Directions:

1. Marinate the chicken thighs with the salt, pepper, soy sauce and garlic for at least 4 hours.
2. Preheat the Air Fryer to 400°F/200°C.
3. Place the chicken with the marinade sauce into the Air Fryer Baking Pan.
4. Top with the lemongrass and butter.
5. Set the timer for 40 minutes and brush the chicken every 10 minutes with the drippings in the Air Fryer Baking Pan.
6. Serve and top with the spring onions.

150 - Garlic-Herbed Pork Chops

Servings: 4
Preparation time: 10 minutes
Cooking Time: 17 minutes

Ingredients:

- 1 cup breadcrumbs
- ¼ cup fresh parsley, chopped
- 2 tablespoons chives, chopped
- 1 teaspoon dried rosemary
- 1 tablespoon garlic, minced
- ½ teaspoon garlic powder
- salt and pepper, to taste
- 2 eggs
- 4 butterfly pork chops

Directions:

1. Preheat the Air Fryer to 350°F/180°C.
2. Mix together the breadcrumbs, fresh parsley, chives, dried rosemary, minced garlic, garlic powder, salt and pepper and set aside.
3. Whisk the eggs with some salt and pepper.
4. Dip the pork chops in the egg mixture and coat evenly with the breadcrumbs.
5. Shake off any excess breadcrumbs and arrange the pork chops in the Air Fryer Basket. Use the Air Fryer Double Layer Rack if needed.
6. Set the timer for 12 minutes.
7. Flip the chops and set the timer for another 5 minutes or until the meat is cooked through.
8. Once cooked through, serve up!

151 - Classic Chicken and Asparagus

Servings: 2
Preparation time: 15 minutes
Cooking Time: 12 minutes

Ingredients:
- 2 chicken breast fillets, cut into strips
- 1 teaspoon garlic powder
- 1 teaspoon onion powder
- salt and pepper, to taste
- 2 tablespoons butter
- 1 tablespoon olive oil
- ½ cup onions, sliced
- 6 spears of asparagus, cut into small stalks
- ½ cup milk
- 1 cup chicken stock
- 1 tablespoon Dijon mustard
- 2 teaspoons cornstarch

Directions:
1. Preheat the Air Fryer to 325°F/170°C.
2. Season the chicken strips with the garlic powder, onion powder, salt and pepper.
3. Place the chicken strips in the Air Fryer Basket and spray with some cooking spray.
4. Set the timer for 12 minutes.
5. While the chicken is cooking, melt the butter and olive oil in a non-stick frying pan.
6. Add the onions and asparagus and sauté for 5 minutes or until the onions are translucent and the asparagus are softened.
7. Stir in the milk and chicken stock and bring to a boil.
8. Reduce the heat, stir in the Dijon mustard and let the sauce simmer for 2 minutes.
9. Mix the cornstarch with a little of the sauce until it forms a paste and add slowly to the sauce.
10. Continue stirring while simmering until the sauce thickens.
11. Remove the chicken from the Air Fryer and serve up while topping over with the sauce.

152 - Crispy Pork Belly

Servings: 2
Preparation time: 10 minutes
Cooking Time: 55 minutes

Ingredients:

- ½ pound whole pork belly, with skin
- 2 teaspoons garlic powder
- 2 teaspoons onion powder
- 1 teaspoon paprika
- ¼ cup fresh rosemary, chopped
- 3 garlic cloves, smashed
- ¼ cup onions, sliced

Directions:

1. Preheat the Air Fryer to 400°F/200°C.
2. Remove excess water from the pork belly with paper towels.
3. Mix together the garlic powder, onion powder, paprika and fresh rosemary and rub the mixture evenly on the pork belly.
4. Line with pork belly with the garlic and onion slices.
5. Roll the belly into a log and secure it with kitchen yarn.
6. Place the log in the Air Fryer and set the timer for 30 minutes.
7. Flip over the log and set the timer for 25 minutes more or until the skin is crispy.
8. Once crispy, serve and enjoy!

153 - Air Fryer Fish Stew

Servings: 2
Preparation time: 5 minutes plus 30 minutes marinating time
Cooking Time: 15 minutes

Instructions:

- 2 cod fillets, cut into small cubes
- 1 tablespoon sesame oil
- 1 tablespoon soy sauce
- pepper, to taste
- 1 tablespoon fish sauce
- 2 tablespoons garlic, sliced
- ¼ cup onions, sliced
- 2 tablespoons ginger slices
- ¼ cup carrots, sliced
- 2 tomatoes, cut into small wedges
- 3 cups fish stock
- 2 heads bok choy

Directions:

1. Marinate the fish cubes with the sesame oil, soy sauce, pepper and fish sauce. Set aside for 30 minutes.
2. Preheat the Air Fryer to 350°F/180°C.
3. Place the fish cubes in the Air Fryer Basket and spray lightly with cooking spray.
4. Set the timer for 7 minutes.
5. Remove the Air Fryer Basket and increase the temperature to 400°F/200°C.
6. Flip over the fish fillets and set the timer for 5 more minutes.
7. While the fish is cooking, pour the remaining marinade into a saucepan.
8. Add the garlic, onions, ginger, carrots, tomatoes, stock and bring to a boil.
9. Reduce the heat and add the fish cubes to the stew.
10. Simmer for 2 minutes and add the bok choy.
11. Serve up in a bowl.

154 - Spicy Chicken & Fried Potatoes

Servings: 2
Preparation time: 5 minutes
Cooking Time: 15 minutes

Ingredients:

- 2 tablespoons Dijon mustard
- 1 teaspoon chili flakes
- 1 teaspoon cayenne pepper
- 2 tablespoons olive oil
- 3 large potatoes, diced and soaked in water for 10 minutes
- 1 large chicken breast, cut into strips

Directions:

1. Preheat the Air Fryer to 350°F/180°C.
2. Mix together the Dijon mustard, chili flakes, cayenne pepper, and olive oil.
3. Drain and pat the potatoes dry with paper towels.
4. Coat the chicken strips and potatoes with the marinade.
5. Place the chicken and potatoes into the Air Fryer Basket and set the timer for 15 minutes.
6. Check the chicken is properly cooked through and serve up!

155 - Roast Chicken in Tomato Cream Sauce

Servings: 2
Preparation Time: 5 minutes
Cooking Time: 27 minutes

Ingredients:

- 4 chicken thighs
- salt and pepper, to taste
- 3 tablespoons all-purpose flour
- 2 tablespoons olive oil
- 2 tablespoons garlic, sliced
- ¼ cup onions, sliced
- ½ cup sliced button mushrooms
- ½ cup tomato sauce
- ¼ cup cream
- 2 tablespoons fresh basil, chopped

Directions:

1. Preheat the Air Fryer to 350°F/180°C.
2. Season the chicken thighs with salt and pepper.
3. Dust the chicken lightly with flour and arrange them skin side up in the Air Fryer Basket.
4. Set the timer for 10 minutes.
5. Increase the temperature to 400°F/200°C and set the timer for another 5 minutes.
6. While the chicken thighs are cooking, make the tomato cream sauce.
7. Heat the olive oil in a non-stick frying pan and sauté the garlic, onions and mushrooms until they are soft.
8. Transfer the chicken thighs to the pan and add the tomato sauce and cream.
9. Simmer for 2 minutes.
10. Coat the chicken with the sauce and braise for 10 minutes.
11. Serve and top with the fresh basil.

156 - Chicken Schnitzel

Servings: 2
Preparation time: 10 minutes
Cooking Time: 12 minutes

Ingredients:
- 3 tablespoons breadcrumbs
- 1 teaspoon paprika
- 1 teaspoon garlic powder
- 1 egg
- salt and pepper, to taste
- 2 chicken breast fillets, pounded

Directions:
1. Preheat the Air Fryer to 350°F/180°C.
2. Mix together the breadcrumbs, paprika and garlic powder and set aside.
3. Whisk the egg with the salt and pepper and set aside.
4. Dip the chicken slices into the egg mixture and coat evenly with the breadcrumbs.
5. Shake off any excess breadcrumbs and place them in the Air Fryer Basket. Use the Air Fryer Double Layer Rack if needed.
6. Spray the chicken schnitzels with some cooking spray.
7. Set the timer for 12 minutes or until the breadcrumbs become golden brown. Ready to serve!

157 - Cod Fillet with Melted Mozzarella

Servings: 2
Preparation time: 5 minutes
Cooking Time: 20 minutes

Ingredients:
- 2 cod fillets
- salt and pepper, to taste
- ¼ cup tomato sauce
- ¼ cup tomatoes, diced
- ½ cup mozzarella cheese, grated
- 2 tablespoons fresh parsley, chopped

Directions:
1. Attach the Air Fryer Grill Pan and preheat the Air Fryer to 350°F/180°C.
2. Season the cod fillets with salt and pepper and place them on the Air Fryer Grill Pan.
3. Set the timer for 15 minutes.
4. Spoon some tomato sauce on the cod fillet and top with diced tomatoes and mozzarella cheese.
5. Set the timer for another 5 minutes.
6. Serve and top with the fresh parsley.

158 - Mushroom and Ham Stuffed Peppers

Servings: 4
Preparation time: 5 minutes
Cooking Time: 25 minutes

Ingredients:
- 1 teaspoon olive oil
- 1 clove garlic, crushed
- ¼ cup onions, diced
- ½ cup mushrooms, sliced
- 1 teaspoon paprika
- 1 teaspoon ground allspice
- salt and pepper, to taste
- 4 medium bell peppers
- 8 slices of deli ham

Directions:
1. Preheat the Air Fryer to 350°F/180°C.
2. Place the olive oil, garlic, onions and mushrooms in the Air Fryer Baking Pan and place the Air Fryer Baking Pan in the Air Fryer Basket.
3. Set the timer for 5 minutes or until the onions are translucent.
4. Remove from the Air Fryer and season with paprika, ground allspice, salt and pepper and set aside.
5. Cut off the tops of the bell peppers and remove the seeds.
6. Line the bell pepper cups with the ham slices.
7. Fill the bell peppers with the mushrooms and arrange the peppers in the Air Fryer Basket.
8. Set the timer for 20 minutes.
9. Serve once timer goes off!

159 - Mini Baguette Pizzas

Servings: 2
Preparation time: 10 minutes
Cooking Time: 5 minutes

Ingredients:
- 2 mini baguettes, halved lengthwise
- ¼ cup tomato sauce
- ½ cup mozzarella cheese, grated
- 20 slices mini salamis

Directions:
1. Preheat the Air Fryer to 350°F/180°C.
2. Spread some tomato sauce on the baguettes and top with the mozzarella cheese.
3. Arrange the salami slices on the mozzarella cheese and place the baguettes in the Air Fryer Basket.
4. Set the timer for 5 minutes or until the cheese has melted.
5. Once cheese is melted, serve and enjoy!

160 - Bacon, Spinach and Artichoke stuffed Mushrooms

Servings: 2
Preparation time: 5 minutes
Cooking Time: 16 minutes

Ingredients:
- 4 bacon slices, chopped
- ½ cup onions, chopped
- 1 tablespoon garlic, minced
- ½ cup artichokes, chopped
- ¼ cup bell peppers, chopped
- 1 cup baby spinach leaves
- 4 large portobello mushrooms, stems removed
- ¼ cup feta cheese

Directions:
1. Preheat the Air Fryer to 350°F/180°C.
2. Fry the bacon in a non-stick frying pan.
3. Add the onions, garlic, artichokes and bell peppers and cook for 4 minutes.
4. Add the spinach and cook for 2 more minutes.
5. Stuff the mushroom heads with the vegetable and bacon filling and top with some feta cheese.
6. Place the mushroom heads in the Air Fryer and set the timer for 10 minutes.
7. Serve up after the timer strikes!

161 - Jacket Potatoes

Servings: 2
Preparation time: 10 minutes
Cooking Time: 21 minutes

Ingredients:
- 4 medium potatoes
- 4 rashers bacon, chopped
- ½ cup onions, finely diced
- ½ cup mozzarella cheese
- 2 tablespoons chives, chopped

Directions:
1. Preheat the Air Fryer to 350°F/180°C.
2. Score each potato with an 'X' at its top.
3. Spray the potatoes with cooking spray and arrange them in the Air Fryer Basket.
4. Set the timer for 15 minutes.
5. Press the bottom of the potatoes which will open up the top of the potatoes where the incisions were.
6. While the potatoes are cooking, fry the bacon and onions in a non-stick frying pan.
7. Top the potatoes with the mozzarella cheese and then with the onion and bacon mixture.
8. Return to the Air Fryer and set the timer for 6 minutes or until the cheese has melted.
9. Serve and top with the chives.

162 - Veggie Stuffed Butternut Squash

Servings: 2
Preparation time: 15 minutes
Cooking Time: 30 minutes

Ingredients:
- ½ medium butternut squash
- ¼ cup onions, chopped
- ¼ cup carrots, grated
- 2 cloves garlic, minced
- ½ cup snow peas
- 2 teaspoons Italian seasoning
- 1 egg
- salt and pepper, to taste

Directions:
1. Preheat the Air Fryer to 350°F/180°C.
2. Scrape and remove the core and seeds out of the butternut squash.
3. Mix the onions, carrots, garlic, snow peas and Italian seasoning,
4. Whisk the egg with the salt and pepper.
5. Add the egg into the vegetable mixture and stir well to combine.
6. Pour into the squash and place the squash carefully into the Air Fryer Basket.
7. Set the timer for 30 minutes.
8. Once timer goes off, serve up.

163 - Tomato and Cream Crispy Prawns

Servings: 2
Preparation time: 10 minutes
Cooking Time: 10 minutes

Ingredients:
- 1 tablespoon butter
- 3 cloves garlic, minced
- ½ cup tomato sauce
- ¼ cup cream
- salt and pepper, to taste
- 20 prawns, peeled and deveined
- 1 teaspoon lemon juice

Directions:
1. Heat the butter in a non-stick frying pan and add the minced garlic.
2. Add the tomato sauce and cream to the pan and season with the salt and pepper.
3. Bring to a slow simmer and remove from the heat. Set aside.
4. Line the base of the Air Fryer with aluminum foil and preheat the Air Fryer to 180°F/350°C.
5. Spray some cooking spray on the prawns and season with salt and pepper.
6. Drizzle over the lemon juice on the prawns and arrange them in the Air Fryer Basket.
7. Set the timer for 5 minutes or until the prawns are crispy.
8. Pour the tomato cream sauce over the prawns and set the timer for 2 more minutes.
9. After timer goes off, serve up.

164 - Stuffed Tomatoes

Servings: 4
Preparation time: 10 minutes
Cooking Time: 8 minutes

Ingredients:

- 4 large tomatoes
- 12 slices of salami
- ½ cup mozzarella cheese, grated
- 2 cloves garlic, minced
- ¼ cup onions, chopped
- 2 teaspoons Italian seasoning
- salt and pepper, to taste
- 2 tablespoons fresh basil, chopped

Directions:

1. Preheat the Air Fryer to 350°F/180°C.
2. Cut the tops off the tomatoes. Remove the tomato flesh and juice and set aside.
3. Line tomato cups with the salami slices.
4. Mix together the mozzarella cheese, minced garlic, chopped onions, Italian seasoning, salt and pepper.
5. Fill the tomatoes with the cheese mixture and top with the chopped basil.
6. Place the tomatoes in the Air Fryer Basket and set the timer for 8 minutes.
7. After timer goes off, serve up!

165 - Roasted Cheesy Pesto Chicken

Servings: 2
Preparation Time: 10 minutes
Cooking Time: 25 minutes

Ingredients:

- 4 chicken thighs
- salt and pepper, to taste
- 2 tablespoons olive oil
- 2 tablespoons garlic, sliced
- ¼ cup onions, sliced
- ½ cup button mushrooms, sliced
- ½ cup pesto sauce
- 2 tablespoon olives, pits removed
- 2 tablespoons fresh basil, finely chopped
- 1 tablespoon parmesan cheese, grated

Directions:

1. Preheat the Air Fryer to 350°F/180°C.
2. Season the chicken thighs with salt and pepper.
3. Arrange the chicken thighs skin side up in the Air Fryer Basket and use the Air Fryer Double Layer Rack if needed.
4. Set the timer for 10 minutes.
5. Increase the temperature to 400°F/200°C and set the timer for 5 more minutes.
6. While the chicken is cooking, heat the olive oil in a non-stick deep frying pan and sauté the garlic, onions and mushrooms until they are soft.
7. Remove the chicken thighs from the Air Fryer and transfer them to the frying pan.
8. Add the pesto sauce and olives and simmer for 10 minutes.
9. Serve and top with the fresh basil and parmesan cheese.

166 - Honey Lemon Chicken

Servings: 2
Preparation Time: 15 minutes
Cooking Time: 30 minutes

Ingredients:
- 6 small chicken thighs
- salt and pepper, to taste
- ½ cup honey
- 2 tablespoons olive oil
- 2 tablespoons lemon juice
- 1 teaspoon garlic powder
- 1 tablespoon sesame seeds
- 2 tablespoons spring onions, chopped

Directions:
1. Preheat the Air Fryer to 350°F/180°C.
2. Season the chicken with salt and pepper.
3. marinate the chicken with the honey, olive oil, lemon juice, garlic powder and sesame seeds for 10 minutes.
4. Place the chicken and the marinade in the Air Fryer Baking Pan and place the Air Fryer Baking Pan in the Air Fryer Basket.
5. Set the timer for 15 minutes.
6. Flip the chicken over and set the timer for 15 more minutes.
7. Serve and top with the spring onions.

167 - Steam Garlic Soy Mahi Mahi

Servings: 2
Preparation Time: 15 minutes
Cooking Time: 30 minutes

Ingredients:
- 2 mahi mahi fillets
- salt and pepper, to taste
- ½ cup soy sauce
- 2 tablespoons olive oil
- 2 tablespoons garlic, minced
- 2 tablespoons spring onions, chopped

Directions:
1. Preheat the Air Fryer at 350°F/180°C.
2. Season the fish with salt and pepper.
3. Marinate the fish with the soy sauce, olive oil and garlic for 10 minutes.
4. Place the fish with the marinade in the Air Fryer Baking Pan.
5. Place the Air Fryer Baking Pan in the Air Fryer Basket.
6. Set the timer for 15 minutes.
7. Serve and top with spring onions.

168 - Teriyaki Beef Strips

Servings: 2
Preparation Time: 15 minutes
Cooking Time: 18 minutes

Ingredients:
- ¾ pound beef loin, cut into strips
- salt and pepper, to taste
- ½ cup teriyaki sauce
- 2 tablespoons olive oil
- 2 tablespoons garlic, minced
- 1 teaspoon sesame seeds
- 2 cups bean sprouts
- 2 tablespoons spring onions, chopped

Directions:
1. Preheat the Air Fryer to 350°F/180°C.
2. Season the beef strips with salt and pepper.
3. Marinate the beef strips with the teriyaki sauce, olive oil, garlic and sesame seeds for 10 minutes.
4. Place the beef and marinade in the Air Fryer Baking Pan and place the Air Fryer Baking Pan in the Air Fryer Basket.
5. Set the timer for 15 minutes.
6. Add the bean sprouts to the Air Fryer Baking Pan and set the timer for 3 more minutes.
7. Serve and top with the spring onions.

169 - BBQ Short Ribs

Servings: 2
Preparation Time: 5 minutes
Cooking Time: 25 minutes

Ingredients:
- ¾ pound short ribs
- salt and pepper, to taste
- ½ cup ketchup
- 2 tablespoons garlic, minced
- 2 tablespoons olive oil
- 1 teaspoon soy sauce
- 2 tablespoons honey
- 2 tablespoons chives, chopped

Directions:
1. Preheat the Air Fryer to 350°F/180°C and line the base of the Air Fryer Basket with aluminum foil.
2. Season the short ribs with salt and pepper.
3. Marinate the ribs with the ketchup, minced garlic, olive oil, soy sauce and honey.
4. Place the ribs on the foil and set the timer for 15 minutes.
5. Flip the ribs over and set the timer for another 10 minutes.
6. Serve and top with chives.

170 - Steamed Salmon with Ginger Soy

Servings: 2
Preparation Time: 5 minutes
Cooking Time: 25 minutes

Ingredients:
- 2 salmon fillets
- salt and pepper, to taste
- 2 tablespoons garlic, minced
- 4 tablespoons ginger, minced
- 4 tablespoons olive oil
- 1 teaspoon soy sauce
- 2 tablespoons fresh dill, chopped

Directions:
1. Preheat the Air Fryer to 350°F/180°C.
2. Season the salmon filets with salt and pepper.
3. Marinate the salmon with the minced garlic, minced ginger, olive oil and soy sauce and place them in the Air Fryer Baking Pan.
4. Place the Air Fryer Baking Pan in the Air Fryer Basket and set the timer for 25 minutes.
5. Serve and top with the dill.

171 - Rum Mushroom and Potato

Servings: 4
Preparation Time: 5 minutes
Cooking Time: 25 minutes

Ingredients:
- 2 cups button mushrooms
- 2 medium potatoes, diced
- ¼ cup onions, sliced
- 1 tablespoon garlic, minced
- 1 tablespoon olive oil
- ¼ cup rum
- 1 teaspoon paprika
- 1 teaspoon garlic powder
- salt and pepper, to taste

Directions:
1. Preheat the Air Fryer to 300°F/150°C.
2. Place the mushrooms, potatoes, onions and garlic in the Air Fryer Baking Pan.
3. Stir together the olive oil, rum, paprika, garlic powder, salt and pepper and pour over the vegetables. Mix well.
4. Set the timer for 25 minutes.
5. Serve up once the timer strikes!

172 - Braised Chicken Tequila

Servings: 2
Preparation Time: 5 minutes
Cooking Time: 35 minutes

Ingredients:
- 2 chicken breasts, sliced
- 1 teaspoon olive oil
- ½ tablespoon garlic, minced
- ¼ cup onions, sliced
- 1 teaspoon garlic powder
- 1 teaspoon paprika
- salt and pepper, to taste
- ¼ cup tequila
- 1 small potato, diced
- 1 small carrot, diced
- ¼ cup fresh flat-leaf parsley, chopped

Directions:
1. Preheat the Air Fryer to 350°F/180°C.
2. Place the chicken slices, olive oil, garlic and onions in the Air Fryer Baking Pan.
3. Season with the garlic powder, paprika salt and pepper.
4. Place the Air Fryer Baking Pan in the Air Fryer Basket and set the timer to 15 minutes.
5. Remove the Air Fryer Baking Pan from the Air Fryer and lower the temperature to 300°F/150°C.
6. Add the tequila, potatoes, carrots and parsley to the Air Fryer Baking Pan and stir to mix well.
7. Return to the Air Fryer and set the timer for 20 more minutes.
8. Once timer goes off, serve up.

---

173 - Drunken' Lamb Chops

Servings: 2
Preparation Time: 5 minutes plus 5 hour marinating time
Cooking Time: 25 minutes

Ingredients:
- 6 small lamb chops
- ¼ cup whiskey
- 2 tablespoons garlic, sliced
- 1 teaspoon garlic powder
- 1 tablespoon olive oil
- 1 teaspoon paprika
- ¼ cup fresh rosemary, chopped

Directions:
1. Marinate the lamb chops with the whisky, garlic, garlic powder, olive oil, paprika and fresh rosemary in a large ziplock bag for at least 5 hours in the fridge.
2. Preheat the Air Fryer to 350°F/180°C.
3. Place the lamb chops on the Air Fryer Basket and use the Air Fryer Double Layer Rack if needed.
4. Set the timer for 25 minutes.

5. Check to see if it's properly cooked through and serve up!

---

174 - Spinach and Artichokes Oh! My!

Servings: 2
Preparation Time: 10 minutes
Cooking Time: 25 minutes

Ingredients:
- 1 cup baby spinach leaves
- 1 cup artichokes, chopped
- 1 tablespoon garlic, minced
- 1 teaspoon olive oil
- 1 teaspoon garlic powder
- 1 teaspoon paprika
- ½ cup cream
- salt and pepper, to taste
- ¼ cup feta cheese, crumbled

Directions:
1. Preheat the Air Fryer to 300°F/150°C.
2. Place the baby spinach leaves, artichokes, minced garlic, olive oil, garlic powder and paprika in the Air Fryer Baking Pan.
3. Mix well and place the Air Fryer Baking Pan in the Air Fryer Basket.
4. Set the timer for 20 minutes.
5. Pour in the cream and season with salt and pepper.
6. Set the timer for another 5 minutes.
7. Serve and top with the crumbled feta cheese.

---

175 - Snow Peas and Shrimps

Servings: 4
Preparation Time: 10 minutes
Cooking Time: 15 minutes

Ingredients:
- 1 cup shrimps, peeled and deveined
- salt and pepper, to taste
- 2 cups snow peas
- 1 teaspoon paprika
- 2 tablespoons garlic, minced
- 1 teaspoon garlic powder
- 1 teaspoon olive oil
- 2 tablespoons oyster sauce
- ¼ cup almond flakes

Directions:
1. Place the Air Fryer Food Separator in the Air Fryer Basket and preheat the Air Fryer to 300°F/150°C.
2. Season the shrimps with salt and pepper and place at one section of the Air Fryer Basket.
3. Mix together the snow peas, paprika, garlic, garlic powder, olive oil and oyster sauce and place on the other section of the Air Fryer Basket.

4. Set the timer for 15 minutes.
5. Place the peas in a serving bowl and top with the shrimps and almond flakes.

---

176 - Shrimps with Bacon Mornay

Servings: 2
Preparation Time: 15 minutes
Cooking Time: 15 minutes

Ingredients:
- ½ cup cream
- ½ cup pepper jack cheese, grated
- ½ tablespoon garlic, minced
- 2 tablespoons butter
- 10 large shrimps
- ¼ cup bacon bits

Directions:
1. In a saucepan over medium-high heat, heat together the cream, pepper jack cheese and garlic. When the cheese has melted, stir in the butter. Set aside.
2. Prepare the shrimps: Cut the shrimps from below its head to the tail but do not cut all the way through. You want to just open it up a bit to stuff it with the cheese sauce. Season with salt and pepper and set aside.
3. Line the Air Fryer Basket of the Air Fryer with foil and preheat the Air Fryer to 400°F/200°C.
4. To assemble: Dollop some cheese sauce into the opening of the shrimps and arrange them in the Air Fryer Basket. Use the Air Fryer Double Layer Rack if needed.
5. Top with bacon and set the timer for 10 minutes.
6. After timer sounds, serve up.

---

177 - Seafood Potato Chowder

Servings: 2
Preparation Time: 5 minutes
Cooking Time: 28 minutes

Ingredients:

- ¼ cup baby squid rings
- ¼ cup shrimps, peeled and deveined
- 1 cod fillet, cut into small cubes
- salt and pepper, to taste
- 1 teaspoon garlic powder
- 2 tablespoons butter
- ½ cup onions, chopped
- 1 tablespoon garlic, minced
- 2 cups potatoes, finely diced
- 2 tablespoons fresh rosemary, chopped
- 2 cups chicken stock
- ½ cup cream

Directions:

1. Preheat the Air Fryer to 350°F/180°C.
2. Season the squid, shrimps and cod with salt, pepper and garlic powder. Set aside.
3. Place the butter and onions in the Air Fryer Baking Pan. Place the Air Fryer Baking Pan in the Air Fryer Basket and set the timer for 2 minutes.
4. Stir in the minced garlic.
5. Add the potatoes and season with good amount of pepper and salt.
6. Set the timer for 10 minutes.
7. Add the rosemary and seafood and cook for a minute.
8. Pour in the chicken stock and cream and set the timer for 15 minutes. Serve when ready.

178 - Seared Cod with Chorizo Potatoes

Servings: 2
Preparation Time: 10 minutes
Cooking Time: 10 minutes

Ingredients:
- 2 cod fillets
- salt and pepper, to taste
- 1 teaspoon garlic powder
- 2 teaspoons lemon juice
- 2 tablespoons butter
- ½ cup onions, chopped
- 1 cup Spanish chorizo, casings removed and diccd
- 1 cup potatoes, diced
- 1 tablespoon garlic, minced

Directions:
1. Preheat the Air Fryer to 350°F/180°C.
2. Season the chorizos and potatoes with salt and pepper and place them in the Air Fryer Basket.
3. Season the cod fillets with salt, pepper & garlic powder.
4. Drizzle over the lemon juice and place them on the Air Fryer Grill Pan.
5. Place the cod fillets on the Air Fryer Grill Pan and top with the butter and onions.
6. Set the timer for 10 minutes.
7. Serve when ready.

179 - Steamed Tomato Mussels

Servings: 2
Preparation Time: 5 minutes
Cooking Time: 15 minutes

Ingredients:
- 1 cup canned tomatoes
- ½ tablespoon tomato paste
- ½ cup onions, chopped
- 1 tablespoon garlic, minced
- 1 pound mussels, cleaned
- salt and pepper, to taste
- 1 teaspoon garlic powder
- 2 tablespoons fresh basil, chopped

Directions:
1. Preheat the Air Fryer to 350°F/180°C.
2. Pour a little water in the Air Fryer.
3. Place the canned tomatoes, tomato paste, onions, garlic, mussels, salt, pepper and garlic powder in the Air Fryer Baking Pan.
4. Set the timer for 15 minutes.
5. Serve and top with the fresh basil.

180 - Garlic Parmesan Crusted Chicken

Servings: 2
Preparation Time: 10 minutes
Cooking Time: 25 minutes

Ingredients:
- ½ cup breadcrumbs
- 2 tablespoons garlic, minced
- ¼ parmesan cheese, grated
- 2 teaspoons paprika
- 2 teaspoons garlic powder
- 2 teaspoons onion powder
- 2 skinless chicken breast fillets
- salt and pepper, to taste
- 2 tablespoons olive oil

Directions:
1. Preheat the Air Fryer to 350°F/180°C.
2. Mix together the breadcrumbs, minced garlic, parmesan cheese, paprika, garlic powder and onion powder and set aside.
3. Season the chicken with salt and pepper.
4. Drizzle over some olive oil on the chicken and press down one side of the chicken into the breadcrumbs.
5. Place the chicken crumbed side up in the Air Fryer and set the timer for 25 minutes or until the chicken is cooked through and the breadcrumbs turn golden brown.
6. Serve when ready.

181 - Homemade Crispy Chicken

Servings: 2
Preparation Time: 5 minutes
Cooking Time: 25 minutes

Ingredients:
- ½ cup flour
- 1 teaspoon paprika
- 1 teaspoon garlic powder
- 1 teaspoon onion powder
- 1 teaspoon ground nutmeg
- 1 teaspoon ground allspice
- salt and pepper, to taste
- 2 skinless chicken breast fillets, cut in small cubes

Directions:
1. Preheat the Air Fryer to 350°F/180°C.
2. Mix the flour with the paprika, garlic powder, onion powder, ground nutmeg, ground allspice, salt and pepper.
3. Coat the chicken cubes with the seasoned flour, shake off any excess and place them in the Air Fryer Basket.
4. Spray the chicken with some cooking spray and set the timer for 25 minutes or until the chicken is cooked through and turn golden brown. Give the Air Fryer Basket a shake halfway through the cooking time so that the chicken can cook and brown evenly.
5. Serve and enjoy!

182 - Moroccan Beef Stew

Servings: 2
Preparation Time: 5 minutes
Cooking Time: 30 minutes

Ingredients:
- 1 pound beef shank, cut in cubes
- salt and pepper, to taste
- 1 teaspoon paprika
- 1 teaspoon garlic powder
- 3 cups beef stock
- 1 teaspoon onion powder
- 2 tablespoons garlic, minced
- 1 cup baby carrots
- ¼ cup fresh coriander, chopped

Directions:
1. Preheat the Air Fryer to 350°F/180°C.
2. Place the beef shanks in the Air Fryer Baking Pan and season with salt, pepper, paprika and garlic powder.
3. Spray the beef with cooking spray and set the timer for 5 minutes.
4. Add the beef stock, onion powder, minced garlic, baby carrots and fresh coriander.
5. Set the timer for 25 minutes. Once timer strikes, serve up!

183 - Roasted Brussels Sprouts and Chorizos

Servings: 2
Preparation Time: 5 minutes
Cooking Time: 25 minutes

Ingredients:
- 2 cups brussels sprouts
- 1 cup Spanish chorizos, sliced
- 1 tablespoon garlic, minced
- 1 teaspoon ground nutmeg
- 1 teaspoon garlic powder
- salt and pepper, to taste

Directions:
1. Preheat the Air Fryer to 400°F/200°C.
2. Place the brussels sprouts, chorizos, minced garlic, ground nutmeg, garlic powder, salt and pepper in a large bowl and mix well to combine.
3. Pour into the Air Fryer Basket and set the timer for 25 minutes.
4. Serve was timer goes off.

184 - Lemon & Thyme Grilled Chicken

Servings: 2
Preparation Time: 5 minutes plus 3 hours marinating time
Cooking Time: 30 minutes

Ingredients:
- 2 chicken breast fillets
- 2 tablespoons lemon juice
- 2 tablespoons olive oil
- 2 tablespoons fresh thyme, chopped
- salt and pepper, to taste
- 4 lemon slices

Directions:
1. Marinate the chicken in the lemon juice, olive oil, thyme, salt and pepper for 3 hours.
2. Attach the Air Fryer Grill Pan and preheat the Air Fryer to 350°F/180°C.
3. Place the chicken breasts on the Air Fryer Grill Pan and set the timer for 20 minutes.
4. Flip the chicken and top with the lemon slices.
5. Set the timer for 10 more minutes or until the chicken is cooked through.
6. Serve once properly cooked.

185 - Grilled Chicken with Cucumber Mint Salsa

Servings: 2
Preparation Time: 10 minutes
Cooking Time: 20 minutes

Ingredients:
- 2 chicken breast fillets
- salt and pepper, to taste
- ½ cup cucumbers, diced
- ¼ cup onions, finely chopped
- ¼ cup mint leaves, chopped
- 1 teaspoon garlic, minced
- 2 teaspoons apple cider vinegar

Directions:
1. Attach the Air Fryer Grill Pan to the Air Fryer and preheat the Air Fryer to 350°F/180°C.
2. Season the chicken with salt and pepper and place on the Air Fryer Grill Pan.
3. Set the timer for 15 minutes.
4. Flip the chicken over and set the timer for another 5 minutes or until the chicken is cooked through.
5. To make the cucumber mint salsa: Mix your chopped cucumbers, onions, mint leaves, garlic and apple cider vinegar and set aside.
6. Remove the chicken from the Air Fryer and top with the salsa.
7. Serve and enjoy!

186 - Beurre Blanc Scallops

Servings: 2
Preparation Time: 5 minutes
Cooking Time: 23 minutes

Ingredients:
- 8 large scallops
- salt and pepper, to taste
- ½ cup white wine
- 2 tablespoons butter
- 1 tablespoon cream
- 1 teaspoon garlic, minced
- ¼ cup shallots, sliced
- 2 tablespoons fresh parsley, chopped

Directions:
1. Preheat the Air Fryer to 350°F/180°C.
2. Season the scallops with salt and pepper and set aside.
3. Mix together the white wine, butter, cream, garlic and shallots in the Air Fryer Baking Pan and place the Air Fryer Baking Pan in the Air Fryer Basket.
4. Set the timer for 10 minutes.
5. Add the scallops to the Air Fryer Baking Pan and set the timer for 8 minutes.
6. Stir the Air Fryer Baking Pan and top with fresh parsley.
7. Set the timer for another 5 minutes. Serve once timer goes off.

187 - Vinegar & Soy Pork Belly

Servings: 2
Preparation Time: 5 minutes
Cooking Time: 25 minutes

Ingredients:
- ¾ pound pork belly, cut in cubes
- salt and pepper, to taste
- ¼ cup soy sauce
- 2 tablespoons vinegar
- ¼ cup chicken stock
- 2 tablespoons sugar
- 1 tablespoon peppercorns
- ¼ cup garlic cloves, smashed
- 4 bay leaves

Directions:
1. Preheat the Air Fryer to 350°F/180°C.
2. Place the pork belly cubes in the Air Fryer Baking Pan and season with the salt and pepper.
3. Place the Air Fryer Baking Pan in the Air Fryer Basket and set the timer for 5 minutes.
4. Stir in the soy sauce, vinegar, chicken stock, sugar, peppercorns, garlic cloves and bay leaves.
5. Set the timer for 20 more minutes.
6. Once timer strikes, serve up!

188- No Fuss Kimchi Chicken Drums

Servings: 2
Preparation Time: 5 minutes plus 3 hours marinating time
Cooking Time: 15 minutes

Ingredients:
- 4 chicken drumsticks
- salt and pepper, to taste
- 1 cup ready-made kimchi

Directions:
1. Season the chicken drums with salt and pepper and place in a ziplock bag.
2. Add in the kimchi to the bag and marinate for 3 hours.
3. Preheat the Air Fryer to 350°F/180°C.
4. Place the chicken and kimchi in the Air Fryer Baking Pan and place in the Air Fryer Basket.
5. Set the timer for 15 minutes or until the chicken is cooked through.
6. Check to make sure it's properly cooked though and serve up.

189 - Beef strips, Tomatoes and Corn

Servings: 2
Preparation Time: 5 minutes
Cooking Time: 8 minutes

Ingredients:
- ½ pound beef tenderloins, cut into strips
- 2 tablespoons olive oil
- 2 tablespoons soy sauce
- 1 tablespoon garlic, minced
- salt and pepper, to taste
- 1 cup cherry tomatoes, stems removed and halved
- 1 cup corn kernels

Directions:
1. Attach the Air Fryer Grill Pan and preheat the Air Fryer to 350°F/180°C.
2. Season the beef strips with the olive oil, soy sauce, garlic, salt and pepper and place on the Air Fryer Grill Pan.
3. Add the tomatoes and corn kernels to the Air Fryer Grill Pan.
4. Set the timer for 8 minutes or until desired doneness of the meat.
5. Serve once desired doneness of the meat is achieved.

190 - Sweet Chili Chicken

Servings: 2
Preparation Time: 5 minutes
Cooking Time: 25 minutes

Ingredients:
- 2 chicken breasts
- 1 cup sweet chili sauce
- ground red pepper, to taste
- 1 tablespoon olive oil
- 1 tablespoon garlic, minced
- 1 tablespoon paprika
- ¼ cup chives, chopped

Directions:
1. Preheat the Air Fryer to 350°F/180°C.
2. Season the chicken slices with the sweet chili sauce, red pepper, olive oil, minced garlic, paprika and chives.
3. Place the chicken breasts in the Air Fryer Basket and set the timer for 25 minutes or until the chicken is cooked through.
4. Serve an enjoy!

191 - Chicken, Bacon and Tomato

Servings: 2
Preparation Time: 10 minutes
Cooking Time: 30 minutes

Ingredients:
- 2 chicken breast fillets, halved horizontally
- salt and pepper, to taste
- 6 rashers bacon
- 4 slices tomato
- 4 slices cheddar cheese
- 4 slices mozzarella cheese

Directions:
1. Preheat the Air Fryer to 350°F/180°C.
2. Season the chicken fillets with salt & pepper and place them in the Air Fryer Basket.
3. Set the timer for 15 minutes.
4. Flip the chicken and place the bacon on the chicken fillets.
5. Set the timer for 10 more minutes.
6. When the chicken is cooked through, top with 2 slices each of the tomatoes, cheddar cheese and mozzarella cheese.
7. Top with the other half of the chicken breast and secure with toothpicks
8. Spray the chicken breasts with cooking spray and return to the Air Fryer.
9. Set the timer for 5 minutes or until the cheese melts.
10. Serve and enjoy.

192 - Texan Zucchini, Carrots and Potatoes

Servings: 2
Preparation Time: 5 minutes
Cooking Time: 15 minutes

Ingredients:
- 1 zucchini, diced
- 1 cup baby carrots
- 1 cup baby potatoes, halved
- 1 tablespoon taco seasoning
- 1 teaspoon garlic powder
- 1 teaspoon olive oil
- ¼ cup fresh parsley, chopped
- salt and pepper, to taste

Directions:
1. Preheat the Air Fryer to 350°F/180°C.
2. Mix together all the ingredients and pour into the Air Fryer Baking Pan.
3. Place the Air Fryer Baking Pan in the Air Fryer Basket and set the timer for 15 minutes.
4. Serve once the timer goes off.

193 - Chicken Penne Piccata

Servings: 2
Preparation Time: 10 minutes plus 3 hours marinating time
Cooking Time: 20 minutes

Ingredients:

- 1 chicken breast fillet, cut into strips
- salt and pepper, to taste
- 2 tablespoons butter
- ¼ cup white wine
- ¼ cup chicken stock
- 2 tablespoons capers
- 2 cups cooked penne
- 2 tablespoons fresh parsley, chopped

Directions:

1. Preheat the Air Fryer to 350°F/180°C.
2. Place the chicken strips in the Air Fryer Baking Pan and season with salt and pepper.
3. Place the Air Fryer Baking Pan in the Air Fryer Basket and set the timer for 10 minutes.
4. Add the butter, white wine, chicken stock and capers and set the time for another 10 minutes.
5. Remove from the Air Fryer and top over the cooked pasta.
6. Serve and top with the fresh parsley.

194 - Grilled Chicken and Apple Mint Sauce

Servings: 2
Preparation Time: 10 minutes
Cooking Time: 30 minutes

Ingredients:

- 2 cups granny smith apples, peeled, cored and sliced
- 2 chicken breast fillets
- salt and pepper, to taste
- ¼ cup mint leaves, chopped

Directions:

1. Preheat the Air Fryer and to 350°F/180°C.
2. Place the apples in the Air Fryer Basket and attach the Air Fryer Grill Pan.
3. Season the chicken with salt and pepper and place the chicken on the Air Fryer Grill Pan.
4. Spray the chicken with cooking spray and set the time for 20 minutes.
5. Remove the apples from the Air Fryer Basket.
6. Flip the chicken and set the timer for another 10 minutes.
7. Mash the apples with a fork and add to the chopped mint.
8. Remove the chicken fillets from the Air Fryer and top over with the apple mint sauce.
9. Serve up!

195 - Garlic Creamy Broccoli

Servings: 2
Preparation Time: 5 minutes
Cooking Time: 25 minutes

Ingredients:
- 1 cup cream
- 2 tablespoons garlic, minced
- 1 teaspoon garlic powder
- 3 cups broccoli florets
- ½ cup onions, sliced

Directions:
1. Preheat the Air Fryer to 350°F/180°C.
2. Place the cream, garlic and garlic powder in the Air Fryer Baking Pan and set the timer for 5 minutes.
3. Add the broccoli and onions to the Air Fryer Baking Pan.
4. Return the Air Fryer Baking Pan to the Air Fryer Basket and set the timer for 20 minutes.
5. Serve up once the timer goes off.

196 - Coriander Lime Chicken

Servings: 2
Preparation Time: 5 minutes
Cooking Time: 35 minutes

Ingredients:
- 2 chicken breast fillets
- salt and pepper, to taste
- ½ cup chicken stock
- 1 tablespoon garlic, sliced
- 1 tablespoon lime juice
- 3 sprigs fresh thyme
- 2 lemon wedges
- 2 tablespoons fresh coriander, chopped

Directions:
1. Preheat the Air Fryer to 350°F/180°C.
2. Season the chicken breast fillets with salt and pepper.
3. Place the chicken in the Air Fryer Baking Pan.
4. Pour in the chicken stock, garlic, lime juice and thyme and season with more pepper.
5. Add the lemon wedges and coriander and place the Air Fryer Baking Pan in the Air Fryer Basket and set the timer for 25 minutes.
6. Flip the chicken fillets and set the timer for another 10 minutes.
7. Check to see if the chicken fillets are properly cooked through and serve up.

197 - Mexican Roasted Zucchinis

Servings: 4
Preparation Time: 5 minutes
Cooking Time: 8 minutes

Ingredients:
- 2 large zucchinis, diced
- 2 tablespoons taco seasoning
- 1 teaspoon paprika
- salt and pepper, to taste
- ½ onion, diced
- 1 medium red bell pepper, seeds removed and diced
- 2 cloves garlic, halved

Directions:
1. Preheat the Air Fryer to 350°F/180°C.
2. Season the zucchinis with the taco seasoning, paprika, salt and pepper and place them in the Air Fryer Basket.
3. Add in the onions, red bell peppers and garlic.
4. Spray the vegetables with some cooking spray and set the timer for 8 minutes.
5. Serve and enjoy!

198 - Grilled Vegetables

Servings: 2
Preparation Time: 5 minutes
Cooking Time: 15 minutes

Ingredients:
- 1 cup squash, diced
- 1 teaspoon garlic powder
- ½ teaspoon turmeric
- salt and pepper, to taste
- ½ teaspoon paprika
- ½ cup fennel
- ½ cup green beans
- ¼ cup mozzarella cheese

Directions:
1. Attach the Air Fryer Grill Pan and preheat the Air Fryer to 350°F/180°C.
2. Season the squash with the garlic powder, turmeric, salt, pepper and paprika and place them on the Air Fryer Grill Pan.
3. Set the timer for 8 minutes or until they are tender.
4. Add the fennel and beans to the Air Fryer Grill Pan and set the timer for another 5 minutes.
5. Top the vegetables with mozzarella cheese and return to the Air Fryer for 2 more minutes or until the cheese is melted.
6. Serve when ready!

199 - Baked Baby Potatoes

Servings: 2
Preparation Time: 5 minutes
Cooking Time: 15 minutes

Ingredients:
- 2 cups baby potatoes, halved
- 1 tablespoon of olive oil
- 1 teaspoon paprika
- 1 teaspoon garlic powder
- salt and pepper, to taste
- ½ cup parmesan cheese, shavings
- 1 tablespoon chives, chopped

Directions:
1. Preheat the Air Fryer to 350°F/180°C.
2. Season the potatoes with the olive oil, paprika, garlic powder, salt and pepper.
3. Place the potatoes in the Air Fryer and set the timer for 15 minutes.
4. Serve and top with parmesan cheese and chives.

200 - Molten Sweet Purple Potatoes

Servings: 2
Preparation Time: 5 minutes
Cooking Time: 17 minutes

Ingredients:
- 2 cups baby potatoes, halved
- 1 cup purple yam, cubed
- 1 tablespoon of olive oil
- 1 teaspoon paprika
- 1 teaspoon garlic powder
- 1 teaspoon onion powder
- salt and pepper, to taste
- ½ cup mozzarella cheese, grated
- ¼ cup feta cheese, crumbled
- ½ cup parmesan, shavings
- 1 tablespoon chives, chopped

Directions:
1. Preheat the Air Fryer to 350°F/180°C.
2. Season the potatoes and purple yam with the olive oil, paprika, garlic powder, onion powder, salt and pepper and place in the Air Fryer Basket.
3. Set the timer for 15 minutes and give the vegetables a shake halfway through the cooking time.
4. Top with the mozzarella cheese and feta cheese and return to the Air Fryer for 2 more minutes or until the cheese has melted.
5. Serve and top with the parmesan cheese and chives.

201 - Honey Mustard Chicken and Turkey Meatballs

Servings: 4
Preparation Time: 10 minutes
Cooking Time: 15 minutes plus overnight chilling

Ingredients:

- ½ pound ground chicken
- ½ pound ground turkey
- ¼ cup onions, minced
- 1 tablespoon mustard
- 1 tablespoon honey
- 1 teaspoon garlic powder
- 1 tablespoon garlic, minced
- 1 tablespoon cheddar cheese, grated
- ¼ cup fresh basil, chopped
- salt and pepper, to taste

Directions:

1. Mix the ground chicken, ground turkey, onions, mustard, honey, garlic powder, minced garlic, cheddar cheese, fresh basil, salt and pepper in a large bowl.
2. Cover with plastic wrap and chill overnight.
3. Preheat the Air Fryer to 400°F/200°C.
4. Form meatballs of your desired size and arrange them in the Air Fryer Basket. Use the Air Fryer Double Layer Rack if needed.
5. Set the timer for 15 minutes.
6. Serve up once the timer strikes.

202 - Veggie Balls

Servings: 4
Preparation Time: 10 minutes plus overnight chilling time
Cooking Time: 15 minutes

Ingredients:

- 2 heads cauliflower, cut into florets
- ¼ cup onions, minced
- 1 tablespoon garlic, minced
- 1 teaspoon garlic powder
- 1 teaspoon onion powder
- 1 teaspoon paprika
- salt and pepper, to taste
- 1 cup cornstarch

Directions:

1. Pulse the cauliflower florets in a food processor until they resemble a grain-like texture.
2. Mix the ground cauliflower, onions, garlic, garlic powder, onion powder, paprika, salt and pepper.
3. Cover with a plastic wrap and chill overnight.
4. Preheat the Air Fryer to 400°F/200°C.
5. Season the cornstarch with salt and pepper.
6. Form balls from the mixture and dust them with the cornstarch.
7. Arrange the balls in the Air Fryer and set the timer for 15 minutes.
8. Serve when ready.

203 - Indian Samosas

Servings: 4
Preparation Time: 15 minutes plus 30 minutes chilling time
Cooking Time: 10 minutes

Ingredients:
- 1 cup onions, chopped
- 1 cup cooked rice
- 2 green chilis, finely chopped
- 1 teaspoon chili powder
- ½ cup fresh coriander, finely chopped
- 1 tablespoon masala powder
- 1 tablespoon grated carrots
- salt and pepper, to taste
- 1 quantity whole wheat pastry dough

Directions:
1. Mix the onions, cooked rice, green chilis, chili powder, fresh coriander, masala powder, carrots, salt and pepper in a bowl and chill for 30 minutes.
2. Cut the pastry dough into triangles.
3. Use 1 tablespoon of filling for each triangle and fold in half. Seal the edges with water.
4. Preheat the Air Fryer to 350°F/180°C.
5. Arrange the samosas in the Air Fryer Basket and use the Air Fryer Double Layer Rack if needed.
6. Spray the samosas with cooking spray and set the timer for 10 minutes. Flip the samosas halfway through the cooking time so that they can cook and brown evenly.
7. Serve once timer goes off.

204 - Leftover Mac and Cheese Balls

Servings: 4
Preparation Time: 10 minutes
Cooking Time: 10 minutes

Ingredients:
- 2 cups leftover mac and cheese
- ¼ cup cheddar cheese, grated
- 1 cup breadcrumbs
- 1 teaspoon paprika
- salt and pepper, to taste
- 3 eggs
- 2 tablespoons milk
- ½ cup flour

Directions:
1. Preheat the Air Fryer to 400°F/200°C.
2. Mix together the leftover mac and cheese with the cheddar cheese in a bowl and set aside.
3. Mix together the breadcrumbs, paprika, salt and pepper and set aside.
4. Whisk the eggs with the milk and season with salt and pepper.
5. Form balls from the mac and cheese mixture and dust in some flour.
6. Dip the balls in the egg mixture and coat evenly in the breadcrumbs.
7. Set the timer for 10 minutes. Serve once done!

205 - Easy Turkey Leg Roast

Servings: 6
Preparation Time: 5 minutes plus 30 minutes chilling time
Cooking Time: 40 minutes

Ingredients:

- 6 turkey legs, with bones
- ¼ cup olive oil
- 1 tablespoon onion powder
- 1 tablespoon garlic powder
- 1 tablespoon fresh rosemary
- 1 tablespoon fresh tarragon
- salt and pepper, to taste

Directions:

1. Marinate the turkey legs with the olive oil, onion powder, garlic powder, fresh rosemary, fresh tarragon, salt and pepper and chill for 30 minutes in the fridge.
2. Preheat the Air Fryer to 350°F/180°C.
3. Arrange the turkey legs in the Air Fryer Basket and use the Air Fryer Double Layer Rack if needed.
4. Set the timer for 20 minutes.
5. When timer is done, flip over the turkey legs and set the timer for 20 more minutes.
6. Serve up after the timer strikes.

206 - Pandan Chicken Thighs

Servings: 4
Preparation Time: 15 minutes plus 30 minutes chilling time
Cooking Time: 35 minutes

Ingredients:

- 6 chicken thighs, deboned
- ¼ cup olive oil
- 1 tablespoon soy sauce
- 1 tablespoon onion powder
- 1 tablespoon garlic powder
- salt and pepper
- 12 pandan (screwpine) leaves

Directions:

1. Marinate the chicken thighs with the olive oil, soy sauce, onion powder, garlic powder, salt and pepper and chill for 30 minutes in the fridge.
2. Preheat the Air Fryer to 350°F/180°C.
3. Wrap the chicken thighs in the pandan leaves and secure with a toothpick.
4. Arrange the chicken in the Air Fryer and set the timer for 20 minutes.
5. Flip the chicken and set the timer for 15 more minutes.
6. Serve up on a plate.

207 - Roast Chicken with Apples

Servings: 2
Preparation Time: 5 minutes
Cooking Time: 16 minutes

Ingredients:
- 2 chicken breast fillets, cubed
- salt and pepper, to taste
- 2 tablespoons fresh rosemary, chopped
- 2 granny smith apples, peeled and diced
- 2 tablespoons cider vinegar
- 2 tablespoons butter
- ¼ cup chicken stock

Directions:
1. Preheat the Air Fryer to 350°F/180°C.
2. Place the chicken cubes in the Air Fryer Baking Pan and season them with salt, pepper and fresh rosemary.
3. Place the Air Fryer Baking Pan in the Air Fryer Basket and set the timer for 8 minutes.
4. Add the apples, cider vinegar, butter and chicken stock to the Air Fryer Baking Pan and season with more salt and pepper.
5. Set the timer for 8 more minutes or until the chicken is cooked through.
6. Check the chicken is properly cooked through and serve up.

208 - Grilled Pork Chops with Sweet Potatoes

Servings: 4
Preparation Time: 5 minutes plus marinating overnight
Cooking Time: 16 minutes

Ingredients:
- 4 pork loin chops, 1-inch thick
- 1 tablespoon lemon juice
- 4 tablespoons olive oil
- 2 tablespoons garlic, minced
- 3 tablespoons fresh oregano, chopped
- salt and pepper, to taste
- 2 cups sweet potatoes, cubed
- 1 large zucchini, diced
- ¼ cup fresh parsley, chopped

Directions:
1. Marinate the pork chops with the lemon juice, olive oil, minced garlic, fresh oregano, salt and pepper. Cover with plastic wrap and chill overnight.
2. Preheat the Air Fryer to 350°F/180°C.
3. Mix the sweet potatoes and zucchinis with the olive oil and the fresh parsley.
4. Arrange the pork chops in the Air Fryer Basket and set the timer for 8 minutes.
5. Add in the potatoes and zucchinis and cook for another 8 minutes.
6. Serve and top with the fresh parsley.

209 - Apple and Broccoli Chops!

Servings: 4
Preparation Time: 5 minutes
Cooking Time: 22 minutes

Ingredients:

- 4 pork chops, 1-inch thick with bone
- 1 teaspoon paprika
- 1 teaspoon chili powder
- 1 teaspoon garlic salt
- ⅛ teaspoon ground red pepper
- ⅛ teaspoon ground cinnamon
- salt and pepper, to taste
- 2 granny smith apples, peeled and diced
- 1 head broccoli, cut into florets
- 3 tablespoons apple cider vinegar
- 3 tablespoons light brown sugar
- 2 teaspoons fresh rosemary, chopped

Directions:

1. Preheat the Air Fryer to 350°F/180°C.
2. Marinate the chops with the paprika, chili powder, garlic salt, red pepper, ground cinnamon, salt and pepper.
3. Toss the apples and broccoli florets with the apple cider vinegar, brown sugar, fresh rosemary, salt, and pepper.
4. Place pork chops in the Air Fryer and set the timer for 12 minutes.
5. Turn over the chops and add the apples and broccoli florets.
6. Set the timer for 10 more minutes. Serve when done.

210 - Catfish and Chips

Servings: 2
Preparation Time: 10 minutes
Cooking Time: 22 minutes

Ingredients:

- 2 medium potatoes, peeled, cubed and soaked in water for 30 minutes
- 2 catfish fillets
- 1 tablespoon lemon juice
- ½ cup breadcrumbs
- ½ tablespoon fresh parsley, chopped
- 1 tablespoon garlic powder
- salt and pepper, to taste
- 1 egg, beaten

Directions:

1. Attach the Air Fryer Food Separator and preheat the Air Fryer to 350°F/180°C.
2. Drain and pat dry the potatoes. Season with salt and pepper and place in one section of the Air Fryer.
3. Spray some cooking spray onto the potatoes and set the timer for 7 minutes.
4. While the potatoes are cooking, prepare the catfish.
5. Pour the lemon juice onto the catfish.
6. Mix together the breadcrumbs, fresh parsley, garlic powder, salt and pepper.
7. Dip the fish fillets in the egg and coat evenly with the breadcrumbs.
8. Remove the potatoes from the Air Fryer and shake the potatoes.
9. Add the catfish fillets to the other section of the Air Fryer.
10. Set the timer for 15 minutes. Shake the fries again halfway through the cooking time to ensure that they are evenly browned.
11. Serve and enjoy!

211 - Cod Fillets with Honey Glazed Greens and Mandarins

Servings: 4
Preparation Time: 10 minutes
Cooking Time: 20 minutes

Ingredients:

- 10 spears asparagus
- 8 ounces fresh green beans, trimmed
- 4 tablespoons honey
- 1 tablespoon soy sauce
- 1 tablespoon Dijon mustard
- 1 teaspoon rice wine vinegar
- 4 cod fillets
- salt and pepper, to taste
- 2 mandarins, segmented

Directions:

1. Toss the asparagus and green beans in a bowl with the honey, soy sauce, mustard and rice wine vinegar and set aside.
2. Preheat the Air Fryer to 350°F/180°C.
3. Season the cod fillets with the salt and pepper.
4. Place the cod fillets into the Air Fryer and spray with a little cooking spray.
5. Set the timer for 10 minutes.
6. Flip the fish and add the vegetables to the Air Fryer Basket.
7. Cook for 10 more minutes.
8. Remove from Air Fryer and mix in the mandarin segments.
9. Serve and enjoy!

212 - Duckie Pie

Servings: 4
Preparation Time: 20 minutes
Cooking Time: 10 minutes

Ingredients:
- 2 cups leftover roast duck
- ¼ cup green onions, chopped
- 2 tablespoons hoisin sauce
- 1 cup flour
- 3 tablespoons butter
- 2 tablespoons water
- 1 egg

Directions:
1. Preheat air fryer to 300°F/150°C.
2. Mix together the roast duck, green onions and hoisin sauce and place into the Air Fryer Baking Pan.
3. Mix together the flour, butter and water and knead until a dough forms.
4. Roll out the dough until it is large enough to cover the Air Fryer Baking Pan.
5. Crimp the edges onto the rim of the Air Fryer Baking Pan.
6. Whisk the egg and brush the pie crust.
7. Place the Air Fryer Baking Pan into the Air Fryer Basket and set the timer for 10 minutes.
8. Serve once the timer strikes.

213 - Chicken and Sausage Pie

Servings: 2
Preparation Time: 10 minutes
Cooking Time: 14 minutes

Ingredients:
- ¾ cup cooked chicken breast, shredded
- 1 beef sausage, sliced
- ½ cup potatoes, diced
- ¼ cup green peas
- ¼ cup carrots, diced
- ½ teaspoon paprika
- ½ teaspoon garlic powder
- ½ teaspoon onion powder
- salt and pepper, to taste
- 1 pastry pie dough
- 1 egg

Directions:
1. Preheat the Air Fryer to 300°F/150°C.
2. Place the shredded chicken, sliced beef sausages, potatoes, green peas and carrots in the Air Fryer Baking Pan.
3. Season with the paprika, garlic powder, onion powder, salt and pepper.
4. Place the Air Fryer Baking Pan in the Air Fryer and set the timer for 4 minutes.
5. Remove from the Air Fryer and allow to cool.
6. Roll out the dough to be large enough to cover the Air Fryer Baking Pan.
7. Seal the edges so they rest on the rim of the Air Fryer Baking Pan.
8. Whisk the egg and brush the pie crust.
9. Return to the Air Fryer and set the timer for 10 minutes.
10. Serve and enjoy!

214 - Oriental Shrimps and Tofu

Servings: 2
Preparation Time: 5 minutes
Cooking Time: 10 minutes

Ingredients:

- 6 ounces tofu, drained and cut into 1-inch cubes
- pepper, to taste
- 3 tablespoons hoisin sauce
- 2 tablespoons rice vinegar
- 2 tablespoons water
- 2 teaspoons sugar
- ½ teaspoon ground ginger
- ½ teaspoon cornstarch
- ⅛ teaspoon crushed red pepper flakes
- 1 teaspoon vegetable oil
- ½ cup medium shrimps, peeled and deveined
- 1 clove garlic, minced
- ½ cup onions, cut lengthwise
- 1 cup snow peas

Directions:

1. Preheat air fryer to 350°F/150°C.
2. Season the tofu cubes with pepper and place them in the Air Fryer Baking Pan.
3. Place Air Fryer Baking Pan in the Air Fryer basket and set the time for 4 minutes. Shake the Air Fryer Baking Pan halfway through the cooking time.
4. Remove tofu cubes from the Air Fryer Baking Pan and set aside.
5. Combine the hoisin sauce, rice vinegar, water, sugar, ginger, cornstarch, red pepper flakes, vegetable oil, shrimps, garlic and onions and pour into the Air Fryer Baking Pan.
6. Add in the snow peas.
7. Set the timer for 6 minutes or until the shrimps are cooked through.
8. Remove the Air Fryer Baking Pan from the Air Fryer and stir in the tofu cubes.
9. Serve up on a plate or in a bowl.

215 - Coconut Seafood Delight

Servings: 4
Preparation Time: 5 minutes
Cooking Time: 30 minutes

Ingredients:
- 1 cup shrimps, peeled and deveined
- 1 cup squid rings
- salt and pepper, to taste
- 1 medium onion, chopped
- 1 teaspoon garlic, minced
- 2 teaspoons shrimp paste
- ½ tablespoon water
- 3 pieces dried Thai chilis
- 2 cups coconut milk

Directions:
1. Preheat the Air Fryer to 300°F/150°C.
2. Place the shrimps and squids in the Air Fryer Baking Pan and season with salt and pepper.
3. Add the onions, garlic, shrimp paste, water and chilis and mix well to combine.
4. Place the Air Fryer Baking Pan in the Air Fryer Basket and set the timer for 20 minutes.
5. Pour in coconut milk and cook for another 10 minutes. Serve and enjoy!

216 - Under the Sea Curry

Servings: 4
Preparation Time: 5 minutes
Cooking Time: 15 minutes

Ingredients:
- 1 teaspoon vegetable oil
- 1 medium onion, halved and sliced
- 1 tablespoon fresh ginger, minced
- 1 tablespoon garlic, minced
- 1 cup light coconut milk
- 3 tablespoons lime juice
- 2 tablespoons curry paste
- 12 medium shrimps, peeled and deveined
- 12 sea scallops, halved
- 10 spears asparagus, cut into 2-inch pieces
- 2 tablespoon cilantro, chopped

Directions:
1. Preheat the Air Fryer to 300°F/150°C.
2. Mix together the oil, onions, ginger, garlic, coconut milk, lime juice and curry paste and pour into the Air Fryer Baking Pan.
3. Add the shrimp, scallops, asparagus and fresh cilantro.
4. Place the Air Fryer Baking Pan in the Air Fryer Basket and set the timer for 15 minutes.
5. Once timer goes off, serve up.

217 - Parmesan Crusted Chicken

Servings: 2
Preparation Time: 10 minutes
Cooking Time: 8 minutes

Ingredients:
- 2 chicken breast fillets, pounded
- salt and pepper, to taste
- 1 egg
- 2 cups bread crumbs
- ½ cup parmesan cheese, grated
- 2 tablespoons all-purpose flour

Directions:
1. Preheat the Air Fryer to 350°F/180°C.
2. Season the chicken fillets with salt and pepper.
3. Whisk the egg with pepper and set aside.
4. Mix together the breadcrumbs and parmesan cheese.
5. Dust the chicken in flour, dip in the seasoned egg and coat evenly with breadcrumbs.
6. Spray with some cooking spray and place the chicken in the Air Fryer Basket. Use the Air Fryer Double Layer Rack if needed.
7. Set the timer for 8 minutes or until the chicken is cooked through and the breadcrumbs turn golden brown.
8. Serve and enjoy.

218 - Mexican Salsa and Chicken Thighs

Servings: 2
Preparation Time: 5 minutes
Cooking Time: 25 minutes

Ingredients:
- 4 pcs chicken thighs
- 2 tablespoons taco seasoning
- ½ cup ready-made salsa
- ½ cup cheddar cheese, grated
- 1 tablespoon sour cream

Directions:
1. Preheat the Air Fryer to 400°F/200°C.
2. Marinade the chicken thighs with taco seasoning and arrange in the Air Fryer Basket. Use the Air Fryer Double Layer Rack if needed.
3. Top with the salsa and set the timer for 20 minutes.
4. Top with the cheese and set the timer for 5 more minutes or until the cheese melts.
5. Remove from the Air Fryer and serve while drizzling over with sour cream.

219 - Easy Wild Mushroom and Rice

Servings: 2
Preparation Time: 5 minutes
Cooking Time: 25 minutes

Ingredients:
- 1 chicken breast fillets, cooked shredded
- ½ cup wild mushrooms, sliced
- 1 teaspoon paprika
- salt and pepper, to taste
- 2 cups chicken stock
- ½ cup long grain rice
- 1 cup heavy cream

Directions:
1. Preheat the Air Fryer to 400°F/200°C.
2. Place the chicken and mushrooms in the Air Fryer Baking Pan.
3. Season with paprika, salt and pepper.
4. Add in the chicken stock and rice.
5. Place the Air Fryer Baking Pan in the Air Fryer Basket and set the timer for 20 minutes
6. Add in the heavy cream and season with salt and pepper.
7. Fluff the rice and set the timer for 5 more minutes.
8. Once timer strikes, serve up.

220 - Quick Italian Chicken Marsala

Servings: 2
Preparation Time: 5 minutes
Cooking Time: 30 minutes

Ingredients:
- ⅛ cup all-purpose flour
- salt and pepper, to taste
- ½ teaspoon dried oregano
- 4 chicken thighs
- 1 cup button mushrooms, sliced
- ½ cup marsala wine

Directions:
1. Attach the Air Fryer Grill Pan and preheat the Air Fryer to 400°F/200°C.
2. Mix together the flour, salt, pepper and oregano.
3. Coat the chicken in the flour mix and arrange them on the Air Fryer Grill Pan.
4. Spray the chicken with some cooking spray and set the timer for 20 minutes.
5. Add the mushrooms and marsala wine to the Air Fryer Grill Pan and set the timer for 10 more minutes.
6. Serve and enjoy!

221 - Cadienne Chicken Pasta

Servings: 4
Preparation Time: 5 minutes
Cooking Time: 20 minutes

Ingredients:

- 2 chicken breasts, cut into thin strips
- 2 tablespoons Cajun seasoning
- 1 tablespoon butter
- 1 green bell pepper, seeds removed and chopped
- ¼ cup red bell pepper, seeds removed and chopped
- ¼ cup mushrooms, sliced
- ¼ cup onions, sliced
- ¼ cup parmesan cheese, shavings
- 12 oz linguine, cooked

Directions:

1. Attach the Air Fryer Grill Pan and preheat the Air Fryer to 350°F/180°C.
2. Season the chicken with Cajun seasoning and place them on the Air Fryer Grill Pan.
3. Set the timer for 10 minutes. Turn the chicken halfway through the cooking time.
4. Add the butter, bell peppers, mushrooms and onions to the Air Fryer Grill Pan and set the timer for 5 minutes.
5. Add the parmesan cheese and set the timer for 5 more minutes.
6. Remove from the Air Fryer, pour over pasta and toss well to combine.
7. Serve and enjoy!

222 - Chicken Thigh Hainanese

Servings: 4
Preparation Time: 10 minutes plus marinating overnight
Cooking Time: 15 minutes

Ingredients:
- 4 skinless chicken thighs, deboned
- 1 teaspoon five spice powder
- 2 teaspoons sesame oil
- 5 cloves garlic, minced
- 2 tablespoon cornstarch, diluted with 4 tablespoons water
- 2 eggs
- 10 cream crackers, crushed
- 1 tablespoon Worcestershire sauce
- 1 tablespoon A1 steak sauce
- ⅛ cup ketchup
- ½ tablespoons light soy sauce
- 1 teaspoon white pepper
- 1 cup of chicken stock

Directions:
1. Marinate the chicken with the five spice powder, sesame oil, minced garlic and cornstarch in a ziplock bag and chill overnight.
2. Preheat the Air Fryer to 350°F/180°C.
3. Dip the chicken pieces in the egg and coat evenly with the crushed crackers.
4. Arrange the thighs in the Air Fryer and set the timer for 15 minutes or until the chicken is cooked through.
5. While the chicken is cooking, combine the Worcestershire sauce, A1 steak sauce, ketchup, light soy sauce, white pepper and chicken stock in a saucepan and bring to a boil until thickened.
6. Remove the chicken from the Air Fryer and serve while topping with the sauce.

223 - Sweet Potato, Sprouts and Beets

Servings: 4
Preparation Time: 5 minutes
Cooking Time: 20 minutes

Ingredients:

- 6 rashers bacon, chopped
- 2 cups brussels sprouts, halved
- 1 cup sweet potatoes, diced
- 1 cup beets, diced
- ½ cup white onions, chopped
- 4 cloves garlic, sliced
- 1 teaspoon garlic powder
- 1 teaspoon cayenne pepper
- ¼ cup chives, chopped
- 2 tablespoons parmesan cheese, shavings

Directions:

1. Preheat the Air Fryer to 350°F/180°C.
2. Place the bacon in the Air Fryer Baking Pan and set the timer for 10 minutes or until they are crisp.
3. Remove the bacon from the Air Fryer Baking Pan and set aside.
4. Add the brussels sprouts, sweet potatoes, beets and white onions in the Air Fryer Baking Pan with the bacon fat.
5. Add the garlic, garlic powder and cayenne pepper and set the timer for 10 minutes or until the vegetables are cooked.
6. Stir in the chives and top with the parmesan shavings and bacon bits. Serve up!

224 - Chicken with Coriander and Brussels Sprouts

Servings: 4
Preparation Time: 5 minutes
Cooking Time: 16 minutes

Ingredients:

- 6 chicken breast fillets, cubed
- 2 cups brussels sprouts, halved
- salt and pepper, to taste
- ½ cup fresh coriander, chopped
- 5 cloves garlic, minced

- 1 large onion, cut into thick slices
- 2 tablespoons cider vinegar
- 2 tablespoons butter
- ½ cup chicken stock

Directions:

1. Preheat the Air Fryer to 350°F/180°C.
2. Place the chicken cubes and brussels sprouts in the Air Fryer Baking Pan.
3. Season with salt and pepper.
4. Mix in the coriander.
5. Place the Air Fryer Baking Pan in the Air Fryer Basket and set the timer for 8 minutes.
6. Add the garlic, onions, cider vinegar, butter and chicken stock to the dish and season with more salt and pepper.
7. Set the timer for another 8 minutes or until the chicken is cooked through. Serve up!

225 - Pesto Lamb Chops

Servings: 4
Preparation Time: 10 minutes
Cooking Time: 15 minutes

Ingredients:

- 2 cups fresh basil, torn
- ½ cup fresh cilantro, torn
- 5 cloves garlic, peeled
- ¼ cup extra virgin olive oil

- ½ cup pine nuts, toasted
- salt and pepper, to taste
- 12 lamb chops

Directions:

1. Preheat the Air Fryer to 300°F/150°C.
2. Blend the fresh basil, fresh cilantro, garlic cloves, pine nuts and extra virgin olive oil in a food processor.
3. Season with salt and pepper to taste.
4. Spread the pesto on the lamb chops, applying a thicker layer on the upper side.
5. Arrange the chops in the Air Fryer Basket and use the Air Fryer Double Layer Rack if needed.
6. Set the timer for 15 minutes.
7. Remove from the Air Fryer and drizzle over with olive oil. Serve and enjoy!

226 - Roast Rosemary Chicken Thighs

Servings: 4
Preparation Time: 5 minutes
Cooking Time: 25 minutes

Ingredients:
- 12 small chicken thighs
- salt and pepper, to taste
- 1 teaspoon garlic powder
- 1 teaspoon paprika
- 6 cloves garlic, minced
- 3 sprigs fresh rosemary

Directions:
1. Preheat the Air Fryer to 300°F/150°C.
2. Marinate the chicken thighs with the salt, pepper, garlic powder, paprika and minced garlic.
3. Place the rosemary sprigs in the Air Fryer Basket and arrange the chicken thighs on them. Use the Air Fryer Double Layer Rack if needed.
4. Set the timer for 15 minutes.
5. Flip the chicken thighs over and set the timer for 10 more minutes.
6. Remove the chicken thighs and drizzle over with olive oil.
7. Serve and enjoy!

227 - Nana's Cinnamon Beef Stew

Servings: 2
Preparation Time: 5 minutes
Cooking Time: 35 minutes

Ingredients:
- ½ pound beef loin, cut into cubes
- ½ teaspoon ground cinnamon
- ½ teaspoon garlic powder
- ½ teaspoon onion powder
- salt and pepper, to taste
- 3 cloves garlic, minced
- 1 tablespoon onions, diced
- 1 tablespoon carrots, diced
- 1 whole celery stalks, chopped
- 1½ cups beef stock
- 1 tablespoon fresh parsley, chopped

Directions:
1. Preheat the Air Fryer to 400°F/200°C.
2. Season the beef cubes with the ground cinnamon, garlic powder, onion powder, salt and pepper.
3. Rub the minced garlic onto the meat and spray the beef cubes with cooking spray.
4. Place the meat in the Air Fryer Baking Pan and set the timer for 10 minutes.
5. Lower the temperature to 300°F/150°C.
6. Add the onions, carrots, celery and beef stock to the Air Fryer Baking Pan and season with more salt and pepper.
7. Set the timer for 25 minutes.
8. Remove from the Air Fryer and top with fresh parsley.
9. Serve and enjoy!

228 - Lemon and Lime Lamb Patties

Servings: 4
Preparation Time: 10 minutes plus marinating overnight
Cooking Time: 15 minutes

Ingredients:

- 2 cups ground lamb
- 1 large yellow onion, finely diced
- 2 large cloves garlic, minced
- 1 cup matzo meal
- salt and pepper, to taste
- 2 eggs
- 10 sprigs flat-leaf parsley, finely chopped
- 1 tablespoon lime rind

Lemon Sauce

- ½ cup extra virgin olive oil
- ½ cup lemon juice
- ½ teaspoon coarse kosher salt
- 4 egg yolks
- ⅛ teaspoon turmeric
- salt and pepper, to taste

Directions:

1. Knead together the ground meat, onions, garlic, matzo meal, salt, pepper, egg, fresh parsley and lime rind and chill overnight.
2. Preheat the Air Fryer to 300°F/150°C.
3. Form patties from the lamb mixture and place them in the Air Fryer Basket.
4. Set the timer for 15 minutes.
5. While the lamb patties are cooking, blend together the lemon sauce ingredients in a food processor until smooth.
6. Remove the lamb patties from the Air Fryer and top with the lemon sauce.
7. Serve and enjoy!

229 - Pork Belly and Peppered Chocolate Sauce

Servings: 3
Preparation Time: 5 minutes
Cooking Time: 40 minutes

Ingredients:
- 1½ pounds pork belly, cut into cubes
- salt and pepper, to taste
- 1 cup beef stock
- ½ cup 70% chocolate, chopped

Directions:
1. Preheat the Air Fryer to 350°F/180°C.
2. Season the pork cubes with salt and pepper.
3. Place the pork cubes in the Air Fryer and spray with some cooking spray.
4. Set the timer for 20 minutes.
5. Remove the pork cubes and allow to cool.
6. Mix together the beef stock and chocolate in the Air Fryer Baking Pan.
7. Season generously with pepper and set the timer for 20 minutes.
8. Serve and pour the sauce over the pork cubes.

230 - Greek Chicken Pasta

Servings: 3
Preparation Time: 5 minutes
Cooking Time: 12 minutes

Ingredients:
- 2 large chicken breast, cut into strips
- 1 tablespoon olive oil
- red pepper flakes, optional
- 1 pound zucchini, about 2 medium, cut into 1-inch chunks
- 1 cup kalamata olives, sliced
- salt and pepper, to taste
- 2 cups macaroni, cooked
- 6 ounces feta cheese, crumbled

Directions:
1. Preheat the Air Fryer to 300°F/150°C.
2. Toss together the chicken, olive oil, pepper flakes, zucchini, olives, salt and pepper in the Air Fryer Baking Pan.
3. Place the Air Fryer Baking Pan in the Air Fryer and set the timer for 12 minutes
4. Serve and pour over the cooked pasta and top with the feta cheese.

231 - Cod Patties

Servings: 3
Preparation Time: 10 minutes plus 1 hour chilling time
Cooking Time: 20 minutes

Ingredients:
- 4 cod fillets
- salt and pepper, to taste
- 1 teaspoon red pepper flakes
- 1 teaspoon lemon zest
- 1 tablespoon lemon juice
- 2 tablespoons fresh parsley, chopped
- 2 tablespoons chives, chopped
- 1 teaspoon tabasco
- 1 raw egg, lightly beaten
- 2 tablespoons olive oil

Directions:
1. Preheat the Air Fryer to 300°F/150°C.
2. Season the cod fillets with salt and pepper and place in the Air Fryer Basket.
3. Set the timer for 5 minutes.
4. Remove the fillets from the Air Fryer and mash them with a fork.
5. Mix in the pepper flakes, lemon zest, lemon juice, parsley, chives, salt and pepper.
6. Add the tabasco, egg and olive oil.
7. Form into patties and chill for an hour or overnight.
8. Preheat the Air Fryer to 300°F/150°C.
9. Put patties in the Air Fryer and spray with some cooking spray.
10. Set the timer for 15 minutes.
11. Serve once timer goes off.

232 - Vietnamese Chicken and Pickled Vegetables Sandwich

Servings: 1
Preparation Time: 5 minutes
Cooking Time: 17 minutes

Ingredients:
- 1 small chicken breast
- salt and pepper, to taste
- ½ teaspoon caster sugar
- 1 teaspoon olive oil
- 1 teaspoon rice vinegar
- ½ teaspoon lime juice
- ½ small carrot, peeled and grated
- 2 spring onions, thinly sliced
- ¼ cup cucumbers, cubed
- ½ red chili, thinly sliced
- 2 slices bread
- 3-4 lettuce leaves

Directions:
1. Preheat the Air Fryer to 300°F/150°C.
2. Season the chicken breast with salt and pepper.
3. Place the chicken in the Air Fryer Basket and set the timer for 15 minutes.
4. Remove the chicken and allow to cool a little. Shred the chicken and set aside.
5. To make the pickled vegetables: Dilute the sugar in the olive oil, rice vinegar and lime juice. Add the carrots, onions, cucumbers and chilis into the bowl. Set aside.
6. Place the bread slices in the Air Fryer and set the timer for 2 minutes.
7. Top a bread slice with the lettuce, shredded chicken and the vegetable mixture. Top with the other slice of bread.
8. Serve and enjoy!

233 - One-Pot Creamy Tomato Basil Penne

Servings: 2
Preparation Time: 5 minutes
Cooking Time: 25 minutes

Ingredients:
- 1 cup tomatoes, diced
- 1 cup chicken stock
- 1 cup tomato sauce
- ¼ cup cream
- ½ medium onion, sliced
- 4 cloves garlic, minced
- 1 teaspoon dried oregano
- 1 teaspoon olive oil
- salt and pepper, to taste
- 6 oz uncooked penne
- ⅓ cup fresh basil leaves, chopped
- 1 tablespoon parmesan cheese, grated

Directions:
1. Preheat the Air Fryer to 300°F/150°C.
2. Mix the diced tomatoes, chicken stock, tomato sauce, cream, onions, minced garlic, dried oregano, olive oil, salt and pepper in the Air Fryer Baking Pan.
3. Mix in the pasta and place the Air Fryer Baking Pan in the Air Fryer Basket.
4. Set the timer for 15 minutes.
5. Remove from the Air Fryer, stir well, place back in the Air Fryer and set the timer for 10 more minutes.
6. Mix in the fresh basil.
7. Serve top with grated parmesan cheese.

234 - Coriander Fried Tofu

Servings: 2
Preparation Time: 5 minutes plus 30 minutes marinating time
Cooking Time: 20 minutes

Ingredients:
- 1½ cups low-fat extra firm tofu, cubed
- 1 teaspoon sesame oil
- 1 tablespoon coriander paste
- 2 tablespoon fish sauce
- 2 tablespoon low sodium soy sauce
- 1 teaspoon duck fat

Directions:
1. Preheat the Air Fryer to 300°F/150°C.
2. Mix together the tofu cubes, sesame oil, coriander paste, fish sauce and soy sauce in the Air Fryer Baking Pan. Set aside for 30 minutes.
3. Mix the duck fat into the Air Fryer Baking Pan and place the Air Fryer Baking Pan in the Air Fryer Basket.
4. Set the timer for 20 minutes.
5. Serve once the timer sounds.

235 - Tofu and Minced Meat

Servings: 4
Preparation Time: 5 minutes
Cooking Time: 30 minutes

Ingredients:

- 1 cup firm tofu, cubed
- 1 cup ground chicken
- 2 teaspoons oyster sauce
- 2 teaspoons white pepper
- ½ teaspoon salt
- ½ teaspoon sesame oil
- ¼ cup chicken stock
- 2 shiitake mushrooms, chopped
- 2 teaspoons spring onions, chopped
- 2 teaspoons ginger, minced
- 1 teaspoon minced garlic
- ¼ cup carrots, thinly sliced
- 1 red chili, seeds removed and thinly sliced

Directions:

1. Preheat the Air Fryer to 300°F/150°C.
2. Pat dry the excess water from the tofu cubes and arrange them in the Air Fryer Basket.
3. Set the timer for 20 minutes.
4. Remove the tofu cubes and set aside.
5. Mix together the minced chicken, oyster sauce, white pepper, salt, sesame oil, chicken stock, mushrooms, spring onions, ginger, garlic, carrots and chilis in the Air Fryer Baking Pan.
6. Place the Air Fryer Baking Pan in the Air Fryer Basket and set the timer for 10 minutes or until the chicken is fully cooked.
7. Mix the tofu cubes with the minced chicken until the tofu cubes are well coated with the sauce.
8. Serve up!

236 - Easy Tofu and Vegetables

Servings: 4
Preparation Time: 5 minutes
Cooking Time: 25 minutes

Ingredients:
- 12 ounces firm tofu, cubed
- 1 tablespoon cornstarch
- 3 tablespoons water
- 1 cup broccoli, cut into small florets
- ½ cup red bell peppers, thinly sliced
- 2 tablespoons sesame oil
- 3 tablespoons dark soy sauce
- 2 tablespoons rice wine vinegar
- 2 tablespoons hoisin sauce
- 1 teaspoon brown sugar

Directions:
1. Preheat the Air Fryer to 300°F/150°C.
2. Remove excess water from the tofu cubes with a kitchen towel.
3. Mix the cornstarch with the water and set aside.
4. Mix together the tofu cubes, broccoli, bell peppers, sesame oil, dark soy sauce, rice wine vinegar, hoisin sauce and brown sugar in the Air Fryer Baking Pan.
5. Stir in the cornstarch mixture.
6. Place the Air Fryer Baking Pan in the Air Fryer Basket and set the timer for 10 minutes.
7. Stir and set the timer for another 15 minutes
8. Serve once the timer goes off.

237 - Vegetable and Fish Noodle Stew

Servings: 2
Preparation Time: 5 minutes
Cooking Time: 20 minutes

Ingredients:
- 2 cod fillets, cubed
- 3 tablespoons soba sauce
- ¼ cup cherry tomatoes, halved
- ½ cup broccoli florets
- salt and pepper, to taste
- 3 cups fish stock
- ½ cup firm tofu, cubed
- 1 pack soba noodles

Directions:
1. Preheat the Air Fryer to 350°F/180°C.
2. Mix together the fish cubes, soba sauce, cherry tomatoes and broccoli florets in the Air Fryer Baking Pan.
3. Season with salt and pepper and set the timer for 10 minutes.
4. Cook the soba noodles in boiling water. Drain and set aside.
5. Add the fish stock, tofu and soba noodles to the Air Fryer Baking Pan and set the timer for 10 more minutes, stirring halfway through the cooking time. Serve after the timer strikes.

238 - Crispy Noodles with Crunchy Veggies

Servings: 2
Preparation Time: 10 minutes
Cooking Time: 15 minutes

Ingredients:
- 6 oz egg noodles
- 1 teaspoon vegetable oil
- 1 large onion, thinly sliced
- 1 cup cabbage, shredded
- 1 large red bell pepper, seeds removed and thinly sliced
- 1 large carrot, grated
- 1 tomato, finely diced
- 1 tablespoon date tamarind chutney
- 2 tablespoons hoisin sauce

Directions:
1. Preheat the Air Fryer to 300°F/150°C.
2. Blanch the egg noodles in hot water for 30 seconds until just half-cooked. Drain and leave to cool.
3. Toss noodles into Air Fryer Baking Pan with the vegetable oil.
4. Place the Air Fryer Baking Pan in the Air Fryer Basket and set the timer for 15 minutes.
5. Remove from the Air Fryer and toss with the onions, cabbage, bell peppers, carrots and tomatoes.
6. Season with the chutney and hoisin sauce, toss until well mixed before serving.

239 - Broccoli Mac N' Cheese

Servings: 2
Preparation Time: 2 minutes plus 5 minutes resting time
Cooking Time: 15 minutes

Ingredients:
- ½ cup milk, warmed
- 1½ cups cheddar cheese, grated
- ½ cup broccoli, cut into small florets
- 1 cup elbow macaroni, cooked
- 1 tablespoon parmesan cheese, grated

Directions:
1. Preheat the Air Fryer to 350°F/180°C.
2. Add the milk, cheddar cheese, broccoli and macaroni in the Air Fryer Baking Pan.
3. Top with parmesan cheese.
4. Place the Air Fryer Baking Pan in the Air Fryer Basket and set the timer for 15 minutes.
5. Remove from the Air Fryer and allow to rest for 5 minutes.
6. Once rested, serve up!

240 - Rosemary Cream Salmon Pasta

Servings: 2
Preparation Time: 10 minutes
Cooking Time: 18 minutes

Ingredients:
- 3 cloves garlic, minced
- 1 large onion, finely chopped
- 2 tomatoes, diced
- 1½ cups tomato sauce
- ¼ cup cream
- 2 cups fusilli, cooked
- 2 salmon fillets, skins removed
- 2 lemon slices
- 2 fresh rosemary sprigs, chopped
- 2 tablespoons parmesan cheese, grated

Directions:
1. Preheat the Air Fryer to 325°F/170°C.
2. Place the minced garlic, onions and tomatoes in the Air Fryer Baking Pan.
3. Place the Air Fryer Baking Pan in the Air Fryer Basket and set the timer for 5 minutes.
4. Add the tomato sauce and cream to the Air Fryer Baking Pan.
5. Return to the Air Fryer and set the timer for 5 more minutes
6. Toss the pasta into the Air Fryer Baking Pan and mix well.
7. Place the salmon fillet on the pasta.
8. Place a slice of lemon and the chopped rosemary on each salmon fillet and top with the parmesan cheese.
9. Return to the Air Fryer and set the timer for 8 more minutes or until the fish is cooked through.

241 - Chorizo Meatballs

Servings: 4
Preparation time: 15 minutes plus 30 minutes chilling time
Cooking Time: 15 minutes

Ingredients:
- 1 pound Spanish chorizos
- 2 German sausages, finely chopped
- ½ cup onions, minced
- 2 tablespoons red bell peppers finely chopped
- 2 tablespoons chives, chopped
- 3 tablespoons breadcrumbs
- 1 tablespoon paprika

Directions:
1. Remove the chorizos from their casings.
2. Mix the chorizos with the sausages, onions, bell peppers and chives.
3. Knead until well combined and form meatballs.
4. Chill the meatballs for 30 minutes.
5. Preheat the Air Fryer to 350°F/180°C.
6. Mix together the breadcrumbs and paprika and coat the meatballs with the breadcrumbs.
7. Arrange the meatballs in the Air Fryer Basket and use the Double Layer Rack if needed.
8. Set the timer for 15 minutes or until the meatballs are cooked through.

242 - Kimchi Stuffed Squid

Servings: 2
Preparation time: 5 minutes
Cooking Time: 12 minutes

Ingredients:
- 1 whole squid, membranes removed and thoroughly cleaned
- salt and pepper, to taste
- 1 teaspoon garlic powder
- 1 cup ready-made kimchi

Directions:
1. Preheat the Air Fryer to 350°F/180°C.
2. Season the squid with the salt, pepper and garlic powder.
3. Stuff the squid with the kimchi.
4. Set the timer for 12 minutes.

243 - Chicken and Chorizos with Tomatoes

Servings: 2
Preparation time: 10 minutes plus 30 minutes chilling time
Cooking Time: 16 minutes

Ingredients:
- 2 chicken thighs
- salt and pepper, to taste
- 1 tablespoon onion powder
- 1 teaspoon garlic powder
- 1 tablespoon olive oil
- 1 cup tomato sauce
- ¼ cup whole olives, seedless
- ½ cup chorizos, chopped
- 2 tablespoons fresh basil, chopped

Directions:
1. Preheat the Air Fryer to 350°F/180°C.
2. Season the chicken thighs with the salt, pepper, onion powder, garlic powder and olive oil.
3. Chill the chicken in the fridge for 30 minutes.
4. Arrange the chicken in the Air Fryer Baking Pan and place the Air Fryer Baking Pan in the Air Fryer Basket.
5. Set the timer for 10 minutes.
6. Add the tomato sauce, olives and chorizos to the Air Fryer Baking Pan and set the timer for 6 more minutes or until the chicken is cooked through.
7. Serve and top with the fresh basil.

244 - Italian Crabby Patty

Servings: 2
Preparation time: 15 minutes plus 30 minutes chilling time
Cooking Time: 12 minutes

Ingredients:
- 2 cups crab meat
- 1 teaspoon ground allspice
- 1 teaspoon Italian seasoning
- 1 teaspoon dried sage
- salt and pepper, to taste
- 3 eggs
- 2 tablespoons milk
- 1 cup flour
- 1½ cups breadcrumbs

Directions:
1. Preheat the Air Fryer to 325°F/170°C.
2. Mix together the crab meat with the ground allspice, Italian seasoning, dried sage, salt and pepper.
3. Form crab meat patties and chill for 30 minutes.
4. Whisk the eggs with the milk to make an egg wash and season with pepper.
5. Dust the patties in flour and dip in the egg mixture.
6. Coat evenly with the breadcrumbs and arrange in the Air Fryer Basket.
7. Set the timer for 12 minutes and flip the crab patties with every few minutes during cooking.
8. Serve up once the timer strikes!

245 - Mr. Potato Jack!

Servings: 2
Preparation time: 10 minutes
Cooking Time: 23 minutes

Ingredients:
- 2 large potatoes, halved
- 1 cup mozzarella cheese, grated
- 2 tablespoons bacon bits
- 2 tablespoons chives, chopped
- ¼ cup sour cream

Directions:
1. Preheat the Air Fryer to 400°F/200°C.
2. Arrange the potatoes in the Air Fryer Basket.
3. Set the timer for 15 minutes or until the potatoes are tender.
4. Top the potatoes with the grated cheese and bacon bits.
5. Return to the Air Fryer and set the timer for 8 more minutes.
6. Remove from the Air Fryer and serve while topping with chives and sour cream.

246 - Green Mango and Garlic Squid

Servings: 2
Preparation time: 5 minutes
Cooking Time: 12 minutes

Ingredients:
- 1 cup green mangoes, diced
- 4 cloves garlic, sliced
- ¼ cup onions, sliced
- salt and pepper, to taste
- 1 whole squid, membranes removed and thoroughly cleaned

Directions:
1. Preheat the Air Fryer to 350°F/180°C.
2. Mix together the green mangoes, garlic and onions.
3. Season with a little salt and pepper.
4. Stuff the squid with the mango mixture.
5. Place the squid in the Air Fryer Basket and set the timer for 12 minutes.
6. Serve and enjoy!

247 - Chicken Marinara

Servings: 2
Preparation time: 5 minutes
Cooking Time: 18 minutes

Ingredients:
- 4 chicken thighs
- salt and pepper, to taste
- 1 cup ready-made marinara sauce
- 2 teaspoons garlic, minced
- 2 tablespoons fresh basil, chopped

Directions:
1. Preheat the Air Fryer to 400°F/200°C.
2. Place the chicken thighs in the Air Fryer Baking Pan and season with salt and pepper.
3. Spray the chicken with cooking spray.
4. Place the Air Fryer Baking Pan in the Air Fryer Basket and set the timer for 10 minutes.
5. Pour in the marinara sauce and add the minced garlic and fresh basil.
6. Return to the Air Fryer and set the timer for 8 more minutes or until the chicken is cooked through.
7. Serve and enjoy!

248 - Chicken Enchilada

Servings: 2
Preparation time: 5 minutes
Cooking Time: 18 minutes

Ingredients:

- 4 chicken thigh fillets, sliced
- 1 teaspoon taco seasoning
- salt and pepper, to taste
- 2 teaspoons garlic, minced
- ½ cup onions, chopped
- ½ cup tomatoes, diced
- 1 tablespoon jalapeños
- 1 teaspoon olive oil
- 1 cup tomato sauce
- 2 tablespoons fresh basil, chopped

Directions:

1. Preheat the Air Fryer to 350°F/180°C.
2. Place the chicken slices in the Air Fryer Baking Pan and season with the taco seasoning, salt and pepper.
3. Add the garlic, onions, tomatoes, jalapeños and olive oil.
4. Place the Air Fryer Baking Pan in the Air Fryer Basket and set the timer for 10 minutes.
5. Pour in the tomato sauce and fresh basil and stir well.
6. Return to the Air Fryer and set the timer for 8 more minutes or until the chicken is cooked through.
7. Serve and enjoy!

249 - Pizza Peppers

Servings: 2
Preparation time: 10 minutes
Cooking Time: 8 minutes

Ingredients:

- 4 medium bell peppers
- 8 slices deli ham
- 1 cup cheddar cheese
- 1 cup pineapple chunks
- ¼ cup onions, finely chopped
- 1 cup tomato sauce
- ½ cup feta cheese, crumbled
- 1 cup mozzarella cheese, grated
- 2 tablespoons fresh basil, finely chopped

Directions:

1. Preheat the Air Fryer to 400°F/200°C.
2. Slice off the tops of the bell peppers and remove the seeds.
3. Place two slices of deli ham inside each bell pepper.
4. Divide the cheddar cheese, pineapple chunks and onions between the bell peppers.
5. Divide the tomato sauce between the bell peppers and top with the feta cheese and mozzarella cheese.
6. Top with the fresh basil and arrange the peppers inside the Air Fryer Basket.
7. Set the timer for 8 minutes. Serve once timer strikes.

250 - Lamb Chops with Tomatoes and Olives

Servings: 2
Preparation time: 5 minutes
Cooking Time: 15 minutes

Ingredients:
- 1 pound lamb chops
- 1 teaspoon garlic powder
- 1 teaspoon ground anise
- 1 tablespoon paprika
- 1 teaspoon olive oil
- 1 cup tomato sauce
- 1 cup vegetable stock
- ¼ cup whole olives, seedless
- 1 cup tomatoes, diced
- ¼ cup onions, chopped
- 2 tablespoons fresh basil, chopped

Directions:
1. Preheat the Air Fryer to 350°F/180°C.
2. Mix together the lamb chops, garlic powder, ground anise, paprika and olive oil.
3. Place the lamb chops in Air Fryer Baking Pan.
4. Place the Air Fryer Baking Pan in the Air Fryer Basket and set the timer for 5 minutes.
5. Pour in the tomato sauce, vegetable stock, olives, tomatoes and onions and return to the Air Fryer.
6. Set the timer for 10 more minutes or until desired doneness of the lamb chops.
7. Serve and top with the fresh basil.

251 - Pork Cordon Bleu

Servings: 2
Preparation time: 10 minutes
Cooking Time: 12 minutes

Ingredients:
- 3 tablespoons breadcrumbs
- 1 teaspoon paprika
- 1 teaspoon garlic powder
- 1 egg, beaten
- salt and pepper, to taste
- 2 slices deli ham
- 2 slices cheese
- 2 pork steaks, pounded

Directions:
1. Preheat the Air Fryer to 350°F/180°C.
2. Mix together the breadcrumbs, paprika, and garlic powder.
3. Whisk the eggs with some salt and pepper.
4. Place a slice of ham and a slice of cheese onto a slice of pork and fold them in half.
5. Dip into the egg mixture and then coat evenly in breadcrumbs.
6. Shake off the excess breadcrumbs and arrange in the Air Fryer Basket.
7. Air fry for 12 minutes and serve when done.

252 - Chicken Mozzarella Melt

Servings: 2
Preparation time: 5 minutes
Cooking Time: 20 minutes

Ingredients:
- 2 chicken breast fillets, sliced
- salt and pepper, to taste
- ¼ cup onions, sliced
- ¼ cup mushrooms, sliced
- ¼ cup tomato, diced
- ½ cup mozzarella cheese, grated
- 2 tablespoons fresh parsley, chopped

Directions:
1. Preheat the Air Fryer to 350°F/180°C.
2. Place the chicken slices in the Air Fryer Baking Pan and season with salt and pepper.
3. Add the onions and mushrooms.
4. Place the Air Fryer Baking Pan in the Air Fryer Basket and set the timer for 15 minutes.
5. Remove from the Air Fryer and cover completely with the tomatoes and mozzarella cheese.
6. Return to the Air Fryer and set the timer for 5 more minutes or until the cheese has melted.
7. Serve and top with the fresh parsley.

253 - Sea Bass en Papillote

Servings: 4
Preparation time: 10 minutes
Cooking Time: 8 minutes

Ingredients:
- 4 sea bass fillets
- salt and pepper, to taste
- 1 cup corn kernels
- 1 cup green beans, chopped
- 1 cup tomatoes, diced
- ½ cup mushrooms, sliced
- 2 tablespoons lemon juice
- 4 sprigs rosemary

Directions:
1. Preheat the Air Fryer to 350°F/180°C.
2. Cut 4 sheets of foil large enough to make parcels for the sea bass fillets.
3. Season both sides of the sea bass fillets with salt and pepper and place in the middle of the foil.
4. Top each fillet with the corn kernels, green beans, tomatoes, mushrooms and rosemary sprigs.
5. Drizzle over the lemon juice and season with more pepper.
6. Seal the foil sheets to form parcels so that the fillets are completely encased.
7. Arrange the parcels in the Air Fryer Basket and use the Air Fryer Double Layer Rack if needed.
8. Set the timer for 8 minutes.
9. Once timer goes off, serve.

254 - Puttanesca Stuff Tomatoes

Servings: 2 servings
Preparation time: 10 minutes
Cooking Time: 10 minutes

Ingredients:
- 4 large tomatoes
- salt and pepper, to taste
- 1 cup canned tomatoes
- 2 teaspoons anchovies
- 1 tablespoon capers
- 2 cups cooked spaghetti
- ½ cup feta cheese
- 8 bacon slices, chopped
- 2 tablespoons parsley, chopped

Directions:
1. Preheat the Air Fryer to 350°F/180°C.
2. Slice the top of the tomatoes and remove the flesh and seeds into a bowl.
3. Season the empty tomato cups with salt and pepper.
4. Mix the tomato flesh and seeds with the canned tomatoes, anchovies, capers and cooked pasta.
5. Season with pepper and mix until well combined.
6. Fill the tomatoes cups with the pasta mixture and top with feta cheese and chopped bacon.
7. Arrange in the Air Fryer Basket and set the timer for 10 minutes.
8. Serve and garnish with the fresh parsley.

255 - One Pan Chicken Chipotle

Servings: 2
Preparation Time: 10 minutes
Cooking Time: 10 minutes

Ingredients:
- 2 chicken breasts, sliced
- salt and pepper, to taste
- 1 teaspoon taco seasoning
- 1 tablespoon garlic, minced
- 2 tablespoons chipotles, chopped
- ½ cup mushrooms, sliced
- ¼ cup fresh coriander, chopped
- 2 teaspoons lime juice
- ¼ cup parmesan cheese, shavings

Directions:
1. Preheat the Air Fryer to 350°F/180°C.
2. Place the chicken slices in the Air Fryer Baking Pan and season with the salt, pepper and taco seasoning.
3. Spray with cooking spray and place the Air Fryer Baking Pan in the Air Fryer Basket.
4. Add in the minced garlic, chipotles, mushrooms and fresh coriander.
5. Add the lime juice and season with more pepper.
6. Set the timer for 10 minutes or until the chicken is cooked through.
7. Serve and top with the parmesan cheese.

256 - Fresh Tortellini with Sausages in Tomato Sauce

Servings: 2
Preparation Time: 5 minutes
Cooking Time: 15 minutes

Ingredients:
- 1 cup Italian sausages, sliced
- 1 cup tomato sauce
- 1 cup chicken stock
- 1 teaspoon Italian seasoning
- 2 cups fresh tortellini
- pepper, to taste
- ¼ cup fresh basil, chopped
- 1 cup mozzarella cheese, grated

Directions:
1. Preheat the Air Fryer to 350°F/180°C.
2. Place the sliced sausages in the Air Fryer Baking Pan.
3. Add the tomato sauce, chicken stock, Italian seasoning and tortellini's.
4. Season with pepper and mix until well combined.
5. Place the Air Fryer Baking Pan in the Air Fryer Basket and set the timer for 10 minutes.
6. Stir in the fresh basil and grated mozzarella.
7. Set the timer for 5 more minutes.
8. Serve when ready.

257 - Herbed-Crusted Flank Steaks

Servings: 4
Preparation Time: 10 minutes
Cooking Time: 8 minutes

Ingredients:
- 4 flank steaks
- salt and pepper, to taste
- ⅓ cup breadcrumbs
- 1 teaspoon dried rosemary
- 1 teaspoon dried sage
- 1 teaspoon paprika

Directions:
1. Preheat the Air Fryer to 350°F/180°C.
2. Season the steaks with salt and pepper and spray with some cooking spray.
3. Mix together the breadcrumbs, dried rosemary, dried sage and paprika.
4. Coat only one side of the steaks.
5. Arrange the steaks crumbed side up in the Air Fryer Basket.
6. Set the timer for 8 minutes or until desired doneness of meat.
7. Serve when ready.

258 - Spaghetti with Shrimps, Spinach and Asparagus

Servings: 2
Preparation time: 5 minutes
Cooking Time: 10 minutes

Ingredients:
- 1 tablespoon butter, melted
- 2 tablespoons garlic, minced
- ½ cup shrimps, peeled and deveined
- 1 cup asparagus, cut into small pieces
- 6 oz spaghetti, cooked
- salt and pepper, to taste
- 1 cup baby spinach leaves

Directions:
1. Preheat the Air Fryer to 350°F/180°C.
2. Place the butter, minced garlic, shrimps and asparagus the Air Fryer Baking Pan.
3. Place the Air Fryer Baking Pan in the Air Fryer Basket and set the timer for 6 minutes.
4. Add the cooked pasta to the Air Fryer Baking Pan and season with salt and pepper.
5. Return to the Air Fryer and set the timer for 4 more minutes.
6. Stir in the spinach.
7. Serve on a plate or bowl.

259 - Shrimps, Tomatoes and Cauliflower

Servings: 2
Preparation time: 5 minutes
Cooking Time: 10 minutes

Ingredients:
- 2 cups cauliflower, cut into florets
- 1 cup shrimps, peeled and deveined
- pepper, to taste
- 1 teaspoon paprika
- 2 tablespoons garlic, minced
- 1 cup tomato sauce
- 1 cup tomatoes, diced

Directions:
1. Preheat the Air Fryer to 350°F/180°C.
2. Place the cauliflower florets in the Air Fryer Baking Pan.
3. Add the shrimps and season with pepper and paprika.
4. Add the garlic and place the Air Fryer Baking Pan in the Air Fryer Basket.
5. Set the timer for 4 minutes.
6. Pour in the tomato sauce and diced tomatoes.
7. Stir until well combined.
8. Return to the Air Fryer and set the timer for 6 more minutes or until the shrimps are cooked.
9. Serve once done.

260 - Cheesy Chicken, Bacon and Zucchini

Servings: 2
Preparation Time: 5 minutes
Cooking Time: 30 minutes

Ingredients:
- 2 chicken breast fillets, sliced
- salt and pepper, to taste
- 6 rashers bacon, chopped
- 1 medium zucchini, sliced
- 4 slices tomato
- 4 slices cheddar cheese
- 4 slices mozzarella cheese
- ¼ cup chives, chopped

Directions:
1. Preheat the Air Fryer to 350°F/180°C.
2. Season the chicken slices with salt & pepper.
3. Place the chopped bacon and chicken slices in the Air Fryer Baking Pan and place the Air Fryer Baking Pan in the Air Fryer Basket.
4. Set the timer for 15 minutes.
5. Flip the chicken slices and add the zucchinis.
6. Set the timer for 10 minutes or until the chicken is cooked through.
7. Add the tomato, cheddar cheese and mozzarella slices and set the timer for 5 more minutes until the cheeses have melted.
8. Serve and top with chives.

261 - Lemon Butter King Crab

Servings: 4
Preparation Time: 5 minutes
Cooking Time: 8 minutes

Ingredients:
- 2 cans King Crab
- ½ cup butter, melted
- ½ teaspoon garlic salt
- 2 tablespoons garlic, minced
- 2 tablespoons lemon juice
- 2 tablespoons fresh cilantro, chopped

Directions:
1. Preheat the Air Fryer to 300°F/150°C.
2. Place the King Crab in the Air Fryer Baking Pan.
3. Add the butter, garlic salt, minced garlic and lemon juice.
4. Place the Air Fryer Baking Pan in the Air Fryer Basket and set the timer for 8 minutes.
5. Top with the fresh cilantro.
6. Serve and enjoy.

262 - Chicken Chickpea and Potatoes

Servings: 2
Preparation Time: 10 minutes
Cooking Time: 15 minutes

Ingredients:
- 2 chicken breast fillet, cubed
- 1 teaspoon garlic powder
- 1 teaspoon dried sage
- salt and pepper, to taste
- 1 cup canned chickpeas
- 1 cup potatoes, diced

Directions:
1. Preheat the Air Fryer to 350°F/180°C.
2. Place the chicken cubes in the Air Fryer Baking Pan and season with the garlic powder, sage, salt & pepper.
3. Add the chickpeas and potatoes to the Air Fryer Baking Pan.
4. Season with pepper and spray with cooking spray.
5. Place the Air Fryer Baking Pan in the Air Fryer Basket and set the timer for 15 minutes or until the chicken is cooked through.
6. Serve once done.

263 - Guacamole Chicken Wraps

Servings: 2
Preparation time: 10 minutes
Cooking Time: 8 minutes

Ingredients:
- 2 large chicken breasts, sliced
- 1 teaspoon cayenne pepper
- 1 teaspoon garlic powder
- salt and pepper, to taste
- ¼ cup onions, chopped
- 2 tortilla wraps
- 1 cup guacamole
- 1 cup tomatoes, chopped
- ¼ cup fresh coriander, chopped

Directions:
1. Preheat the Air Fryer to 350°F/180°C.
2. Season the chicken slices with cayenne pepper, garlic powder, salt and pepper.
3. Place the chicken and onions in the Air Fryer Baking Pan and spray with cooking spray.
4. Place the Air Fryer Baking Pan in the Air Fryer Basket and set the timer for 8 minutes or until the chicken is cooked through.
5. Place the chicken and onions on the tortilla wraps and top with a dollop of guacamole.
6. Top with chopped tomatoes and fresh coriander.
7. Roll and twist to encase the filling.
8. Serve and enjoy!

264 - Chickpea and Tomato Stew

Servings: 2
Preparation time: 10 minutes
Cooking Time: 10 minutes

Ingredients:
- 2 onions, chopped
- 1 stalk celery, chopped
- 1 cup chickpeas
- ¼ cup red lentils, soaked overnight, rinsed and drained
- 1 teaspoon ginger, sliced
- 1 teaspoon turmeric
- 1 teaspoon paprika
- salt and pepper, to taste
- 4 cups chicken stock
- 3 big tomatoes, diced
- ¼ cup fresh cilantro, chopped
- 1 cup cooked long grain rice, optional

Directions:
1. Preheat the Air Fryer to 350°F/180°C.
2. Place the onions, celery, chickpeas, lentils and ginger in the Air Fryer Baking Pan.
3. Season with the turmeric, paprika, salt and pepper.
4. Place the Air Fryer Baking Pan in the Air Fryer Basket and set the timer for 5 minutes.
5. Add the chicken stock and tomatoes and stir until well combined.
6. Return to the Air Fryer and set the timer for another 5 minutes.
7. Top with fresh cilantro.
8. Serve with rice if desired and enjoy!

265 - Chicken Tomato Vodka Pasta

Servings: 2
Preparation Time: 10 minutes
Cooking Time: 13 minutes

Ingredients:

- 2 chicken breasts, sliced
- 1 teaspoon paprika
- salt and pepper, to taste
- 1 cup tomato sauce
- 1 shot of vodka
- ¼ cup onions, diced
- ¼ cup fresh basil, chopped
- 2 cups of cooked penne
- ½ cup mozzarella, grated
- 1 tablespoon fresh basil, chopped

Directions:

1. Preheat the Air Fryer to 350°F/180°C.
2. Place the chicken slices in the Air Fryer Baking Pan and season with paprika, salt and pepper.
3. Spray with some cooking spray and place the Air Fryer Baking Pan in the Air Fryer Basket.
4. Set the timer for 8 minutes.
5. Remove from the Air Fryer and pour in the tomato sauce and vodka.
6. Add the onions and return the Air Fryer.
7. Set the timer for 5 more minutes or until the chicken is cooked through.
8. Pour the chicken over the cooked pasta and stir in the mozzarella cheese.
9. Serve and top with the fresh basil.

266 - Hemp Trout with Tropical Salad

Servings: 2
Preparation Time: 10 minutes
Cooking Time: 8 minutes

Ingredients:

- 2 trout fillets
- salt and pepper, to taste
- 2 tablespoons lemon juice
- 3 tablespoons hemp oil
- ½ tablespoon balsamic vinegar
- 1 teaspoon garlic, minced
- 3 tablespoons alfalfa sprouts
- ¼ cup mangoes, diced
- ¼ cup mandarin segments
- 1 teaspoon hemp seeds

Directions:

1. Preheat the Air Fryer to 350°F/180°C.
2. Season the trout fillets with salt, pepper and 1 tablespoon of lemon juice.
3. Place the fillets in the Air Fryer Basket and spray with cooking spray.
4. Set the timer for 8 minutes.
5. To make the tropical salad: Mix together the hemp oil, the remaining lemon juice, balsamic vinegar and minced garlic in a bowl. Add the alfalfa sprouts, mangoes and mandarin segments. Season with pepper and mix well to combine.
6. Remove the trout fillets from the Air Fryer and place on a plate with the tropical salad.
7. Serve and top with the hemp seeds.

267 - Apple and Potato Salad with Chili and Lime Dressing

Servings: 2
Preparation Time: 10 minutes plus cooling time
Cooking Time: 10 minutes

Ingredients:
- 2 cups baby potatoes, halved
- 2 cups apples, diced
- 1 teaspoon lime juice
- ¼ cup celery, chopped
- 1 teaspoon chili flakes
- ½ cup mayonnaise
- salt and pepper, to taste
- 1 tablespoon fresh cilantro, chopped

Directions:
1. Preheat the Air Fryer to 350°F/180°C.
2. Place in the potatoes in the Air Fryer Basket and set the timer for 10 minutes or until the potatoes are tender.
3. Remove the potatoes from the Air Fryer and transfer to a large bowl leave to cool.
4. Add the apples and lime juice to the potatoes.
5. Add the celery, chili flakes and mayonnaise.
6. Season with salt and pepper and toss until well combined.
7. Serve and top with the fresh cilantro.

268 - Mandarin Lemon Chicken Drums

Servings: 2
Preparation Time: 10 minutes
Cooking Time: 13 minutes

Ingredients:
- 4 chicken drumsticks
- 1 teaspoon paprika
- salt and pepper, to taste
- ½ cup mandarin slices
- ¼ cup onions, diced
- 2 tablespoons lemon juice
- ¼ cup fresh parsley, chopped

Directions:
1. Preheat the Air Fryer to 350°F/180°C.
2. Place the chicken drumsticks in the Air Fryer Baking Pan and season with paprika, salt and pepper.
3. Spray with some cooking spray if desired and set the timer for 8 minutes.
4. Add the mandarin slices, onions, lemon juice and more pepper.
5. Return to the Air Fryer and set the timer for another 5 minutes or until the chicken is cooked through.
6. Serve and garnish with some fresh parsley.

269 - Salmon Fillets with Arugula and Strawberries Salad

Servings: 2
Preparation Time: 10 minutes
Cooking Time: 8 minutes

Ingredients:
- 2 salmon fillets
- salt and pepper, to taste
- 2 tablespoons lemon juice
- 1 cup arugula leaves
- ¼ cup strawberries, sliced
- ¼ cup feta cheese, crumbled
- ½ tablespoon balsamic vinegar
- 3 tablespoons olive oil

Directions:
1. Preheat the Air Fryer to 350°F/180°C.
2. Season the salmon fillets with salt, pepper and lemon juice.
3. Place the salmon in the Air Fryer Basket and set the timer for 8 minutes.
4. To make the salad: Mix together the arugula leaves, strawberries and feta cheese. Drizzle with the balsamic vinegar and olive oil and season well with the pepper.
5. Remove the salmon fillets from the Air Fryer and serve on a plate with the salad.

270 - Rosemary, Bacon and Gruyere Sausages

Servings: 2
Preparation Time: 10 minutes
Cooking Time: 12 minutes

Ingredients:
- 6 sausage patties
- 1 teaspoon paprika
- salt and pepper, to taste
- 8 rashers bacon, chopped
- ½ cup gruyere cheese, grated

Directions:
1. Preheat the Air Fryer to 350°F/180°C.
2. Season the sausage patties with the paprika, salt and pepper.
3. Place them in the Air Fryer Basket and use the Air Fryer Double Layer Rack if needed.
4. Top with the chopped bacon and set the timer for 10 minutes.
5. Remove from the Air Fryer and top the patties with the gruyere cheese.
6. Set the timer for another 2 minutes until the cheese has melted.
7. Serve once cheese has melted!

271 - Deconstructed Chicken Caesar

Servings: 2
Preparation Time: 15 minutes
Cooking Time: 12 minutes

Ingredients:

- 2 chicken breast fillets, sliced
- 1 teaspoon paprika
- salt and pepper, to taste
- 1 tablespoon mustard
- 1 teaspoon lemon juice
- 2 egg yolks
- 1 teaspoon anchovies
- 2 teaspoons garlic, minced
- 4 tablespoons olive oil
- ¼ cup parmesan cheese, shavings

Directions:

1. Preheat the Air Fryer at 350°F/180°C.
2. Season the chicken with paprika, salt and pepper.
3. Whisk together the mustard, lemon juice and egg yolks.
4. Whisk in the anchovies and minced garlic.
5. Gradually whisk in the olive oil until the sauce is thickened.
6. Marinate the chicken slices with the Caesar mixture until the chicken is well coated.
7. Place the chicken slices in the Air Fryer Basket and set the timer for 12 minutes or until the chicken is cooked through.
8. Remove from the Air Fryer and top with the parmesan shavings before serving.

272 - Chicken with Artichokes and Mushrooms

Servings: 2
Preparation Time: 5 minutes
Cooking Time: 13 minutes

Ingredients:

- 1 chicken breast, sliced
- salt and pepper, to taste
- ½ cup artichokes, chopped
- ¼ cup button mushrooms, sliced
- ¼ cup goat cheese
- 2 tablespoons fresh parsley, chopped

Directions:

1. Preheat the Air Fryer to 350°F/180°C.
2. Place the chicken slices in the Air Fryer Baking Pan and season with salt and pepper to taste.
3. Spray the chicken with a little cooking spray and place the Air Fryer Baking Pan in the Air Fryer Basket.
4. Set the timer for 8 minutes.
5. Add the artichokes and mushrooms and set the timer for another 5 minutes.
6. Remove from the Air Fryer and top with the goat cheese and fresh parsley before serving.

273 - Chicken Cilantro with Beets

Servings: 2
Preparation Time: 5 minutes
Cooking Time: 11 minutes

Ingredients:
- 1 chicken breast, cubed
- salt and pepper, to taste
- ¼ cup red bell peppers, diced
- 1 large beet, thinly sliced
- ¼ cup radish, sliced
- ¼ cup goat cheese
- ¼ cup fresh cilantro, chopped

Directions:
1. Preheat the Air Fryer to 350°F/180°C.
2. Place the chicken cubes in the Air Fryer Baking Pan and season with salt and pepper.
3. Place the Air Fryer Baking Pan in the Air Fryer Basket and set the timer for 8 minutes.
4. Add the bell peppers, beets and radish to the Air Fryer Baking Pan and set the timer for 3 more minutes or until the chicken is cooked through.
5. Serve and top with the goat cheese and fresh cilantro.

274 - Sausages with Broccoli and Cheese

Servings: 2
Preparation Time: 10 minutes
Cooking Time: 12 minutes

Ingredients:
- 4 small sausage patties
- 4 rashers bacon, chopped
- 1 cup broccoli, cut into small florets
- ¼ cup butter, cubed
- ¼ cup cheddar cheese, grated
- 1 tablespoon cream cheese
- ¼ cup mozzarella cheese, grated
- ¼ cup low-fat milk
- 1 tablespoon fresh parsley, chopped
- 1 teaspoon anchovies

Directions:
1. Preheat the Air Fryer to 350°F/180°C.
2. Arrange the sausages and bacon in the Air Fryer Baking Pan.
3. Place the Air Fryer Baking Pan in the Air Fryer Basket and set the timer for 6 minutes.
4. Add the broccoli florets and set the timer for 3 minutes.
5. Dot the meat and broccoli with the butter cubes.
6. Combine the cheddar cheese, cream cheese and mozzarella cheese with the low-fat milk and pour into the Air Fryer Baking Pan.
7. Stir in the chopped fresh parsley and anchovies.
8. Set the timer for 3 more minutes or until the cheese has melted.
9. Serve once cheese has melted.

275 - Veggie Overload

Servings: 4
Preparation Time: 5 minutes
Cooking Time: 7 minutes

Ingredients:

- 1 teaspoon olive oil
- 1 cup broccoli florets, cut into small florets
- 1 cup baby brussels sprouts, halved
- ¼ cup onions, sliced
- garlic salt and pepper, to taste
- 1 teaspoon paprika
- 1 cup baby spinach leaves, chopped
- ¼ cup parmesan cheese, grated
- ¼ cup chives, chopped

Directions:

1. Preheat the Air Fryer to 350°F/180°C.
2. Add the olive oil in the Air Fryer Baking Pan and mix in the broccoli florets, brussels sprouts and onions.
3. Season the vegetables with the garlic salt, pepper and paprika.
4. Place the Air Fryer Baking Pan in the Air Fryer Basket and set the timer for 5 minutes.
5. Mix in the baby spinach leaves and set the timer for 2 more minutes or until the vegetables are cooked to your desired crunchiness.
6. Serve and top with the parmesan cheese and chives.

276 - Herbed Stuffed Mushroom Cups

Servings: 2
Preparation Time: 10 minutes
Cooking Time: 6 minutes

Ingredients:
- 1 cup ricotta cheese
- 1 teaspoon Italian seasoning
- 1 teaspoon garlic powder
- 1 tablespoon chives, chopped
- 1 tablespoon fresh cilantro, chopped
- salt and pepper, to taste
- 4 large shiitake mushrooms, cleaned and stems removed

Directions:
1. Preheat the Air Fryer to 350°F/180°C.
2. Mix the ricotta cheese with the Italian seasoning, garlic powder, chives and fresh cilantro.
3. Season with salt and pepper.
4. Stuff the mushrooms with the ricotta mixture and arrange them in the Air Fryer Basket. Use the Air Fryer Double Layer Rack if needed.
5. Set the timer for 6 minutes or until the mushrooms are cooked.
6. Serve once mushrooms are cooked.

277 - Tomatoes Stuffed with Peppers

Servings: 4
Preparation Time: 15 minutes
Cooking Time: 8 minutes

Ingredients:
- 4 large tomatoes
- 1 cup mozzarella cheese, grated
- ¼ cup fresh basil, chopped
- ¼ cup onions, finely chopped
- 1 teaspoon Italian seasoning
- salt and pepper, to taste
- 2 large bell peppers, stems removed and each cut into 2 rings

Directions:
1. Preheat the Air Fryer to 350°F/180°C.
2. To prepare the tomatoes, cut the tops off the tomatoes and remove the pulps and seeds. Reserve the pulps and seeds in a bowl and set aside.
3. Mix the mozzarella, basil and onions with the tomato pulp and season with the Italian seasoning, salt and pepper.
4. Place each bell pepper ring into each tomato, so that the peppers line the inside walls of the tomatoes.
5. Fill the tomatoes with the cheese mixture and arrange them in the Air Fryer Basket.
6. Set the timer for 8 minutes.
7. Serve once done.

278 - Garlic Lemon Chicken and Shrimps

Servings: 2
Preparation Time: 5 minutes
Cooking Time: 20 minutes

Ingredients:
- 1 tablespoon butter
- 1 tablespoon garlic, minced
- 1 tablespoon lemon juice
- 1 chicken breast, cubed
- salt and pepper, to taste
- 1 teaspoon paprika
- 1 cup shrimps, shells removed and deveined
- 2 tablespoons fresh cilantro, chopped

Directions:
1. Preheat the Air Fryer to 350°F/180°C.
2. Place the butter, garlic and lemon juice in the Air Fryer Baking Pan.
3. Add the chicken cubes and season with salt and pepper.
4. Place the Air Fryer Baking Pan in the Air Fryer Basket and set the timer for 15 minutes.
5. Mix in the paprika, shrimps and fresh cilantro.
6. Set the timer for another 5 minutes or until the chicken and shrimps are cooked through.
7. Once properly cooked through, begin to serve.

279 - Air Fried Garlic Scallops with Baby Spinach

Servings: 2
Preparation Time: 5 minutes
Cooking Time: 7 minutes

Ingredients:
- 1 cup scallops
- 1 teaspoon paprika
- salt and pepper, to taste
- 5 cloves garlic, sliced
- 2 tablespoons ghee
- ½ cup onions, sliced
- ¼ cup fresh cilantro, chopped
- 1 cup baby spinach leaves

Directions:
1. Preheat the Air Fryer to 350°F/180°C.
2. Season the scallops with the paprika, salt and pepper and place them in the Air Fryer Baking Pan with the garlic and ghee.
3. Set the timer for 3 minutes and flip over the scallops.
4. Top the scallops with the onions and fresh cilantro and set the timer for 4 minutes.
5. Remove from the Air Fryer and top with the baby spinach leaves before serving.

280 - Spicy Meatballs

Servings: 4
Preparation Time: 5 minutes plus 25 minutes chilling time
Cooking Time: 15 minutes

Ingredients:
- 1 pound lean ground beef
- ¼ cup onions, finely chopped
- 1 tablespoon garlic, minced
- 2 tablespoons jalapeños
- 2 tablespoons paprika
- 2 tablespoons chili flakes
- Pepper, to taste

Directions:
1. Mix together the ground beef, onions, garlic and jalapeños.
2. Season with the paprika, chili flakes and pepper.
3. Roll into ping pong sized meatballs and chill for 25 minutes.
4. Preheat the Air Fryer to 400°F/200°C.
5. Arrange the meatballs in the Air Fryer Basket. Use the Air Fryer Double Layer Rack if needed.
6. Set the timer for 15 minutes.
7. Serve once done.

281 - Spicy Beef Rice

Servings: 2
Preparation Time: 5 minutes
Cooking Time: 15 minutes

Ingredients:
- 500 grams beef, sliced thinly into strips
- 2 tablespoons olive oil
- Salt and pepper, to taste
- ½ cup shallots, sliced
- 1 teaspoon ginger, minced
- ¼ cup beef stock
- 2 tablespoons hot chili paste
- 2 cups cooked rice

Directions:
1. Preheat the Air Fryer to 350°F/180°C.
2. Place the beef strips in the Air Fryer Baking Pan and season with olive oil and salt and pepper.
3. Add the shallots and ginger to the Air Fryer Baking Pan.
4. Place the Air Fryer Baking Pan in the Air Fryer Basket and set the timer for 10 minutes.
5. Stir in the beef stock and hot chili paste and set the timer for 5 more minutes.
6. Pour contents from the Air Fryer Baking Pan over the cooked rice.
7. Serve and enjoy!

282 - Stuffed Peppers with Bacon and Cheese

Servings: 2
Preparation Time: 10 minutes
Cooking Time: 8 minutes

Ingredients:
- 2 large bell peppers
- ¼ cup bacon, chopped
- ½ cup mozzarella cheese, grated
- 2 cloves garlic, minced
- ½ cup tomatoes, diced
- 1 teaspoon paprika
- Salt and pepper, to taste

Directions:
1. Preheat the Air Fryer to 350°F/180°C.
2. Cut the tops off the bell peppers. Remove the seeds and the rest of the insides of the bell peppers, so they are completely hollow.
3. Mix together the bacon, mozzarella cheese, garlic, tomatoes, paprika, salt and pepper in a medium size bowl.
4. Fill both bell peppers with the bowl mixture.
5. Place the bell peppers in the Air Fryer Basket and set the timer for 8 minutes.
6. Serve once done.

283 - Pumpkin and Mushroom Peppers

Servings: 2
Preparation Time: 10 minutes
Cooking Time: 8 minutes

Ingredients:
- 2 large bell peppers
- ¼ cup pumpkin, diced
- ½ cup mozzarella cheese, grated
- ½ cup wild mushrooms, sliced
- 2 cloves garlic, minced
- Salt and pepper, to taste

Directions:
1. Preheat the Air Fryer to 350°F/180°C.
2. Cut the tops off the bell peppers. Remove the seeds and the rest of the insides of the bell peppers, so they are completely hollow.
3. Mix together the pumpkin, mozzarella cheese, wild mushrooms, garlic, salt and pepper in a medium size bowl.
4. Fill both bell peppers with the bowl mixture.
5. Place the bell peppers in the Air Fryer Basket and set the timer for 8 minutes.

284 - Spicy Beef Stew

Servings: 2
Preparation Time: 5 minutes
Cooking Time: 30 minutes

Ingredients:
- 500 grams beef, cut into chunks
- Salt and pepper, to taste
- 1 teaspoon garlic powder
- 3 cups beef stock
- ½ cup jalapenos
- 1 cup potatoes, cut into cubes
- 1 cup baby carrots
- 1 tablespoon habanero hot sauce

Directions:
1. Preheat the Air Fryer to 350°F/180°C.
2. Place the beef in the Air Fryer Baking Pan and season with salt, pepper and garlic powder.
3. Spray the beef with cooking spray and set the timer for 5 minutes.
4. Add beef stock, jalapenos, potatoes and baby carrots.
5. Stir in the habanero hot sauce.
6. Set the timer for 25 minutes.
7. Serve once done.

285 - Warm Winter Vegetable Soup

Servings: 2
Preparation Time: 5 minutes
Cooking Time: 19 minutes

Ingredients:
- ¼ cup onions, sliced
- ½ cup carrots, diced
- 1 cup tomatoes, cubed
- 1 cup of celery, chopped
- 2 tablespoons garlic, minced
- 3 cups vegetable stock
- ¼ cup fresh flat-leaf parsley leaves, chopped

Directions:
1. Preheat the Air Fryer to 350°F/180°C.
2. Place the onions and carrots in the Air Fryer Baking Pan and set the timer for 4 minutes.
3. Add the tomatoes and celery and set the timer for 5 minutes.
4. Add the minced garlic and set the timer for 5 minutes.
5. Pour in the vegetable stock and set the timer for 5 more minutes.
6. Add the parsley and stir well to combine before serving.

286 - White Wine Garlic Mussels

Servings: 2
Preparation Time: 5 minutes
Cooking Time: 8 minutes

Ingredients:
- 1 pound fresh mussels, cleaned
- 1 tablespoon olive oil
- 5 cloves garlic, minced
- 1 tablespoon onions, sliced
- ½ teaspoon paprika
- salt and pepper, to taste
- ½ cup white wine
- 1 tablespoon fresh cilantro, chopped

Directions:
1. Preheat the Air Fryer to 350°F/180°C.
2. Mix the mussels, olive oil, garlic, onions and paprika in the Air Fryer Baking Pan.
3. Season with salt and pepper and pour in the white wine.
4. Place the Air Fryer Baking Pan in the Air Fryer Basket and set the timer for 5 minutes.
5. Add the cilantro and set the timer for 3 more minutes.
6. Serve once done.

Appetizer Recipes

287 - Air Fried Garlic Mushrooms

Servings: 4
Preparation Time: 5 minutes
Cooking Time: 20 minutes

Ingredients:
- 8 rashers bacon, chopped
- ½ cup onions, sliced
- ¼ cup butter
- 2 tablespoons garlic, minced
- 3 cups button mushrooms, halved
- salt and pepper, to taste
- ¼ cup spring onions, chopped

Directions:
1. Preheat the Air Fryer to 350°F/180°C.
2. Place the bacon in the Air Fryer Baking Pan and set the timer for 10 minutes. Remove the bacon and set aside.
3. Add the onions to the bacon fat and set the timer for 4 minutes or until the onions are slightly browned.
4. Mix in the butter, garlic and mushrooms and set the timer for 6 minutes.
5. Serve and season with salt and pepper and top with the spring onions.

288 - A Minute on Your Lips Wings

Servings: 4
Preparation Time: 15 minutes plus 2 hours marinating time
Cooking Time: 20 minutes

Ingredients:

- 1 pound chicken wings
- 1 tablespoon olive oil
- 1 teaspoon soy sauce
- 1 tablespoon fresh rosemary, chopped
- 3 tablespoons garlic, minced
- 1 tablespoon ghee
- ¼ cup cream
- ¼ cup parmesan cheese, grated
- 1 teaspoon pepper
- ¼ cup parsley, chopped

Directions:

1. Marinate the wings with the combined olive oil, soy sauce, fresh rosemary and 2 tablespoons of garlic for 2 hours.
2. Preheat the Air Fryer to 350°F/180°C.
3. Arrange the wings in the Air Fryer Basket and use the Air Fryer Double Layer Rack if needed.
4. Set the timer for 20 minutes or until the wings are cooked through. Halfway through the cooking time, rearrange the chicken wings to allow even cooking.
5. While the wings are cooking, make the sauce.
6. Melt the ghee in a saucepan and add the remaining garlic. Whisk in the cream and parmesan cheese and season with pepper.
7. Place the fried wings on a plate, pour the sauce over and top with chopped parsley.

289 - Salt and Pepper Squid

Servings: 4
Preparation Time: 5 minutes
Cooking Time: 6 minutes

Ingredients:

- ½ cup flour
- 2 teaspoons pepper
- 2 teaspoons Himalayan salt
- 1 pound squid rings
- 1 teaspoon lime juice
- ¼ cup parsley, chopped

Directions:

1. Preheat the Air Fryer to 350°F/180°C.
2. Mix the flour with a teaspoon each of pepper and salt and set aside.
3. Season the squid rings with the other teaspoons of pepper and salt.
4. Coat the squid rings in the seasoned flour and shake off any excess.
5. Place them in the Air Fryer Basket and drizzle over the lime juice.
6. Set the timer for 6 minutes or until the squid is cooked through.
7. Serve and top with some fresh parsley.

290 - Tuna and Eggplant Bruschetta

Servings: 4
Preparation Time: 10 minutes
Cooking Time: 5 minutes

Ingredients:
- 1 cup tuna flakes in water
- 2 tablespoons organic mayonnaise
- ¼ cup celery, chopped
- ¼ cup onions, chopped
- 1 teaspoon lemon juice
- salt and pepper, to taste
- 1 large eggplant, sliced diagonally into ½-inch thick slices
- 2 tablespoons fresh parsley, chopped

Directions:
1. Preheat the Air Fryer to 350°F/180°C.
2. Combine the tuna, mayonnaise, celery, onions and lemon juice in a bowl.
3. Season with salt and pepper.
4. Top the eggplant with the tuna mixture and spray with cooking spray.
5. Place the eggplant bruschetta's in the Air Fryer Basket and use the Air Fryer Double Layer Rack if needed.
6. Set the timer for 5 minutes or until the eggplant is cooked through.
7. Serve and top with the fresh parsley.

291 - Bacon and Cauliflower Soup

Servings: 2
Preparation Time: 5 minutes
Cooking Time: 20 minutes

Ingredients:

- 3 rashers bacon, chopped
- 1 cup cauliflower, cut into small florets
- ¼ cup white onions, chopped
- 1 tablespoon chives, chopped
- 2 cloves garlic, minced
- ½ teaspoon garlic powder
- ½ teaspoon of cayenne pepper
- 2 cups vegetable stock
- ¼ tablespoon peppercorns
- 1 tablespoon chives, chopped
- 1 tablespoon parmesan shavings

Directions:

1. Preheat the Air Fryer to 350°F/180°C.
2. Place the bacon in Air Fryer Baking Pan and cook for 10 minutes until crisp. Remove from the Air Fryer and set aside.
3. Add the cauliflower florets, white onions, chives, minced garlic, garlic powder and cayenne pepper to the Air Fryer Baking Pan.
4. Set the timer for another 5 minutes.
5. Add the vegetable stock, peppercorns and chives.
6. Cook for additional 5 minutes.
7. Serve and top with the parmesan shavings and bacon bits.

292 - Crispy Garlic Chicken Wings

Servings: 4
Preparation Time: 10 minutes plus 10 minutes resting time
Cooking Time: 15 minutes

Ingredients:
- ¼ cup low-fat buttermilk
- 2 tablespoons Dijon mustard
- 1 cup whole wheat breadcrumbs
- 2 tablespoons chives, chopped
- 2 tablespoons garlic, minced
- 2 teaspoons garlic powder
- ¼ teaspoon paprika
- 1 pound chicken wings
- salt and pepper, to taste

Directions:
1. Combine the buttermilk and mustard in a bowl and set aside.
2. Mix the breadcrumbs, chives, garlic, garlic powder and paprika and set aside.
3. Season the chicken wings with salt and pepper.
4. Dip the wings in the buttermilk and evenly coat with the breadcrumbs by pressing the breadcrumbs firmly onto the wings. Rest to set for about 10 minutes.
5. Preheat the Air Fryer to 350°F/180°C.
6. Arrange the wings in the Air Fryer Basket and use the Air Fryer Double Layer Rack if needed.
7. Spray the wings with cooking spray and air fry wings for 15 minutes (or until cooked though).

293 - Air Fried Gemba's

Servings: 2
Preparation Time: 5 minutes
Cooking Time: 12 minutes

Ingredients:
- 2 cups shrimps, peeled and deveined
- ¼ teaspoon paprika
- garlic salt and pepper, to taste
- ¼ cup ghee
- 2 tablespoons garlic, minced
- 2 teaspoons lemon juice
- 2 tablespoons chives, chopped

Directions:
1. Preheat the Air Fryer to 350°F/180°C.
2. Place the shrimps in the Air Fryer Baking Pan and season with the paprika, garlic salt and pepper.
3. Add the ghee, minced garlic and lemon juice to the Air Fryer Baking Pan.
4. Place the Air Fryer Baking Pan in the Air Fryer Basket and set the timer for 12 minutes.
5. Serve and top with the chopped chives.

294 - Asparagus and Corn Soup

Servings: 2
Preparation Time: 5 minutes
Cooking Time: 16 minutes

Ingredients:
- 1 tablespoon olive oil
- ¼ cup white onions, chopped
- 2 cloves garlic, sliced
- ½ teaspoon garlic powder
- 1¼ cups asparagus, chopped
- ¼ cup corn kernels
- 2 cups vegetable stock
- ¼ tablespoon peppercorns
- 1 tablespoon chives, chopped

Directions:
1. Preheat the Air Fryer to 350°F/180°C.
2. Place the olive oil and white onions into the Air Fryer Baking Pan.
3. Place the Air Fryer Baking Pan in the Air Fryer Basket and set the timer for 2 minutes.
4. Add the garlic, garlic powder, asparagus and corn to the Air Fryer Baking Pan and cook for another 4 minutes.
5. Add the vegetable stock, peppercorns and chives.
6. Set the timer for 10 more minutes.
7. Serve and enjoy!

295 - Chicken and Pumpkin Soup

Servings: 2
Preparation Time: 5 minutes
Cooking Time: 19 minutes

Ingredients:

- 1 cup pumpkins, cut into small cubes
- 1 tablespoon olive oil
- ½ cup cooked chicken, shredded
- ¼ cup white onions, chopped
- 2 cups vegetable stock
- ¼ tablespoon peppercorns

- 2 cloves garlic, sliced
- ½ tablespoon ginger, chopped
- ½ teaspoon garlic powder
- ½ teaspoon paprika
- 1 tablespoon parmesan cheese, shaved
- 1 tablespoon chives, chopped

Directions:

1. Preheat the Air Fryer to 350°F/180°C.
2. Place the pumpkins and olive oil in the Air Fryer Baking Pan.
3. Place the Air Fryer Baking Pan in the Air Fryer Basket and set the timer for 5 minutes.
4. Add the shredded chicken and onions to the Air Fryer Baking Pan and cook for 4 minutes.
5. Add the vegetable stock, peppercorns, garlic, ginger, garlic powder and paprika to the Air Fryer Baking Pan.
6. Cook for 10 more minutes.
7. Serve and top with the parmesan shavings and chives.

296 - French Garlic Soup

Servings: 2
Preparation Time: 5 minutes
Cooking Time: 15 minutes

Ingredients:

- 1 tablespoon olive oil
- 1 cup white onions, chopped
- 2 cloves garlic, sliced
- 2 cups vegetable stock

- ¼ tablespoon peppercorns
- 1 tablespoon fresh parsley, chopped
- 1 tablespoon spring onions, chopped
- 1 tablespoon parmesan cheese, shavings

Directions:

1. Preheat the Air Fryer to 350°F/180°C.
2. Place the olive oil and white onions in the Air Fryer Baking Pan.
3. Place the Air Fryer Baking Pan in the Air Fryer Basket and set the timer for 8 minutes.
4. Add the garlic and cook for another 2 minutes.
5. Add the vegetable stock, peppercorns, fresh parsley and spring onions to the Air Fryer Baking Pan.
6. Set the timer for another 5 minutes. Serve and top with the parmesan shavings.

297 - Cajun Mahi-Mahi Crisp

Servings: 4
Preparation Time: 10 minutes
Cooking Time: 10 minutes

Ingredients:
- 1 cup breadcrumbs
- 1 tablespoon Cajun seasoning
- 1 teaspoon paprika
- 2 eggs
- salt and pepper, to taste
- 4 mahi-mahi fillets, cut into cubes
- ¼ cup fresh cilantro, chopped

Directions:
1. Mix the breadcrumbs, Cajun seasoning and paprika in a bowl and set aside.
2. Whisk the eggs with salt and pepper and set aside.
3. Season the fish fillet cubes with pepper.
4. Dip them in the egg and coat evenly in the breadcrumbs. Allow the breadcrumbs to set.
5. Preheat the Air Fryer to 400°F/200°C.
6. Arrange the fish in the Air Fryer Basket and use the Air Fryer Double Layer Rack if needed.
7. Spray them with cooking spray.
8. Set the timer for 10 minutes or until the breadcrumbs turn golden brown.
9. Serve and top with the fresh cilantro.

298 - Spanish Chorizos with Cauliflower

Servings: 4
Preparation Time: 10 minutes
Cooking Time: 15 minutes

Ingredients:
- 8 Spanish chorizos
- 1 teaspoon paprika
- 1 teaspoon dried thyme
- pepper, to taste
- 2 cups cauliflower, cut into small florets
- 2 tablespoons fresh cilantro, chopped
- 2 tablespoons fresh rosemary, chopped
- ¼ cup parmesan cheese

Directions:
1. Attach the Air Fryer Food Separator and preheat the Air Fryer to 400°F/200°C.
2. Season the chorizos with paprika, thyme and pepper and arrange them in one section of the Air Fryer Basket.
3. Season the cauliflower florets with the pepper, fresh cilantro and fresh rosemary and place them in the other section of the Air Fryer Basket.
4. Top the cauliflowers with the parmesan cheese and spray with some cooking spray.
5. Set the timer for 15 minutes. Serve once timer goes off.

299 - Chicken in Red Wine Reduction

Servings: 2
Preparation Time: 10 minutes
Cooking Time: 25 minutes

Ingredients:
- 2 chicken whole legs
- salt and pepper, to taste
- ½ cup red wine
- 1 tablespoon garlic, sliced
- 1 tablespoon fresh cilantro, chopped
- 1 tablespoon fresh rosemary, chopped
- ⅛ cup sugar

Directions:
1. Preheat the Air Fryer to 350°F/180°C.
2. Place the chicken legs in the Air Fryer Baking Pan and season them with salt and pepper.
3. Add the red wine, sliced garlic, fresh cilantro and fresh rosemary to the Air Fryer Baking Pan.
4. Place the Air Fryer Baking Pan in the Air Fryer Basket and set the timer for 15 minutes or until the chicken is cooked through.
5. Remove the chicken legs from the Air Fryer Baking Pan and set aside.
6. Dissolve the sugar in the red wine sauce and cook for another 10 minutes or until the sauce has thickened.
7. Pour the sauce over the chicken before serving.

300 - Crispy Broccoli and Chicken

Servings: 2
Preparation Time: 10 minutes
Cooking Time: 15 minutes

Ingredients:

- ¼ cup buttermilk
- ½ tablespoon Dijon mustard
- ½ cup whole wheat breadcrumbs
- 1 tablespoon chives, chopped
- 2 tablespoons parmesan cheese, grated
- 1 tablespoon garlic, minced
- 1 teaspoon garlic salt
- 2 chicken breasts, pounded thinly
- ½ cup broccoli florets
- salt and pepper, to taste

Directions:

1. Combine the buttermilk and mustard in a bowl and set aside.
2. Mix the breadcrumbs, chives, parmesan cheese, minced garlic and garlic salt together and set aside
3. Dip the chicken into the buttermilk and coat evenly with the breadcrumbs. Leave for a few minutes to set.
4. Preheat the Air Fryer to 350°F/180°C.
5. Arrange the chicken in the Air Fryer Basket and set the timer for 10 minutes or until the chicken is cooked through. Use the Air Fryer Double Layer Rack if needed.
6. Remove the chicken from the Air Fryer and set aside.
7. Season the broccoli florets with salt and pepper.
8. Place the broccoli in the Air Fryer Basket and set the timer for 5 minutes.
9. Serve once done.

301 - Cod Cakes with Cucumber Mint Dip

Servings: 2
Preparation time: 10 minutes
Cooking Time: 12 minutes

Ingredients:

- 3 cod fillets, mashed
- 1 teaspoon garlic, minced
- 1 teaspoon garlic powder
- salt and pepper, to taste
- ¼ cup fresh cilantro, chopped
- 1 tablespoon lemon juice
- 1 teaspoon olive oil
- 2 tablespoons onions, minced
- 1 cup breadcrumbs
- ½ cup yogurt
- ¼ cup cucumbers, diced
- ¼ cup mint leaves, chopped

Directions:

1. Season the mashed cods with the garlic, garlic powder, salt, pepper, fresh cilantro, lemon juice, olive oil and onions.
2. Form small cakes and coat evenly with the breadcrumbs. Leave to rest for the breadcrumbs to set.
3. Preheat the Air Fryer to 350°F/180°C.
4. Arrange the cod cakes in the Air Fryer Basket and use the Air Fryer Double Layer Rack if needed.
5. Spray with cooking spray and set the timer for 12 minutes.
6. While the cod cakes are cooking, make the cucumber mint dip.
7. To make the cucumber mint dip: Mix the yogurt, cucumbers and mint leaves in a bowl. Season with pepper and chill until the cod cakes are ready.
8. Serve once done!

302 - Salmon Fish Sticks with Marinara Sauce

Servings: 2
Preparation time: 10 minutes
Cooking Time: 15 minutes

Ingredients:
- 1 cup breadcrumbs
- 1 teaspoon paprika
- 1 teaspoon dried sage
- 1 teaspoon dried tarragon
- 3 salmon fillets, cut into 2-inch sticks
- salt and pepper, to taste
- 1 tablespoon lemon juice
- ½ cup marinara sauce

Directions:
1. Preheat the Air Fryer to 350°F/180°C.
2. Mix the breadcrumbs with the paprika, dried sage and dried tarragon and set aside.
3. Season the fish sticks with salt, pepper and lemon juice.
4. Coat them evenly with the breadcrumbs and arrange them in the Air Fryer Basket. Use the Air Fryer Double Layer Rack if needed.
5. Set the timer for 12 minutes.
6. Place the marinara sauce in an ovenproof bowl and warm in the Air Fryer for 2 to 4 minutes.
7. Pour the sauce over the fish sticks and serve.

303 - Avocado Boats

Servings: 2
Preparation time: 5 minutes
Cooking Time: 8 minutes

Ingredients:
- 2 avocados, halved and pits removed
- 1 tablespoon olive oil
- 2 tablespoons lemon juice
- 4 eggs
- pepper, to taste
- ¼ cup feta cheese
- 2 tablespoons chives, chopped.

Directions:
1. Preheat the Air Fryer to 350°F/180°C.
2. Place the avocados in the Air Fryer Basket on their peels.
3. Drizzle with olive oil and lemon juice.
4. Crack an egg into each avocado.
5. Season with pepper.
6. Set the timer for 8 minutes.
7. Serve and top with the feta cheese and chopped chives.

304 - Zucchini Boats

Servings: 2
Preparation time: 10 minutes
Cooking Time: 8 minutes

Ingredients:
- 2 medium zucchinis, halved, flesh removed and reserved
- 1 teaspoon olive oil
- salt and pepper, to taste
- ½ cup tomato sauce
- 1 tomato, diced
- ¼ cup olives, sliced
- 6 slices mozzarella cheese
- 1 tablespoon fresh parsley, chopped

Directions:
1. Preheat the Air Fryer to 350°F/180°C.
2. Place the zucchinis in the Air Fryer Basket.
3. Drizzle over with olive oil and season with salt and pepper.
4. Set the timer for 3 minutes.
5. Dice the reserved zucchini flesh and combine with the tomato sauce, diced tomatoes and olives.
6. Spoon into the zucchini boats and top the zucchini boats with the mozzarella slices.
7. Set the timer for 5 minutes.
8. Serve and top with the fresh parsley.

305 - Mini Margherita Pizza

Servings: 2
Preparation time: 5 minutes
Cooking Time: 8 minutes

Ingredients:
- 2 mini pizza crusts
- ½ cup tomato sauce
- 1 cup mozzarella cheese, sliced
- 10 tomato slices
- ¼ cup olives, sliced
- 1 tablespoon fresh basil, torn

Directions:
1. Preheat the Air Fryer to 350°F/180°C.
2. Place the pizza crusts in the Air Fryer Basket and use the Air Fryer Double Layer Rack if needed.
3. Set the timer for 3 minutes.
4. Spread the tomato sauce over the crust and arrange the mozzarella slices, tomatoes and olives.
5. Set the timer for 5 minutes or until the cheese has melted.
6. Serve and top with the fresh basil.

306 - Bacon Wrapped Hotdogs with Cheese

Servings: 4
Preparation time: 10 minutes
Cooking Time: 12 minutes

Ingredients:
- 12 cocktail hotdogs
- 12 cheddar slices
- 12 rashers bacon

Directions:
1. Preheat the Air Fryer to 400°F/200°C.
2. Wrap each hotdog with a slice of cheese.
3. Wrap tightly with a rasher of bacon and arrange them in the Air Fryer Basket. Use the Air Fryer Double Layer Rack if needed.
4. Set the timer for 12 minutes.
5. Serve once timer goes off!

307 - Caramelized Onions, Mushrooms and Sausages

Servings: 2
Preparation time: 5 minutes
Cooking Time: 13 minutes

Ingredients:
- 2 tablespoons olive oil
- 2 cup onions, sliced
- salt and pepper, to taste
- 1 cup button mushrooms, quartered
- 3 German frankfurters, sliced to bite sizes

Directions:
1. Preheat the Air Fryer to 350°F/180°C.
2. Add the olive oil and onions to the Air Fryer Baking Pan and season with salt and pepper.
3. Set the timer for 8 minutes.
4. Add the mushrooms and frankfurters
5. Set the timer for another 5 minutes and mix well to combine the flavors.
6. Serve when done.

308 - Pecorino and Sage Chicken Fingers

Servings: 2
Preparation time: 10 minutes
Cooking Time: 15 minutes

Ingredients:
- 1 egg
- 1 cup breadcrumbs
- 1 teaspoon dried sage
- 1 cup pecorino cheese, grated
- 2 chicken breasts, cut into strips
- salt and pepper, to taste

Directions:
1. Whisk the egg and set aside.
2. Mix the breadcrumbs, dried sage and pecorino cheese and set aside.
3. Season the chicken fingers with salt and pepper.
4. Dip the chicken fingers in the egg and coat evenly with the breadcrumbs. Leave to set for a few minutes.
5. Preheat the Air Fryer to 350°F/180°C.
6. Arrange the chicken fingers in the Air Fryer Basket and use the Air Fryer Double Layer Rack if needed.
7. Set the timer for 15 minutes or until the chicken is cooked through.
8. Once chicken has properly cooked through, serve your meal!

309 - Corned Beef Nibblers

Servings: 2
Preparation Time: 10 minutes plus 30 minutes chilling time
Cooking Time: 10 minutes

Ingredients:
- 2 tablespoons chives, chopped finely
- ¼ cup onions, minced
- 1 cup canned corned beef, minced finely
- 1 tablespoon garlic, minced
- 1 egg, lightly beaten
- ½ cup breadcrumbs
- ¼ cup parmesan cheese, grated

Directions:
1. Mix the chives, onions, corned beef and garlic with the egg.
2. Shape into balls and chill for 30 minutes.
3. Coat the balls evenly with the combined breadcrumbs and parmesan cheese. Leave to rest for the breadcrumbs to set.
4. Preheat the Air Fryer to 350°F/180°C.
5. Arrange the balls in the Air Fryer Basket and use the Air Fryer Double Layer Rack if needed.
6. Spray the balls with the cooking spray and set the timer for 10 minutes.
7. Serve and enjoy!

310 - Rosemary Cream Chicken Wings

Servings: 2
Preparation time: 10 minutes
Cooking Time: 25 minutes

Ingredients:

- 1 pound chicken wings
- salt and pepper, to taste
- 1 tablespoon onion powder
- 2 tablespoons olive oil
- ¼ cup fresh rosemary, chopped
- ¼ cup onions, chopped
- 1 tablespoon garlic, sliced
- ½ cup mushrooms, sliced
- 1 cup cream
- ¼ cup parmesan cheese, grated

Directions:

1. Preheat the Air Fryer to 350°F/180°C.
2. Season the wings with the salt, pepper, onion powder, olive oil and fresh rosemary.
3. Arrange the wings in the Air Fryer Basket and set the timer for 15 minutes or until the wings are cooked through. Halfway through the cooking time, rearrange the wings to allow even cooking.
4. Remove from the Air Fryer and set aside.
5. Place the onions, garlic and mushrooms in the Air Fryer Baking Pan and set the timer for 4 minutes.
6. Add the cream and parmesan cheese and set the timer for 6 more minutes.
7. Transfer the sauce into a serving dish and coat the wings in the sauce.
8. Serve and enjoy!

311 - Tortilla Chips with Tomatoes

Servings: 2
Preparation time: 5 minutes
Cooking Time: 3 minutes

Ingredients:

- 8 corn tortillas, cut into bite-sized triangles
- 1 large tomato, diced
- ¼ cup sour cream
- ¼ cup cheese sauce
- 1 tablespoon garlic, minced
- 2 teaspoons chives, chopped

Directions:

1. Preheat the Air Fryer to 400°F/200°C.
2. Arrange the tortilla chips in the Air Fryer Basket and spray with cooking spray.
3. Set the timer for 3 minutes.
4. Remove from the Air Fryer and allow to cool.
5. Top the tortillas with the diced tomatoes and drizzle over with the sour cream and cheese sauce.
6. Serve and top with the minced garlic and chopped chives.

312 - Tuna Nibbles

Servings: 2
Preparation Time: 10 minutes
Cooking Time: 15 minutes

Ingredients:
- 4 tablespoons chives, chopped
- 1 tablespoon fresh oregano, chopped
- 4 tablespoons celery, finely chopped
- ¼ cup apples, diced
- 1 tablespoon garlic, minced
- 1 cup tuna flakes in oil, drained
- 1 egg, lightly beaten
- ½ cup breadcrumbs
- ¼ cup parmesan cheese, grated

Directions:
1. Combine the chives, fresh oregano, celery, apples, garlic, tuna and egg.
2. Form balls and coat evenly with the combined breadcrumbs and parmesan cheese.
3. Chill for a few minutes for the breadcrumbs to set.
4. Preheat the Air Fryer to 350°F/180°C.
5. Arrange the tuna balls in the Air Fryer Basket and spray them with some cooking spray.
6. Set the timer for 15 minutes or until they become golden brown.
7. Serve and enjoy!

313 - Sweet Potato Croquettes

Servings: 2
Preparation time: 15 minutes plus 30 minutes chilling time
Cooking Time: 48 minutes

Ingredients:

- 3 large sweet potatoes, peeled and pierced with a fork
- salt and pepper, to taste
- 2 teaspoons garlic powder
- 1 tablespoon fresh parsley, chopped
- ¼ cup butter
- ¼ cup cream
- 1 teaspoon paprika
- 1 cup breadcrumbs
- 1 teaspoon onion powder

Directions:

1. Preheat the Air Fryer to 350°F/180°C.
2. Place the sweet potatoes in the Air Fryer Basket and set the timer for 40 minutes or until fork tender.
3. Mash the sweet potatoes and season with salt, pepper and a teaspoon of garlic powder.
4. Add the parsley, butter, cream and paprika and mix well to combine.
5. Chill for 30 minutes.
6. Form balls from the mashed sweet potatoes.
7. Coat them evenly with the combined breadcrumbs, onion powder and a teaspoon garlic powder. Leave for a few minutes to set.
8. Preheat the Air Fryer to 400°F/200°C.
9. Arrange the croquettes in the Air Fryer Basket and use the Air Fryer Double Layer Rack if needed.
10. Set the timer for 8 minutes.
11. Serve once done.

314 - Soda Calamari Fritters

Servings: 4
Preparation time: 15 minutes
Cooking Time: 12 minutes

Ingredients:
- 1 cup all-purpose flour
- ½ teaspoon garlic salt
- 1 teaspoon onion powder
- ½ teaspoon garlic powder
- ¼ cup 7UP® or Sprite
- 2 cups calamari rings

Directions:
1. Preheat the Air Fryer to 400°F/200°C.
2. Mix the flour, garlic salt, onion powder and garlic powder.
3. Slowly pour in the soda and mix well to combine.
4. Coat the calamari rings with the batter one at a time and drip off any excess.
5. Arrange the calamari rings in the Air Fryer Basket and use the Air Fryer Double Layer Rack if needed.
6. Spray the calamari rings and set the timer for 12 minutes. Halfway through the cooking time, shake Air Fryer Basket to prevent the rings from sticking together and to allow even cooking.
7. Serve once done.

315 - Curried Fish Sticks

Servings: 4
Preparation Time: 10 minutes
Cooking Time: 8 minutes

Ingredients:

- 4 trout fillets, cut into 3-inch strips
- 3 tablespoons curry powder
- 1 teaspoon salt
- 2 teaspoons sugar
- 1 teaspoon ground cumin
- pepper, to taste
- 1 egg, lightly beaten
- ½ cup flour
- 15 curry leaves, chopped

Directions:

1. Preheat the Air Fryer to 350°F/180°C.
2. Season the fish sticks with 2 tablespoons of curry powder, salt, sugar, ground cumin powder and pepper.
3. Dip them in the egg and coat them evenly in the combined flour and remaining curry powder.
4. Arrange the fish sticks in the Air Fryer Basket and use the Air Fryer Double Layer Rack if needed.
5. Set the timer for 8 minutes.
6. Serve and top with the curry leaves.

316 - Peppered Squid Balls

Servings: 4
Preparation Time: 15 minutes plus 20 minutes chilling time
Cooking Time: 10 minutes

Ingredients:

- 1 pound squid
- 2 tablespoons garlic, minced
- 2 tablespoons olive oil
- ¼ cup onions, finely chopped
- ½ teaspoon garlic salt
- 2 teaspoons lemon juice
- ¼ cup chives, chopped
- 2 eggs
- pepper, to taste
- 1 cup gluten-free flour
- 1 teaspoon paprika

Directions:

1. Blend the squid in a food processor until it becomes a thick/lumpy consistency.
2. Transfer to a bowl and combine with the garlic, olive oil, onions, garlic salt, lemon juice and chives.
3. Form small balls and chill for 20 minutes.
4. Whisk the eggs with some pepper and set aside.
5. Mix the flour with some pepper and paprika and set aside.
6. Dip the balls in the egg and coat evenly with the flour mixture.
7. Preheat the Air Fryer to 350°F/180°C.
8. Arrange the squid balls in the Air Fryer Basket and use the Air Fryer Double Layer Rack if needed.
9. Set the timer for 10 minutes. Halfway through the cooking time, rearrange the squid balls with a pair of kitchen tongs to allow even cooking.
10. Serve once squid balls are properly cooked.

317 - Stuffed Onion Rings

Servings: 4
Preparation Time: 15 minutes plus an hour freezing time
Cooking Time: 10 minutes

Ingredients:
- 1 cup cream cheese, softened
- 1 tablespoon garlic, minced
- 1 tablespoon chives, chopped
- salt and pepper, to taste
- 30 onion rings
- ½ cup flour
- ½ teaspoon paprika
- 2 eggs
- 1 cup breadcrumbs

Directions:
1. Fork mash the cream cheese with the garlic and chives and season with salt and pepper.
2. Coat the onion rings with the cream cheese mixture and lay them on a lined baking tray to freeze for an hour.
3. Mix the flour with the paprika.
4. Whisk the eggs and season with salt and pepper.
5. Preheat the Air Fryer to 350°F/180°C.
6. Dip the frozen onion rings in the egg and then dust them with the flour.
7. Coat evenly with the breadcrumbs and arrange them in the Air Fryer Basket.
8. Set the timer for 10 minutes. Halfway through the cooking time, shake the Air Fryer Basket to prevent the rings from sticking together and to allow even cooking.
9. Serve and enjoy!

318 - Bacon Wrapped Squid rings

Servings: 6
Preparation Time: 20 minutes
Cooking Time: 10 minutes

Ingredients:
- 30 squid rings
- ½ teaspoon paprika
- pepper to taste
- 30 rashers bacon
- ¼ cup fresh parsley, chopped

Directions:
1. Preheat the Air Fryer to 350°F/180°C.
2. Season the squid rings with paprika and pepper.
3. Wrap each ring with a slice of bacon and secure with a toothpick.
4. Arrange them in the Air Fryer Basket and use the Air Fryer Double Layer Rack if needed.
5. Set the timer for 10 minutes
6. Serve and top with the fresh parsley.

319 - Crispy Parmesan Salmon Balls

Servings: 2
Preparation Time: 10 minutes
Cooking Time: 10 minutes

Ingredients:
- 1 egg, beaten
- 4 tablespoons chives, chopped
- 1 tablespoon fresh oregano, chopped
- 4 tablespoons celery, finely chopped
- 1 tablespoon garlic, minced
- 1 cup salmon flakes in oil, drained
- ½ cup breadcrumbs
- ¼ cup parmesan cheese, grated

Directions:
1. Preheat the Air Fryer to 350°F/180°C.
2. Mix together the egg, chives, fresh oregano, celery, garlic and salmon.
3. Form balls and coat evenly with the combined breadcrumbs and parmesan cheese.
4. Arrange the balls in the Air Fryer Basket and spray with cooking spray.
5. Set the timer for 10 minutes or until the balls become golden brown.
6. Serve once salmon balls are golden brown.

320 - Easy Baked Shrimp Bites

Servings: 4
Preparation time: 15 minutes
Cooking Time: 10 minutes

Ingredients:
- 1 cup shrimps, peeled, deveined and chopped
- 1 tablespoon dill, finely chopped
- ½ tablespoon lemon juice
- 2 tablespoons olives, chopped
- pepper, to taste
- 8 ounces ready-made puff pastry, cut into 15 squares

Directions:
1. Mix the shrimps with the dill, lemon juice, olives and pepper.
2. Place a full teaspoon of the shrimp mixture onto each pastry square.
3. Fold each pastry square over into a triangle.
4. Moisten the edges with water and use a fork to press the edges firmly together.
5. Preheat the Air Fryer to 400°F/200°C.
6. Arrange the shrimp bites in the Air Fryer Basket and use the Air Fryer Double Layer Rack if needed.
7. Spray the shrimp bites with cooking spray and set the timer for 10 minutes.
8. Serve and enjoy!

321 - Spicy Shrimps with Thousand Island Dressing

Servings: 5
Preparation time: 15 minutes
Cooking Time: 8 minutes

Ingredients:

- ½ cup all-purpose flour
- 1 teaspoon chili flakes
- 1 teaspoon chili powder
- 1 teaspoon cayenne pepper
- 1 egg
- salt and pepper, to taste
- 1 pound shrimps, peeled and deveined
- 3 tablespoons mayonnaise
- 1 tablespoon ketchup
- 1 teaspoon TABASCO®
- 1 tablespoon red wine vinegar

Directions:

1. Preheat the Air Fryer to 350°F/180°C.
2. Mix the flour with the chili flakes, chili powder and cayenne pepper.
3. Whisk the egg with some salt and pepper.
4. Dip the shrimps in the egg and coat evenly with the flour.
5. Arrange the shrimps in the Air Fryer Basket and spray with cooking spray.
6. Set the timer for 8 minutes.
7. While the shrimps are cooking, make the dressing. Mix the mayonnaise, ketchup, TABASCO® and red wine vinegar and chill until the shrimps are ready.
8. Dip shrimps into the dressing.

322 - Sweet Chili Chicken Wings

Servings: 4
Preparation time: 10 minutes plus 20 minutes chilling time
Cooking Time: 15 minutes

Ingredients:
- 1 pound chicken wings
- 2 cloves garlic, minced
- 2 teaspoons ginger powder
- 2 teaspoons garlic powder
- salt and pepper, to taste
- 1 tablespoon chives, chopped
- ¼ cup sweet chili sauce

Directions:
1. Rub the chicken wings with the combined minced garlic, ginger powder, garlic powder, salt and generous amounts of black pepper.
2. Add the chives and chill for 20 minutes.
3. Preheat the Air Fryer to 350°F/180°C.
4. Place the chicken wings in the Air Fryer Basket and use the Air Fryer Double Layer Rack if needed.
5. Set the timer for 15 minutes or until the chicken is cooked through. Halfway through the cooking time, rearrange the chicken wings to allow even cooking.
6. Coat the wings in the sweet chili sauce before serving.

323 - Air Fried Herbed Cheese Sticks

Servings: 4
Preparation time: 15 minutes plus 2 hours chilling time
Cooking Time: 3 minutes

Ingredients:
- ¼ cup feta cheese
- ¼ cup cream cheese
- 1 tablespoon fresh parsley, chopped
- 1 tablespoon fresh cilantro, chopped
- 1 tablespoon chives, chopped
- 1 stalk onion leek, chopped
- pepper, to taste
- 10 spring roll wrappers

Directions:
1. Mix the feta cheese, cream cheese, fresh parsley, fresh cilantro, chives, onion leeks and pepper together in a bowl.
2. Spoon two teaspoons of the feta mixture onto an edge of the spring roll wrapper.
3. Tuck in the ends and roll tightly. Seal with a little water.
4. Repeat with the other spring roll wrappers and chill for 2 hours.
5. Preheat the Air Fryer to 400°F/200°C.
6. Spray the cheese sticks with cooking spray and arrange them in the Air Fryer Basket. Use the Air Fryer Double Layer Rack if needed.
7. Set the timer for 3 minutes or until the sticks turn golden brown.
8. Serve and enjoy!

324 - Pepper Jack Bacon Bites

Servings: 4
Preparation time: 15 minutes plus 2 hours freezing time
Cooking Time: 8 minutes

Ingredients:
- 1 cup breadcrumbs
- 1 teaspoon paprika
- pepper, to taste
- 6 pepper jack cheddar slices, halved
- 6 rashers bacon, halved
- 1 cup all-purpose flour
- 2 eggs, whisked

Directions:
1. Mix the breadcrumbs, paprika and pepper.
2. Wrap the pepper jack cheese slices with the bacon and secure with a toothpick.
3. Dust the cheese bites in the flour and dip in the whisked egg.
4. Coat evenly with the breadcrumbs.
5. Freeze the cheese bites for 2 hours.
6. Preheat the Air Fryer to 400°F/200°C.
7. Place the cheese bites in the Air Fryer Basket.
8. Set the timer for 8 minutes. When the cheese begins to ooze from its crumb coating, remove from the Air Fryer and serve.

325 - Crabby Fingers

Servings: 4
Preparation time: 20 minutes plus 1 hour chilling time
Cooking Time: 8 minutes

Ingredients:

- 1 teaspoon olive oil
- ¼ cup onions, chopped
- ¼ cup red bell peppers, chopped
- 2 tablespoons celery, chopped
- 1 pound crab meat
- ¼ teaspoon chives, chopped
- ½ teaspoon fresh parsley, chopped
- ¼ cup sour cream
- ½ teaspoon lime juice
- 2 eggs
- salt and pepper, to taste
- 1 cup breadcrumbs
- 1 teaspoon paprika
- ½ teaspoon cayenne pepper

Directions:

1. Heat the olive oil in a non-stick frying pan over medium heat and sauté the onions, bell peppers and celery for 5 minutes. Remove from the heat and cool.
2. Add the crab meat, chives, parsley, sour cream and lime juice to the vegetables.
3. Form into 3-inch crab fingers.
4. Whisk the eggs and season with salt and pepper.
5. Mix the breadcrumbs with paprika and cayenne pepper.
6. Dip the crab fingers in the egg and coat evenly with the breadcrumbs. Chill for an hour.
7. Preheat the Air Fryer to 350°F/180°C.
8. Place the crab fingers and vegetables to the Air Fryer Baking Pan. Set the timer for 8 minutes.
9. Serve and enjoy!

326 - Asian Style Chicken Wings

Servings: 4
Preparation time: 10 minutes plus 2 hours marinating time
Cooking Time: 15 minutes

Ingredients:
- ½ cup red wine vinegar
- 5 tablespoons lemon juice
- 2 tablespoons olive oil
- 2 tablespoons soy sauce
- 6 cloves garlic, finely chopped
- 1 tablespoon ground allspice
- 1 teaspoon cayenne pepper
- 1 tablespoon grated ginger
- 1 pound chicken wings
- 1 tablespoon spring onion stalks, finely chopped

Directions:
1. To make the marinade sauce: Whisk together the red wine vinegar, lemon juice, olive oil and soy sauce. Add the garlic, ground allspice, cayenne pepper and ginger and mix well to combine.
2. Marinate the chicken wings in the marinade sauce for 2 hours.
3. Preheat the Air Fryer to 350°F/180°C.
4. Drip off the excess marinade sauce from the wings and arrange them in the Air Fryer Basket. Use the Air Fryer Double Layer Rack if needed.
5. Set the timer for 15 minutes or until the wings are cooked through. Halfway through the cooking time, rearrange the wings to allow even cooking.
6. Serve and top with the spring onions.

327 - Truffle Oil Potato Wedges

Servings: 2
Preparation time: 5 minutes plus 30 minutes soaking time
Cooking Time: 15 minutes

Ingredients:

- 2 medium potatoes, cut into thin wedges
- 1 tablespoon truffle oil
- salt and pepper, to taste
- 1 teaspoon paprika
- ¼ cup parmesan cheese, grated

Directions:

1. Soak the potatoes in water for 30 minutes.
2. Drain and use a paper towel to pat dry.
3. Preheat the Air Fryer to 350°F/180°C.
4. Place the potato wedges into a bowl and mix with the truffle oil, salt and pepper.
5. Transfer the potatoes into the Air Fryer Basket and set the timer for 15 minutes. Halfway through the cooking time, give the Air Fryer Basket a shake to allow even cooking.
6. Remove and cool on a rack.
7. Serve and sprinkle with the paprika and grated parmesan cheese.

328 - Spicy Potato Cubes with Greek Yogurt Dip

Servings: 4
Preparation time: 15 minutes plus 30 minutes soaking time
Cooking Time: 20 minutes

Ingredients:

- 3 large potatoes, cubed
- ½ cup Greek yogurt
- 2 tablespoons extra-virgin olive oil
- 2 tablespoons garlic, minced
- 2 tablespoons fresh parsley, chopped
- salt and pepper, to taste
- 1 teaspoon paprika
- 1 teaspoon garlic powder

Directions:

1. Soak the potatoes for 30 minutes. Drain and pat dry thoroughly with paper towels.
2. Mix the yogurt with a tablespoon of olive oil, the minced garlic and fresh parsley. Chill until the potatoes are ready.
3. Preheat the Air Fryer to 450°F/230°C.
4. Season the potatoes with salt and pepper and place them in the Air Fryer Basket.
5. Spray with some cooking spray and set the timer for 20 minutes.
6. Transfer the potatoes to a serving bowl and toss with the paprika, garlic powder and more pepper.

329 - Ginger Garlic Wings

Servings: 4
Preparation time: 5 minutes plus 2 hours marinating time
Cooking Time: 15 minutes

Ingredients:
- 1 pound chicken wings
- 2 tablespoons lemon juice
- 2 tablespoons honey
- 2 tablespoons soy sauce
- 1 tablespoon ginger, minced
- 2 tablespoons garlic, minced

Directions:
1. Place the wings in a ziplock bag and add the lemon juice, honey, soy sauce, minced ginger and minced garlic.
2. Coat the wings well with the sauce and chill for 2 hours, turning occasionally to ensure the wings are evenly coated.
3. Preheat the Air Fryer to 400°F/200°C.
4. Drip off the excess sauce from the wings and arrange them in the Air Fryer Basket. Use the Air Fryer Double Layer Rack if needed.
5. Set the timer for 15 minutes or until the wings are cooked through. Halfway through the cooking time, rearrange the wings to allow even cooking.
6. Serve once done.

---

330 - Chicken and Mushroom Balls

Servings: 4
Preparation time: 15 minutes plus 1 hour chilling time
Cooking Time: 10 minutes

Ingredients:
- 1 pound ground chicken
- ¼ cup fresh mushrooms, chopped finely
- ¼ cup cooked bacon, chopped
- 1 teaspoon garlic powder
- 1 teaspoon onion powder
- salt and pepper, to taste

Directions:
1. Mix together the ground chicken, mushrooms, bacon, garlic powder and onion powder.
2. Season with salt and pepper and knead well to combine.
3. Form balls and lay them on a tray to chill for an hour.
4. Preheat the Air Fryer to 350°F/180°C.
5. Set the timer for 10 minutes or until the balls are cooked through.
6. Serve once done.

---

331 - Easy Buffalo Wings with Blue Cheese

Servings: 4
Preparation time: 15 minutes
Cooking Time: 20 minutes

Ingredients:

- 3 tablespoons flour
- 1 teaspoon cayenne pepper
- 1 teaspoon paprika
- 1 teaspoon garlic salt
- 1 teaspoon pepper
- 1 pound chicken wings
- ¼ cup BBQ sauce
- 1 tablespoon hot sauce
- ¼ cup sour cream
- ¼ cup blue cheese
- 2 teaspoons garlic, minced

Directions:

1. Preheat the Air Fryer to 400°F/200°C.
2. Combine the flour, cayenne pepper, paprika, garlic salt and pepper.
3. Coat the chicken wings evenly in the flour mixture.
4. Shake off any excess flour and arrange the wings in the Air Fryer Basket. Use the Air Fryer Double Layer Rack if needed.
5. Set the timer for 20 minutes or until the chicken is cooked through.
6. Mix the BBQ sauce with the hot sauce and toss in the wings.
7. Combine the sour cream, blue cheese and minced garlic for the dip.
8. Serve and enjoy!

332 - Spiced Crab Bombs

Servings: 4
Preparation time: 10 minutes plus 30 minutes chilling time
Cooking Time: 12 minutes

Ingredients:
- 2 cups crab meat
- 1 teaspoon ground allspice
- 1 teaspoon paprika
- ½ teaspoon dried sage
- 3 eggs
- 2 tablespoons milk
- salt and pepper, to taste
- 1 cup flour
- 1½ cups breadcrumbs

Directions:
1. Preheat the Air Fryer to 325°F/170°C.
2. Combine the crab meat with the ground allspice, paprika and dried sage.
3. Form balls and chill for 30 minutes.
4. Whisk the eggs with the milk and season with salt and pepper.
5. Dust the balls in the flour and dip in the egg wash.
6. Coat evenly with the breadcrumbs and arrange them in the Air Fryer Basket. Use the Air Fryer Double Layer Rack if needed.
7. Spray with cooking spray and set the timer for 12 minutes. Halfway through the cooking time, rearrange the balls for even cooking.
8. Serve and enjoy!

333 - Crispy BBQ Cauliflower Bites

Servings: 4
Preparation time: 10 minutes
Cooking Time: 20 minutes

Ingredients:
- 1 large head cauliflower, florets
- 2 tablespoons olive oil
- 2 teaspoons garlic powder
- 1 teaspoon paprika
- salt and pepper, to taste
- 1 tablespoon TABASCO®
- 1 teaspoon soy sauce
- ¼ cup ketchup
- 2 tablespoons honey

Directions:
1. Preheat the Air Fryer to 400°F/200°C.
2. Place the cauliflower florets in a big ziplock bag with the olive oil, garlic powder, paprika, salt and pepper.
3. Seal the bag and toss the ingredients so the cauliflower will be evenly coated.
4. Transfer the cauliflower florets to the Air Fryer Basket and set the timer for 15 minutes. Halfway through the cooking time, give the Air Fryer Basket a shake to allow for even cooking.
5. Transfer the cauliflowers to the Air Fryer Baking Pan.
6. Combine the TABASCO®, soy sauce, ketchup and honey and pour over the cauliflower florets.
7. Set the timer for another 5 minutes.
8. Serve and enjoy!

334 - Crispy Radish and Caprese Salad

Servings: 4
Preparation time: 15 minutes
Cooking Time: 30 minutes

Ingredients:

- 1 cup radish, thinly sliced
- salt and pepper, to taste
- 1 cup fresh mini balls of mozzarella cheese
- 1 cup cherry tomatoes
- 1 cup baby arugula leaves
- 1 teaspoon balsamic vinegar
- 2 tablespoons olive oil
- 1 teaspoon garlic, minced
- 1 tablespoon parmesan cheese, shavings

Directions:

1. Preheat the Air Fryer to 350°F/180°C.
2. Season the radish slices with salt and pepper and place them in the Air Fryer Basket.
3. Spray with cooking spray and set the timer for 30 minutes. A few times during the cooking time, give the Air Fryer Basket a shake to allow for even cooking.
4. Just before the radish is done, prepare the caprese salad.
5. Place the mozzarella cheese balls, cherry tomatoes and baby arugula leaves in a salad bowl and toss with a combined dressing of the balsamic vinegar, olive oil, minced garlic and pepper.
6. Serve and top the salad with the crispy radish and parmesan shavings.

335 - Beer Battered Calamari Fritters

Servings: 4
Preparation time: 10 minutes
Cooking Time: 12 minutes

Ingredients:
- 1 cup all-purpose flour
- ½ teaspoon garlic salt
- 1 teaspoon paprika
- 1 teaspoon pepper
- ½ teaspoon garlic powder
- ¼ cup beer
- 2 cups calamari rings

Directions:
1. Preheat the Air Fryer to 400°F/200°C.
2. Mix the flour, garlic salt, paprika, pepper and garlic powder in a bowl.
3. Slowly pour in the beer and mix well to combine.
4. Dip the calamari rings in the batter one at a time and arrange them in the Air Fryer Basket. Use the Air Fryer Double Layer Rack if needed.
5. Spray the calamari with cooking spray and set the timer for 12 minutes.
6. Shake the Air Fryer Basket twice during the cooking time to prevent the calamari's from sticking together.
7. Remove from the Air Fryer and serve once the calamari has turned golden brown.

336 - Calamari and Garlic Mayo Dip

Servings: 4
Preparation time: 15 minutes plus 4 hours marinating time
Cooking Time: 10 minutes

Ingredients:

- 2 cups calamari rings
- 1 cup milk
- 1 cup flour
- 1 teaspoon paprika
- 1 teaspoon garlic powder
- salt and pepper, to taste
- ½ cup mayonnaise
- 2 tablespoons garlic, minced
- 1 teaspoon lemon juice

Directions:

1. Marinate the calamari rings in the milk for 4 hours.
2. Preheat the Air Fryer to 350°F/180°C.
3. Mix the flour, paprika, garlic powder, salt and pepper.
4. Coat the calamari evenly with the flour mixture.
5. Arrange the calamari rings in the Air Fryer Basket and use the Air Fryer Double Layer Rack if needed.
6. Set the timer for 10 minutes. Shake the Air Fryer Basket twice while cooking to prevent the calamari rings from sticking together.
7. Mix the mayonnaise, garlic and lemon juice in a bowl for the dip.
8. Eat up!

337 - Easy Crispy Ravioli with Tomato Salsa

Servings: 4
Preparation time: 15 minutes
Cooking Time: 20 minutes

Ingredients:

- 1 cup canned tomatoes
- ½ cup tomatoes, diced
- ½ cup jalapeños, chopped
- ¼ cup onions, diced
- 2 teaspoons apple cider vinegar
- salt and pepper, to taste
- 2 cups breadcrumbs
- 1 cup parmesan cheese, grated
- 2 eggs, whisked
- 1 teaspoon paprika
- 20 ready-made four cheese raviolis

Directions:

1. To make the tomato salsa: Mix together the canned tomatoes, diced tomatoes, jalapeños, onions and apple cider vinegar. Season with salt and pepper and chill until the raviolis are ready.
2. Preheat the Air Fryer to 350°F/180°C.
3. Mix the breadcrumbs with the parmesan cheese and some pepper.
4. Whisk the eggs and season with the pepper and paprika.
5. Dip the raviolis in the whisked egg and coat evenly with the breadcrumbs.
6. Arrange them in the Air Fryer Basket and spray with cooking spray.
7. Set the timer for 20 minutes.
8. Serve and enjoy!

338 - White Wine Garlic Mushrooms

Servings: 4
Preparation time: 5 minutes
Cooking Time: 32 minutes

Ingredients:

- 1 tablespoon duck fat
- ½ teaspoon garlic powder
- 2 cups button mushrooms, quartered
- ¼ cup white wine
- 1 tablespoon fresh parsley, chopped

Directions:

1. Preheat the Air Fryer to 350°F/180°C.
2. Add the duck fat and garlic powder in the Air Fryer Baking Pan.
3. Set the timer for 2 minutes.
4. Add the mushrooms and cook for another 25 minutes.
5. Add the white wine and fresh parsley and set the timer for 5 more minutes.
6. Serve and enjoy!

339 - Cheesy Crab Stick Poppers

Servings: 2
Preparation time: 10 minutes
Cooking Time: 8 minutes

Ingredients:
- 8 crab sticks
- 8 cheddar sticks
- 8 slices of deli ham
- 8 spring roll wrappers

Directions:
1. Preheat the Air Fryer to 350°F/180°C.
2. Wrap a crab stick and a cheddar stick together with a slice of deli ham.
3. Wrap over with a spring roll wrapper and ensure that it is tight and secure.
4. Repeat for the remaining ingredients.
5. Arrange the poppers in the Air Fryer Basket and use the Air Fryer Double Layer Rack if needed.
6. Set the timer for 8 minutes.
7. Serve and enjoy!

340 - Crispy Shrimps

Servings: 2
Preparation time: 10 minutes
Cooking Time: 8 minutes

Ingredients:
- 1 cup breadcrumbs
- 1 teaspoon paprika
- 1 teaspoon pepper
- 1 teaspoon garlic salt
- 2 eggs
- 2 cups shrimps, peeled and deveined

Directions:
1. Preheat the Air Fryer to 350°F/180°C.
2. Mix the breadcrumbs, paprika, pepper and garlic salt and set aside.
3. Whisk the eggs and season with pepper.
4. Dip the shrimps in the whisked eggs and coat with the breadcrumb mix.
5. Arrange the shrimps in the Air Fryer Basket and use the Air Fryer Double Layer Rack if needed.
6. Set the timer for 8 minutes.
7. Serve and enjoy!

341 - Air Fried Coriander Shrimp Cakes

Servings: Makes 15 shrimp cakes
Preparation time: 15 minutes
Cooking Time: 10 minutes

Ingredients:
- 2 cups fresh cilantro
- 2 teaspoons garlic, minced
- 3 stalks onion leeks
- 2 tablespoons olive oil
- 1 teaspoon dried sage
- ½ teaspoon garlic powder
- salt and pepper, to taste
- 2 cups shrimps, peeled and deveined

Directions:
1. Preheat the Air Fryer to 350°F/180°C.
2. Blend the cilantro, garlic, onion leeks and olive oil until they become a paste.
3. Season with the sage, garlic powder, salt and pepper.
4. Add the shrimps and pulse until a smooth mixture forms.
5. Form 15 shrimp cakes from the mixture and arrange them in the Air Fryer Basket. Use the Air Fryer Double Layer Rack if needed.
6. Set the timer for 10 minutes or until the cakes are cooked through.
7. Serve once ready.

342 - Kale and Chicken Bites

Servings: Makes 16 pieces
Preparation time: 15 minutes plus 40 minutes chilling time
Cooking Time: 10 minutes

Ingredients:
- 2 cups ground chicken
- ½ cup carrots, grated
- ½ onions, minced
- 2 tablespoons garlic, minced
- 1 egg, whisked
- 1 cup kale leaves, chopped
- 1 teaspoon garlic powder
- 1 cup cheddar cheese, grated
- 1 tablespoon flour
- salt and pepper, to taste

Directions:
1. Combine all the ingredients in a large bowl and mix well.
2. Divide the mixture into 16 balls and chill for 40 minutes.
3. Preheat the Air Fryer to 350°F/180°C.
4. Arrange the balls in the Air Fryer Basket and use the Air Fryer Double Layer Rack if needed.
5. Spray the balls with cooking spray.
6. Set the timer for 10 minutes or until the balls become golden brown.
7. Serve when done.

343 - Asian Sesame Ginger Wings

Servings: 4
Preparation time: 10 minutes plus 4 hours marinating time
Cooking Time: 20 minutes

Ingredients:
- 16 chicken wings
- 4 tablespoons minced ginger
- 2 tablespoons oyster sauce
- 2 tablespoons soy sauce
- 1 teaspoon fish sauce
- 1 teaspoon sesame oil
- 1 tablespoon sugar
- 1 teaspoon sesame seeds
- 1 cup flour
- 1 teaspoon garlic powder
- 1 teaspoon pepper
- 1 teaspoon paprika

Directions:
1. Marinate the chicken wings in the combined ginger, oyster sauce, soy sauce, fish sauce, sesame oil, sugar and sesame seeds for 4 hours.
2. Preheat the Air Fryer to 350°F/180°C.
3. Mix together the flour, garlic powder, pepper and paprika.
4. Coat the chicken wings in the flour mixture and arrange them in the Air Fryer Basket. Use the Air Fryer Double Layer Rack if needed.
5. Spray the wings with cooking spray and set the timer for 15 minutes.
6. Rearrange the wings to allow even cooking and set the timer for 5 more minutes.
7. Serve once timer goes off.

344 - Roasted Cajun Tomato Soup

Servings: 2
Preparation time: 10 minutes
Cooking Time: 15 minutes

Ingredients:
- 4 large tomatoes, sliced
- 5 cloves garlic, crushed
- 1 medium onion, chopped
- 1 tablespoon Cajun seasoning
- salt and pepper, to taste
- 3 cups chicken stock
- 2 tablespoons tomato paste
- 1 tablespoon fresh parsley, chopped

Directions:
1. Preheat the Air Fryer to 350°F/180°C.
2. Place the sliced tomatoes, garlic and onions in the Air Fryer Baking Pan.
3. Season with the Cajun seasoning, salt and pepper and place the Air Fryer Baking Pan in the Air Fryer Basket.
4. Set the timer for 15 minutes.
5. Transfer the tomatoes into a blender.
6. Pour in the chicken stock, tomato paste and parsley and blend until smooth before serving.

345 - Healthy Spring Rolls

Servings: Makes 20 spring rolls
Preparation time: 20 minutes plus 30 minutes chilling time
Cooking Time: 10 minutes

Ingredients:
- 1 cup shrimps, peeled and deveined
- 1 teaspoon paprika
- salt and pepper, to taste
- 20 rice paper wrappers
- 20 romaine lettuce leaves
- 2 large avocados, sliced
- 20 cucumber sticks
- ¼ cup onions, chopped

Directions:
1. Preheat the Air Fryer to 350°F/180°C.
2. Place the shrimps in the Air Fryer Baking Pan and season with the paprika, salt and pepper
3. Place the Air Fryer Baking Pan in the Air Fryer Basket and set the timer for 8 minutes.
4. To assemble the spring rolls: Lightly dampen the rice paper wrapper to make it more pliable. Place a romaine lettuce leaf, an avocado slice, a cucumber stick, some shrimps and chopped onions on the rice paper. Season with a bit of pepper. Roll tightly, tuck the ends in and seal with some water at the edges.
5. Repeat for the other remaining rolls.
6. Chill the rolls for 30 minutes before serving.

346 - Mozzarella and Garlic Onion Blooms

Servings: 2
Preparation time: 10 minutes
Cooking Time: 32 minutes

Ingredients:
- 2 large onions
- ¼ cup butter, melted
- 2 tablespoons garlic, minced
- 1 teaspoon chives, chopped
- 2 tablespoons of mozzarella cheese, grated

Directions:
1. Slice 1-inch off the tops and bottoms of the onions and peel the skins.
2. To make an onion bloom, cut slices into the onion as far down as possible but not all the way through.
3. Spread what are now the petals of the onion.
4. Preheat the Air Fryer to 350°F/180°C.
5. Mix the melted butter, garlic, and chives and pour over the onions.
6. Arrange the onions in the Air Fryer Basket and spray with some cooking spray.
7. Set the timer for 30 minutes. Remove the outer layers of the onions if they become too dark from cooking.
8. Top with the mozzarella cheese and cook for 2 more minutes to allow the cheese to melt.
9. Serve and enjoy

347 - Herby Fish Fingers with Tartar Dip

Servings: 2
Preparation time: 10 minutes
Cooking Time: 15 minutes

Ingredients:

- ½ cup mayonnaise
- 1 teaspoon lemon juice
- ¼ cup pickles, finely chopped
- 1 cup breadcrumbs
- 1 teaspoon paprika
- 1 teaspoon ground nutmeg
- 1 teaspoon garlic powder
- salt and pepper, to taste
- 2 eggs
- 1 large dory fillet, cut in strips

Directions:

1. Mix the mayonnaise, lemon juice and pickles to make the tartar dip. Chill until the fish fingers are ready.
2. Combine the breadcrumbs, paprika, ground nutmeg, garlic powder, salt and pepper. Set aside.
3. Whisk the eggs and set aside.
4. Dip the fish fingers in the egg then coat evenly with the breadcrumbs.
5. Preheat the Air Fryer to 350°F/180°C.
6. Arrange the fish sticks in the Air Fryer Basket and use the Air Fryer Double Layer Rack if needed.
7. Set the timer for 15 minutes or until they become golden brown before serving.

348 - Garlic Herbed Cheese Sticks

Servings: Makes 20 cheese sticks
Preparation time: 15 minutes
Cooking Time: 8 minutes

Ingredients:
- 1 cup mozzarella cheese, grated
- 1 cup cheddar cheese, grated
- 1 teaspoon paprika
- 2 tablespoons chives, chopped
- 2 tablespoons fresh cilantro, chopped
- ½ teaspoon garlic powder
- salt and pepper, to taste
- 20 spring roll wrappers

Directions:
1. Preheat the Air Fryer to 400°F/200°C.
2. Mix together the mozzarella cheese, cheddar cheese, paprika, chives, fresh cilantro, garlic powder, salt and pepper.
3. Scoop a tablespoon of the cheese mixture onto a spring roll wrapper.
4. Roll tight, tucking in the ends and seal with a dab of water.
5. Arrange the cheese sticks in the Air Fryer Basket and use the Air Fryer Double Layer Rack if needed.
6. Set the timer for 8 minutes.
7. Serve and enjoy

349 - Flaming Mashed Tots

Servings: 2
Preparation time: 15 minutes
Cooking Time: 8 minutes

Ingredients:
- 2 large potatoes, cubed
- 1 teaspoon ground allspice
- ½ teaspoon garlic powder
- salt and pepper, to taste
- 2 tablespoons jalapeños, thinly sliced
- 2 tablespoons chives, chopped
- 1 cup breadcrumbs

Directions:
1. Boil the potatoes until they are fork tender.
2. Mash the potatoes with a fork and season with the ground allspice, garlic powder, salt and pepper.
3. Add the jalapeños and chives.
4. Form small balls and coat them evenly with the breadcrumbs.
5. Chill for an hour.
6. Preheat the Air Fryer to 400°F/200°C.
7. Arrange the potatoes in the Air Fryer Basket and set the timer for 8 minutes.
8. Ready to be served but be careful they're HOT!

350 - Cauliflower Bites with String Cheese

Servings: 2
Preparation time: 10 minutes
Cooking Time: 15 minutes

Ingredients:
- 1 cup breadcrumbs
- ¼ cup parmesan cheese, grated
- 1 tablespoon garlic powder
- 3 cups cauliflower florets
- ½ cup mozzarella cheese, grated
- 1 tablespoon chives, chopped

Directions:
1. Preheat the Air Fryer to 400/200°C.
2. Mix together the breadcrumbs, parmesan cheese and garlic powder and set aside.
3. Spray the cauliflower florets with cooking spray and coat them with the breadcrumbs.
4. Place the cauliflower florets to the Air Fryer Basket and top with the mozzarella cheese and chives.
5. Set the timer for 15 minutes or until golden brown.
6. Serve and enjoy!

351 - Bacon Wrapped Chicken Tenders

Servings: 2
Preparation time: 10 minutes
Cooking Time: 25 minutes

Ingredients:
- 1 cup breadcrumbs
- ¼ cup parmesan cheese, grated
- 1 teaspoon garlic powder
- 2 chicken breasts, each sliced into 6 pieces
- pepper, to taste
- 12 rashers bacon
- 1 tablespoon fresh parsley chopped

Directions:
1. Combine the breadcrumbs, parmesan cheese and garlic powder and set aside.
2. Season the chicken slices with pepper.
3. Wrap each chicken with a rasher of bacon and secure with a toothpick.
4. Coat them with the breadcrumbs and top with the fresh parsley.
5. Preheat the Air Fryer to 400°F/200°C.
6. Arrange the chicken tenders in the Air Fryer Basket and use the Air Fryer Baking Pan if needed.
7. Spray the chicken tenders with cooking spray.
8. Set the timer for 25 minutes or until the chicken tenders become golden brown.
9. Serve and enjoy!

352 - Oysters Kilpatrick

Servings: 4
Preparation time: 10 minutes
Cooking Time: 10 minutes

Ingredients:
- 10 fresh oysters, shucked
- salt and pepper, to taste
- 2 teaspoons lemon juice
- 2 tablespoons Worcestershire sauce
- ½ cup mozzarella cheese, grated
- ½ cup bacon, coarsely chopped

Directions:
1. Preheat the Air Fryer to 400°F/200°C.
2. Season the oysters with salt and pepper and drizzle over with the lemon juice.
3. Drizzle a little Worcestershire sauce on each oyster.
4. Add some mozzarella cheese on each oyster and top with the chopped bacon.
5. Arrange the oysters in the Air Fryer Basket and use the Air Fryer Double Layer Rack if needed.
6. Set the timer for 10 minutes.
7. Serve and enjoy!

353 - Roasted Shrimp Rockefeller

Servings: 2
Preparation time: 10 minutes
Cooking Time: 10 minutes

Ingredients:
- 2 cups large shrimps, peeled and deveined
- salt and pepper, to taste
- 1 tablespoon garlic, minced
- 2 teaspoons lemon juice
- ½ cup baby spinach leaves, chopped
- ¼ cup butter, melted
- ½ cup mozzarella cheese, grated

Directions:
1. Preheat the Air Fryer to 350°F/180°C.
2. Place the shrimps in the Air Fryer Baking Pan and season with salt and pepper.
3. Add the garlic, lemon juice, baby spinach leaves and butter to the Air Fryer Baking Pan.
4. Top with the grated mozzarella cheese and place the Air Fryer Baking Pan in the Air Fryer Basket.
5. Set the timer for 10 minutes.
6. Serve and enjoy!

354 - Coconut Cream Clam Soup

Servings: 2
Preparation time: 10 minutes
Cooking Time: 23 minutes

Ingredients:
- 2 tablespoons butter
- ½ cup onions, chopped
- 1 tablespoon garlic, minced
- ½ cup celery, chopped
- 1 pound clams, cleaned
- salt and pepper, to taste
- 2 teaspoons lemon juice
- 2 cups chicken stock
- ½ cup coconut cream

Directions:
1. Preheat the Air Fryer to 350°F/180°C.
2. Place the butter and onions in the Air Fryer Baking Pan and set the timer for 2 minutes.
3. Stir in the garlic, celery and clams and season well with salt and pepper.
4. Drizzle over with the lemon juice and cook for a minute.
5. Pour in the chicken stock and coconut cream and set the timer for another 15 minutes.
6. Start serving!

355 - Roasted Mint Salad with Hazelnuts

Servings: 2
Preparation time: 5 minutes
Cooking Time: 15 minutes

Ingredients:
- 1 large zucchini, sliced
- 1 cup baby carrots
- 12 baby potatoes, halved
- ½ cup mint leaves, coarsely chopped
- 2 tablespoons olive oil
- 2 teaspoons paprika
- 1 teaspoon ground allspice
- 2 teaspoons garlic powder
- 2 teaspoons onion powder
- ¼ cup hazelnuts, chopped

Directions:
1. Preheat the Air Fryer to 350°F/180°C.
2. Place the zucchinis, baby carrots, potatoes and mint leaves in the Air Fryer Baking Pan.
3. Drizzle over with olive oil and season with the paprika, ground allspice, garlic powder and onion powder.
4. Place the Air Fryer Baking Pan in the Air Fryer Basket and top with the hazelnuts.
5. Set the timer for 15 minutes.
6. Serve once done.

356 - Thai Chicken Soup

Servings: 2
Preparation time: 5 minutes
Cooking Time: 28 minutes

Ingredients:
- 2 chicken breast fillets, sliced
- 1 teaspoon curry powder
- salt and pepper, to taste
- 1 teaspoon lime juice
- 3 cups chicken stock
- ¼ cup coconut cream
- ¼ cup carrots, grated
- 2 tablespoons garlic, minced
- ¼ cup fresh cilantro, chopped

Directions:
1. Preheat the Air Fryer to 350°F/180°C.
2. Season the chicken slices with the curry powder, salt and pepper.
3. Place the chicken in the Air Fryer Baking Pan and drizzle over with the lime juice.
4. Set the timer for 3 minutes.
5. Mix the stock, coconut cream, carrots and minced garlic to the Air Fryer Baking Pan.
6. Add the fresh cilantro and place the Air Fryer Baking Pan in the Air Fryer Basket.
7. Set the timer for 25 minutes.
8. Serve when ready.

357 - Feel Better Chicken Soup

Servings: 2
Preparation time: 5 minutes
Cooking Time: 25 minutes

Ingredients:
- 3 cups chicken stock
- 2 cooked chicken breasts, shredded
- ¼ cup celery, chopped
- 2 tablespoons garlic, sliced
- ¼ cup fresh cilantro, chopped
- ¼ cup onions, sliced
- 1 tablespoon ginger, sliced
- salt and pepper, to taste

Directions:
1. Preheat the Air Fryer to 350°F/180°C.
2. Place the stock, shredded chicken, celery, garlic, fresh cilantro, onions and ginger into the Air Fryer Baking Pan.
3. Season with salt and pepper and set the timer for 25 minutes.
4. Serve once the timer goes off.

358 - Hawaiian Chicken Wings

Servings: 4
Preparation time: 10 minutes plus 3 hours marinating time
Cooking Time: 30 minutes

Ingredients:
- 1 pound chicken wings
- salt and pepper, to taste
- 1 tablespoon garlic powder
- 1 tablespoon garlic, minced
- 1 tablespoon paprika
- 1 cup pineapple chunks
- ¼ cup spring onions

Directions:
1. Season the chicken wings with salt, pepper, garlic powder, garlic and paprika. Chill for 3 hours.
2. Preheat the Air Fryer to 350°F/180°C.
3. Arrange the wings in the Air Fryer Basket and use the Air Fryer Double Layer Rack if needed.
4. Set the timer for 15 minutes or until the chicken is cooked through.
5. Remove the chicken from the Air Fryer and set aside to cool.
6. Add the pineapple chunks and set the timer for another 15 minutes. If the pineapple chunks are cut too small for the Air Fryer Basket holes, place them in an ovenproof bowl and place the bowl in the Air Fryer Basket.
7. Serve and top with spring onions.

359 - Risotto Cheese Balls

Servings: 4
Preparation Time: 20 minutes
Cooking Time: 15 minutes

Ingredients:

- 1 cup breadcrumbs
- 1 cup parmesan cheese, grated
- pepper, to taste
- 1 cup cooked risotto
- 2 tablespoons sweet corns, minced
- 2 tablespoons carrots, grated
- 1 green chili, chopped
- 1 tablespoon cornstarch
- 1 teaspoon garlic powder
- 1 teaspoon dried oregano
- ½ cup mozzarella cheese, cubed
- 1 egg, lightly whisked

Directions:

1. Mix the breadcrumbs with the parmesan cheese and season with pepper. Set aside.
2. Mix together the risotto, sweet corns, carrots, chili, cornstarch, garlic powder and dried oregano.
3. Form balls with the risotto mix and add a mozzarella cheese cube in the middle of each ball.
4. Dip the balls in the egg and coat evenly with the breadcrumbs. Rest the balls for a few minutes to set.
5. Preheat the Air Fryer to 400°F/200°C.
6. Arrange the balls in the Air Fryer Basket and use the Air Fryer Double Layer Rack if needed.
7. Set the timer for 15 minutes.
8. Serve and enjoy!

360 - Pepperoni Pizza Bites

Servings: 4
Preparation Time: 10 minutes
Cooking Time: 10 minutes

Ingredients:
- 4 small sweet potatoes, cut into ½-inch thick slices to make 16 slices
- ¼ cup marinara sauce
- 1 cup mozzarella cheese, grated
- 16 slices of pepperoni
- 1 teaspoon dried tarragon
- salt and pepper, to taste

Directions:
1. Preheat the Air Fryer to 350°F/180°C.
2. Place the sweet potatoes in the Air Fryer Basket and use the Air Fryer Double Layer Rack if needed. Spray the sweet potatoes with cooking spray.
3. Set the timer for 8 minutes.
4. Top each slice with one teaspoon of marinara sauce.
5. Add a layer of grated mozzarella cheese and a slice of pepperoni.
6. Season with the dried tarragon, some salt and pepper.
7. Set the timer for 2 minutes or just until the cheese melts. Serve!

361 - Hawaiian Zucchini Nibbler

Servings: Makes 20 nibblers
Preparation Time: 10 minutes
Cooking Time: 10 minutes

Ingredients:
- ¼ cup tomato sauce
- 1 large zucchini, sliced into 20 slices
- 10 mozzarella slices, halved
- 10 ham slices, halved
- 10 pineapple rings, cut into small pieces
- 20 rashers bacon

Directions:
1. Preheat the Air Fryer to 350°F/180°C.
2. Spread some tomato sauce on each zucchini and layer with a slice of mozzarella and ham.
3. Top with some pineapples.
4. Wrap the zucchinis in bacon and secure with toothpicks.
5. Spray with a little cooking spray.
6. Arrange the zucchinis in the Air Fryer Basket and use the Air Fryer Double Layer Rack if needed.
7. Set the timer for 10 minutes or until the bacon is crisp and the cheese have melted. Serve!

362 - Bacon Wrapped Ribeye Nibbles

Servings: 4
Preparation Time: 10 minutes plus 4 hours marinating time
Cooking Time: 8 minutes

Ingredients:
- 4 ribeye steaks
- 1 teaspoon dried rosemary
- 1 teaspoon garlic salt
- pepper to taste
- 8 rashers bacon

Directions:
1. Rub the steaks with the combined dried rosemary, garlic salt and pepper.
2. Wrap the bacon rashers around each ribeye and secure with a toothpick.
3. Chill for 4 hours.
4. Preheat the Air Fryer to 400°F/200°C.
5. Arrange the ribeye steaks in the Air Fryer Basket and use the Air Fryer Double Layer Rack if needed.
6. Set the timer for 8 minutes or until the bacon is crisp and the meat is cooked to your desired doneness.
7. Allow the meat to rest for 10 minutes before slicing the meat to desired thickness.
8. Once sliced, begin to serve!

363 - Herb Crusted Crab Croquettes

Servings: 2
Preparation Time: 10 minutes
Cooking Time: 7 minutes

Ingredients:
- 2 cups crab meat
- 2 tablespoons green onions, finely chopped
- salt and pepper, to taste
- 1 egg, beaten
- 2 tablespoons fresh basil
- 2 tablespoons fresh thyme
- ½ cup breadcrumbs

Directions:
1. Combine the crab meat, green onions, salt, pepper and chill for 30 minutes.
2. Lightly whisk the egg and season with salt and pepper. Set aside.
3. Combine the fresh basil, fresh thyme and breadcrumbs and set aside.
4. Form balls from the crab meat mixture.
5. Dip the balls in the egg and coat evenly with the breadcrumbs.
6. Preheat the Air Fryer to 350°F/180°C.
7. Set the timer for 7 minutes.
8. Serve and enjoy!

364 - Chicken and Mash Croquettes

Servings: 2
Preparation Time: 20 minutes
Cooking Time: 8 minutes

Ingredients:
- 2 cup mashed potatoes
- 1 large cooked chicken breast, shredded
- 1 teaspoon paprika
- 1 teaspoon garlic powder
- salt and pepper, to taste
- 1 egg
- ¼ cup parmesan cheese, grated
- 1 cup breadcrumbs

Directions:
1. Mix the mashed potatoes and shredded chicken and season with the paprika, garlic powder, salt and pepper. Chill for 30 minutes.
2. Lightly whisk the egg and season with salt and pepper. Set aside.
3. Combine the parmesan cheese and breadcrumbs and set aside.
4. Preheat the Air Fryer to 350°F/180°C.
5. Scoop out balls of the chicken mixture.
6. Dip in the egg and coat evenly with breadcrumbs.
7. Spray with cooking spray and arrange the balls in the Air Fryer Basket. Use the Air Fryer Double Layer Rack if needed.
8. Set the timer for 8 minutes.
9. Serve and enjoy!

365 - Seafood Bites

Servings: 4
Preparation Time: 10 minutes plus 30 minutes chilling time
Cooking Time: 8 minutes

Ingredients:

- ½ cup shrimps, peeled and deveined
- ½ cup squids, cleaned
- 2 mahi-mahi fillets, chopped
- 4 cloves garlic
- salt and pepper, to taste
- 1 egg
- 1 cup flour
- 1 teaspoon paprika
- 1 teaspoon garlic powder
- 1 teaspoon onion powder
- 1 teaspoon ground cumin

Directions:

1. Preheat the Air Fryer to 350°F/180°C.
2. Puree the shrimps, squids, fish, garlic, salt and pepper until smooth.
3. Chill for 30 minutes.
4. Lightly whisk the egg and season with salt and pepper. Set aside.
5. Combine the flour, paprika, garlic powder, onion powder and ground cumin and set aside.
6. Form balls from the seafood mixture.
7. Dip them in the whisked egg and coat evenly with the flour mixture.
8. Arrange the balls in the Air Fryer Basket and use the Air Fryer Double Layer Rack if needed.
9. Spray the balls with cooking spray and set the timer for 8 minutes.
10. Serve and enjoy!

366 - Herbed Lamb Nibblers

Servings: 4
Preparation Time: 10 minutes plus marinating overnight
Cooking Time: 15 minutes

Ingredients:

- 2 cups ground lamb
- 1½ teaspoons salt
- 1 teaspoon ground black pepper
- 1 teaspoon ground cinnamon
- ¼ teaspoon ground nutmeg
- ¼ cup onions, finely chopped
- ¼ cup carrots, finely chopped
- 2 whole celery stalks, finely chopped
- 6 cloves garlic, minced
- ¼ cup fresh parsley, chopped

Directions:

1. Combine all the ingredients together thoroughly in a mixing bowl and chill overnight.
2. Preheat the Air Fryer to 300°F/150°C.
3. Form mini rolls from the mixture.
4. Arrange them in the Air Fryer Basket and use the Air Fryer Double Layer Rack if needed.
5. Set the timer for 15 minutes or until the lamb is cooked through.
6. Serve and enjoy!

367 - Tofu Shrimp Eggs

Servings: 4
Preparation Time: 20 minutes
Cooking Time: 20 minutes

Ingredients:

- 9 ounces firm tofu, cubed
- 1 cup ground pork
- ½ cup shrimps, peeled and deveined
- 3 shiitake mushrooms, softened and sliced
- 1 tablespoon shredded carrots
- ¼ cup fresh cilantro, chopped

- 2 eggs
- 1 tablespoon soy sauce
- ½ tablespoon white sugar
- 4 tablespoons cornstarch
- 1 tablespoon sesame oil
- 4 tablespoons rice flour

Directions:

1. Preheat the Air Fryer to 350°F/180°C.
2. Blend the tofu, pork, shrimps, mushrooms, carrots and fresh cilantro in a food processor for a minute.
3. Add an egg with the soy sauce, sugar, 1 tablespoon of cornstarch and sesame oil then blend for another minute.
4. Transfer to a bowl and form balls shaped like eggs.
5. Dust each egg in the combined rice flour and remaining cornstarch.
6. Dip into the egg mixture and coat again in the flour.
7. Arrange each egg in an ovenproof egg cup.
8. Arrange the egg cups in the Air Fryer Basket and set the timer for 20 minutes.
9. Once the timer sounds, it is time to serve!

368 - Tomato & Celery Soup

Servings: 2
Preparation Time: 5 minutes
Cooking Time: 19 minutes

Ingredients:
- ¼ cup white onions, chopped
- 1 cup tomatoes, chopped
- 1 cup celery, thinly sliced
- 2 tablespoons of garlic, minced
- 1 teaspoon garlic salt
- 3 cups vegetable stock
- ¼ cup fresh flat-leaf parsley leaves, chopped

Directions:
1. Preheat the Air Fryer to 350°F/180°C.
2. Place the white onions in the Air Fryer Baking Pan and set the timer for 4 minutes.
3. Add the tomatoes and celery and set timer for 5 minutes.
4. Add the minced garlic and garlic salt and set the timer for 5 minutes.
5. Pour in the vegetable stock and set the timer for 5 more minutes.
6. Add the parsley and stir well to combine before serving.

369 - Pumpkin and Sweet Potato Soup

Servings: 2
Preparation Time: 5 minutes
Cooking Time: 19 minutes

Ingredients:
- ¼ cup onions, sliced
- ½ cup carrots, diced
- 1 cup pumpkin, cubed
- 1 cup of sweet potato, cubed
- 2 tablespoons garlic, minced
- 1 teaspoon garlic salt
- 3 cups vegetable stock
- ¼ cup fresh flat-leaf parsley leaves, chopped

Directions:
1. Preheat the Air Fryer to 350°F/180°C.
2. Place the onions and carrots in the Air Fryer Baking Pan and set the timer for 4 minutes.
3. Add the pumpkin and sweet potatoes and set the timer for 5 minutes.
4. Add the minced garlic and garlic salt and set the timer for 5 minutes.
5. Pour in the vegetable stock and set the timer for 5 more minutes.
6. Add the parsley and stir well to combine before serving.

370 - Home Chickpea Soup

Servings: 2
Preparation Time: 5 minutes
Cooking Time: 19 minutes

Ingredients:
- ¼ cup brown onions, sliced
- 300 gram can chickpeas, drained and rinsed
- ½ cup carrots, diced
- 1 cup of sweet potato, cubed
- 2 tablespoons garlic, minced
- 2 teaspoons ground cumin
- 3 cups vegetable stock
- ¼ cup basil leaves, chopped

Directions:
1. Preheat the Air Fryer to 350°F/180°C.
2. Place the brown onions, chickpeas and carrots in the Air Fryer Baking Pan and set the timer for 4 minutes.
3. Add the sweet potatoes and set the timer for 5 minutes.
4. Add the minced garlic and ground cumin and set the timer for 5 minutes.
5. Pour in the vegetable stock and set the timer for 5 more minutes.
6. Sprinkle with basil leaves and stir well to combine before serving.

371 - Butternut Pumpkin and Lentil Soup

Servings: 2
Preparation Time: 5 minutes
Cooking Time: 19 minutes

Ingredients:
- 1 brown onions, finely chopped
- 1 ½ cups dried red lentils
- 1 butternut pumpkin, chopped
- 1 cup of sweet potato, cubed
- 2 tablespoons garlic, minced
- 3 cups vegetable stock
- ¼ cup basil leaves, chopped

Directions:
1. Preheat the Air Fryer to 350°F/180°C.
2. Place the brown onions, lentils and butternut pumpkin in the Air Fryer Baking Pan and set the timer for 4 minutes.
3. Add the sweet potatoes and set the timer for 5 minutes.
4. Add the minced garlic and set the timer for 5 minutes.
5. Pour in the vegetable stock and set the timer for 5 more minutes.
6. Sprinkle with basil leaves and stir well to combine before serving.

372 - Sausage Risotto Balls

Servings: 2
Preparation time 15 minutes plus 1 hour chilling time
Cooking Time: 25 minutes

Ingredients:
- 1 tablespoon olive oil
- 1 onion, finely chopped
- 2 Italian sausages, sliced
- ½ cup mushrooms, sliced
- 1 cup Italian short-grain rice
- 1 cup chicken stock
- 2 tablespoons parmesan cheese, grated
- pepper to taste
- 1 egg, whisked
- ½ cup breadcrumbs

Directions:
1. Heat the olive oil in a non-stick frying pan and sauté the onions, sausages and mushrooms.
2. Add the rice and continue stir-frying for 3 to 4 minutes.
3. Add the chicken stock and bring to a boil.
4. Lower the heat to a simmer and continue cooking until the risotto is cooked, about 15 minutes.
5. Remove from the heat and stir in the parmesan cheese and season with pepper.
6. Chill the risotto for at least an hour.
7. Preheat the Air Fryer to 400°F/200°C.
8. Form balls from the risotto.
9. Dip the balls in the egg and coat them evenly with the breadcrumbs.
10. Arrange the balls in the Air Fryer Basket and use the Air Fryer Double Layer Rack if needed.
11. Spray the balls with cooking spray and set the timer for 5 minutes or until the balls are golden brown.
12. Serve and enjoy!

Dinner Recipes

373 - Chicken and Squash Stew

Servings: 2
Preparation Time: 5 minutes
Cooking Time: 17 minutes

Ingredients:
- 2 chicken breasts, cubed
- pepper, to taste
- ½ cup squash, cubed
- 1 tablespoon onions, sliced
- 1 tablespoon garlic, minced
- ½ teaspoon garlic salt
- 1 tablespoon carrots, diced
- 1½ cups chicken stock
- 1 tablespoon fresh cilantro, chopped

Directions:
1. Preheat the Air Fryer to 350°F/180°C.
2. Season the chicken cubes with pepper and place them in the Air Fryer Baking Pan.
3. Spray the chicken with cooking spray and place the Air Fryer Baking Pan in the Air Fryer Basket.
4. Set the timer for 8 minutes.
5. Add the squash, onions, garlic, garlic salt and carrots to the Air Fryer Baking Pan and set the timer for 4 minutes.
6. Pour in the chicken stock and set the timer for five more minutes.
7. Serve and top with the fresh cilantro.

374 - Easy Chili Con Carne

Servings: 2
Preparation Time: 10 minutes
Cooking Time: 20 minutes

Ingredients:

- 5 rashers bacon, chopped
- ½ pound ground beef
- 1 tablespoon onions, chopped
- 1 tablespoon garlic, minced
- 1 tablespoon red bell peppers, chopped
- 1 tablespoon green bell peppers, chopped
- 1 tablespoon tomato paste
- ½ teaspoon garlic salt
- pepper, to taste
- ¼ teaspoon paprika
- ¼ teaspoon chili flakes
- ½ cup tomato sauce
- ¼ cup cheddar cheese, grated
- 1 tablespoon fresh parsley, chopped
- ¼ cup tomatoes, diced

Directions:

1. Preheat the Air Fryer to 400°F/200°C.
2. Place the bacon and ground beef in the Air Fryer Baking Pan and set the timer for 5 minutes.
3. Add the onions, garlic, red and green bell peppers and tomato paste.
4. Season with the garlic salt, pepper, paprika and chili flakes and stir well to combine.
5. Set the timer for 10 minutes. Stir the chili halfway through the cooking time to mix the flavors well together.
6. Stir in the tomato sauce.
7. Top with the cheddar cheese, fresh parsley and the diced tomatoes.
8. Cook for another 5 minutes or until the meat is cooked through.
9. Serve once meat has been properly cooked through.

375 - Cajun Sloppy Joe

Servings: 2
Preparation Time: 10 minutes
Cooking Time: 23 minutes

Ingredients:

- 5 rashers bacon, chopped
- 1 tablespoon onions, sliced
- 1 tablespoon red bell peppers, chopped
- 1 tablespoon garlic, minced
- 1 tablespoon tomato paste
- ½ pound ground beef
- ½ teaspoon garlic salt
- 1 teaspoon Cajun seasoning
- ½ teaspoon paprika
- ½ cup tomato sauce
- 1 tablespoon fresh parsley, chopped
- ¼ cup tomatoes, diced
- 4 burger buns

Directions:

1. Preheat the Air Fryer to 400°F/200°C.
2. Place the bacon in the Air Fryer Baking Pan.
3. Place the Air Fryer Baking Pan in the Air Fryer Basket and set the timer for 4 minutes.
4. Add the onions, red bell peppers, garlic and tomato paste and set the timer for 2 minutes.
5. Add the ground beef, garlic salt, Cajun seasoning and paprika to the Air Fryer Baking Pan and set the timer for 4 minutes or until the meat is browned.
6. Pour in the tomato sauce, fresh parsley and diced tomatoes and stir well to combine.
7. Set the timer for 10 minutes or until the meat and vegetables are cooked through.
8. Remove from the Air Fryer and set aside.
9. Arrange the burger buns in the Air Fryer and use the Air Fryer Double Layer Rack if needed.
10. Set the timer for 3 minutes or until the buns are toasted.
11. Scoop the meat onto the toasted burger buns before serving.

376 - Eggplant and Hungarian Sausage Casserole

Servings: 2
Preparation Time: 5 minutes
Cooking Time: 15 minutes

Ingredients:
- 1 large eggplant, diced
- 2 Hungarian sausages, sliced
- 1 tablespoon onions, chopped
- 1 tablespoon celery, chopped
- ¼ cup tomatoes, diced
- ½ teaspoon paprika
- pepper, to taste
- 1 tablespoon chives, chopped

Directions:
1. Preheat the Air Fryer to 350°F/180°C.
2. Place the diced eggplants, sausages, onions, celery and tomatoes in the Air Fryer Baking Pan.
3. Season with the paprika and pepper.
4. Top with the chives and set the timer for 15 minutes.
5. Serve and enjoy!

377 - Salmon with Zucchini and Fennel

Servings: 2
Preparation Time: 5 minutes
Cooking Time: 11 minutes

Ingredients:
- 1 teaspoon olive oil
- 1 small zucchini, diced
- ½ cup fennel, chopped
- salt and pepper, to taste
- 2 salmon fillets
- ½ teaspoon lemon juice
- ¼ cup feta cheese, crumbled
- 1 tablespoon olives, chopped
- ½ tablespoon dill, chopped

Directions:
1. Preheat the Air Fryer to 350°F/180°C.
2. Place the olive oil, zucchinis and fennel in the Air Fryer Baking Pan and season with salt and pepper.
3. Place the Air Fryer Baking Pan in the Air Fryer Basket and set the timer for 5 minutes.
4. Season the salmon fillets with salt, pepper and lemon juice and arrange them on the vegetables in the Air Fryer Baking Pan.
5. Return the Air Fryer Baking Pan to the Air Fryer and set the timer for 6 minutes or until the fish is cooked through.
6. Serve and top with the feta cheese, olives and dill.

378 - Chicken and Pepper Air Fry

Servings: 2
Preparation Time: 5 minutes
Cooking Time: 13 minutes

Ingredients:

- ¼ cup white onions, chopped
- 1 chicken breast, sliced
- 1 medium red bell pepper, cut into strips
- 2 cloves garlic, minced
- ½ teaspoon garlic powder
- 1 teaspoon soy sauce
- ½ teaspoon paprika
- ¼ cup spring onions, chopped

Directions:

1. Preheat the Air Fryer to 350°F/180°C.
2. Place the white onions and chicken in the Air Fryer Baking Pan and spray with some cooking spray.
3. Set the timer for 3 minutes.
4. Add the red bell peppers and garlic to the Air Fryer Baking Pan.
5. Season with the garlic powder, soy sauce and paprika.
6. Set the timer for 10 minutes or until the chicken is cooked through.
7. Serve and top with the spring onions.

379 - Tarragon Lamb Chops with Sweet Potatoes

Servings: 2
Preparation Time: 10 minutes
Cooking Time: 20 minutes

Ingredients:
- 2 tablespoons fresh tarragon, chopped
- ½ teaspoon paprika
- ½ teaspoon cayenne pepper
- ½ teaspoon ground nutmeg
- 1 tablespoon garlic, minced
- pepper, to taste
- 4 lamb chops
- 2 cups sweet potatoes, diced
- 1 tablespoon chives, chopped
- 1 tablespoon fresh cilantro, chopped

Directions:
1. Preheat the Air Fryer to 400°F/200°C.
2. Mix together the tarragon, paprika, cayenne pepper, ground nutmeg, minced garlic and pepper.
3. Rub the tarragon mix evenly onto the lamb chops and set aside.
4. Place the sweet potatoes in the Air Fryer Basket and spray with cooking spray.
5. Insert the Air Fryer Double Layer Rack into the Air Fryer.
6. Arrange the chops on the rack above the sweet potatoes.
7. Set the timer for 20 minutes or until the meat and sweet potatoes are cooked to your desired doneness. Halfway through the cooking time, remove the rack with the chops and give the Air Fryer Basket of sweet potatoes a shake to allow even cooking. Return the rack to the Air Fryer and flip the chops over.
8. Serve and top the sweet potatoes with the chives and fresh cilantro.

380 - Pork Roast with a Sweet White Wine Applesauce

Servings: 4
Preparation Time: 15 minutes
Cooking Time: 25 minutes

Ingredients:
- 1 pound pork roast
- salt and pepper, to taste
- 2 tablespoons sugar
- ½ cup sweet white wine
- 1 cup apples, peeled, cored and diced
- 2 tablespoons cilantro, chopped

Directions:
1. Preheat the Air Fryer to 400°F/200°C.
2. Season the pork roast with salt and pepper and place it in the Air Fryer Basket.
3. Spray with some cooking spray and set the timer for 25 minutes. Halfway through the cooking time, flip the roast over using a pair of kitchen tongs.
4. While the pork roast is cooking, make the white wine applesauce.
5. To make the white wine applesauce: Place the sugar and the white wine in a small saucepan over medium heat. Stir until the sugar has dissolved and add in the apples. Allow the apples to stew for 8 minutes or until softened.
6. Remove the pork roast from the Air Fryer and pour over with the sweet white wine applesauce.
7. Serve and top with the fresh cilantro.

381 - Grilled Cod with Olives and Avocado Salad

Servings: 4
Preparation Time: 5 minutes
Cooking Time: 8 minutes

Ingredients:
- 4 cod fillets
- salt and pepper, to taste
- 1 teaspoon lemon juice
- ¼ cup feta cheese, crumbled
- ¼ cup olives, sliced
- 2 avocados, diced
- ¼ cup dill, chopped

Directions:

1. Preheat the Air Fryer to 350°F/180°C.
2. Season the cod fillets with salt, pepper and lemon juice.
3. Arrange the fillets in the Air Fryer Basket and use the Air Fryer Double Layer Rack if needed.
4. Set the timer for 8 minutes or until the fish is cooked through.
5. Remove from the Air Fryer and top with the feta cheese, olives, avocados and dill.
6. Serve and enjoy!

382 - Olive and Balsamic Beef Shanks

Servings: 2
Preparation Time: 5 minutes
Cooking Time: 30 minutes

Ingredients:

- ½ pound beef shank, cubed
- 1 tablespoon garlic, minced
- ½ teaspoon paprika
- salt and pepper, to taste
- 1 tablespoon olives, sliced
- 1 tablespoon fresh basil, chopped
- 1 tablespoon fresh cilantro, chopped
- 1 cup tomatoes, diced
- ½ tablespoon balsamic vinegar
- 1 tablespoon olive oil

Directions:

1. Preheat the Air Fryer to 350°F/180°C.
2. Place the beef cubes in the Air Fryer Baking Pan.
3. Season the beef with the minced garlic, paprika, salt, and pepper.
4. Add the olives, fresh basil, fresh cilantro and tomatoes to the Air Fryer Baking Pan.
5. Drizzle over with the balsamic vinegar and olive oil and season with more pepper.
6. Set the timer for 30 minutes. Halfway through the cooking time, stir the beef cubes to allow for even cooking.
7. Serve and enjoy!

383 - Thyme, Feta and Tomato Chicken

Servings: 2
Preparation Time: 5 minutes
Cooking Time: 30 minutes

Ingredients:
- 2 chicken breasts, cubed
- 1 tablespoon tomato paste
- 1 tablespoon garlic, minced
- ½ teaspoon paprika
- ½ teaspoon dried thyme
- salt and pepper, to taste
- ¼ cup chicken stock
- 1 tablespoon fresh basil, chopped
- 1 cup tomatoes, diced
- ¼ cup feta cheese

Directions:
1. Preheat the Air Fryer to 400°F/200°C.
2. Place the chicken cubes in the Air Fryer Baking Pan and add mix well with the tomato paste, minced garlic, paprika, dried thyme, salt and pepper.
3. Add in the chicken stock, fresh basil and diced tomatoes.
4. Top with the feta cheese.
5. Place the Air Fryer Baking Pan in the Air Fryer Basket and set the timer for 30 minutes or until the chicken is cooked through. Halfway through the cooking time, stir the chicken cubes to allow even cooking.
6. Serve and enjoy!

384 - Sweet Chili Pork Bellies

Servings: 4
Preparation Time: 10 minutes
Cooking Time: 20 minutes

Ingredients:
- 2 tablespoons olive oil
- 2 teaspoons lime juice
- 2 teaspoons honey
- 2 tablespoons garlic, minced
- 1 teaspoon paprika
- 1 teaspoon chili flakes
- 2 tablespoons fresh cilantro, chopped
- salt and pepper, to taste
- 1 pound pork belly slices
- 8 lime slices

Directions:
1. Preheat the Air Fryer to 400°F/200°C.
2. To make the sweet chili: Mix together the olive oil, lime juice, honey, minced garlic, paprika, chili flakes, fresh cilantro, salt and pepper.
3. Rub the pork belly slices evenly with the sweet chili.
4. Line the Air Fryer Basket with the lime slices and place the pork bellies on them.
5. Set the timer for 20 minutes or until the pork is cooked through. Halfway through the cooking time, flip the pork belly slices over using a pair of kitchen tongs.
6. Serve and enjoy!

385 - Chicken Alfredo with Kalamata Olives

Servings: 2
Preparation Time: 10 minutes
Cooking Time: 23 minutes

Ingredients:
- 2 rashers bacon, chopped
- 2 tablespoon garlic, minced
- 1 chicken breast, sliced
- 1 tablespoon kalamata olives, sliced
- ½ teaspoon garlic powder
- freshly ground black pepper
- ½ cup low fat cream
- ¼ cup chicken stock
- 1 tablespoon fresh parsley, chopped

Directions:
1. Preheat the Air Fryer to 350°F/180°C.
2. Place the chopped bacon in the Air Fryer Baking Pan and set the timer for 3 minutes.
3. Add the minced garlic, chicken slices and kalamata olives.
4. Season with the garlic powder and pepper.
5. Return to the oven and set the time for 10 minutes.
6. Combine the cream with the chicken stock and stir into the Air Fryer Baking Pan.
7. Set the timer for 10 more minutes. Finally serve and top with the fresh parsley.

386 - Oriental Stuffed Pepper

Servings: 2
Preparation Time: 10 minutes
Cooking Time: 14 minutes

Ingredients:
- ¼ cup zucchinis, diced
- ¼ cup carrots, diced
- 1 tablespoon onions, sliced
- 1 tablespoon mushrooms, sliced
- ½ teaspoon paprika
- ½ teaspoon garlic powder
- ½ tablespoon soy sauce
- white pepper, to taste
- 2 large bell peppers
- 2 cups cooked rice
- ½ tablespoon chives, chopped

Directions:
1. Preheat the Air Fryer to 350°F/180°C.
2. Combine the zucchinis, carrots, onions and mushrooms in the Air Fryer Baking Pan.
3. Season with the paprika, garlic powder, soy sauce and white pepper.
4. Place the Air Fryer Baking Pan in the Air Fryer Basket and set the timer for 8 minutes.
5. While the vegetables are cooking, prepare the bell peppers. Slice the tops off the bell peppers and discard the pith and seeds.
6. Remove the Air Fryer Baking Pan from the Air Fryer and mix in the cooked rice.
7. Fill the peppers with the rice and vegetable mixture and top with the chives.
8. Arrange the bell peppers in the Air Fryer Basket and set the timer for 6 minutes.
9. Serve once the timer goes off.

387 - Chicken Curry in a Hurry!

Servings: 2
Preparation Time: 5 minutes
Cooking Time: 22 minutes

Ingredients:

- 1 teaspoon olive oil
- 1 tablespoon onions, sliced
- 1 tablespoon red bell peppers, chopped
- ½ tablespoon garlic, minced
- 1 chicken breast, cubed
- ¼ tablespoon mustard
- ⅛ teaspoon turmeric
- ½ tablespoon curry powder
- ½ cup coconut milk
- ½ cup canned diced tomatoes, drained
- ½ tablespoon fresh parsley, chopped

Directions:

1. Preheat the Air Fryer to 350°F/180°C.
2. Combine the olive oil, onions, bell peppers, minced garlic and chicken cubes in the Air Fryer Baking Pan.
3. Set the timer for 10 minutes.
4. Mix in the mustard, turmeric, curry powder, coconut milk and diced tomatoes.
5. Set the timer for another 12 minutes or until the chicken is cooked through.
6. Serve and top with the fresh parsley.

388 - Hanger Steaks with Mango Salsa

Servings: 2
Preparation time: 10 minutes plus 10 minutes resting time
Cooking Time: 10 minutes

Ingredients:

- 2 hanger steaks
- 1 teaspoon ground cumin
- 1 teaspoon paprika
- salt and pepper, to taste
- 1 cup mangoes, diced
- ¼ cup red onions, diced
- ¼ cup mint leaves, chopped
- 1 teaspoon lemon juice
- 1 tablespoon olive oil

Directions:

1. Marinate the steaks with the combined ground cumin, paprika, salt and pepper. Set aside for 10 minutes.
2. Preheat the Air Fryer to 350°F/180°C.
3. Spray the steaks with some cooking spray and arrange them in the Air Fryer Basket. Use the Air Fryer Double Layer Rack if needed.
4. Set the timer for 8 minutes or until desired doneness.
5. While the steaks are cooking, make the salsa: Place the mangoes, red onions and mint leaves in a bowl. Add the lemon juice and olive oil and mix well to combine.
6. Remove the steaks from the Air Fryer and top with the mango salsa.
7. Serve and enjoy!

389 - Cod Fillets with Radish and Baby Potatoes

Servings: 2
Preparation time: 5 minutes
Cooking Time: 16 minutes

Ingredients:
- 2 cod fillets
- 1 teaspoon paprika
- 1 teaspoon sage
- 1 teaspoon tarragon
- 1 tablespoon lemon juice
- ½ cup baby potatoes, halved
- ½ cup radish, halved

Directions:
1. Preheat the Air Fryer to 350°F/180°C.
2. Season the cod fillets with the paprika, dried herbs and lemon juice. Set aside.
3. Place the baby potatoes and radish in the Air Fryer Basket.
4. Spray with cooking spray and set the timer for 8 minutes.
5. Arrange the cod fillets on the vegetables and return to the Air Fryer.
6. Set the timer for 8 more minutes or until the vegetables are cooked to desired crunchiness.
7. Serve and enjoy!

390 - Bacon Wrapped Chops

Servings: 2
Preparation time: 5 minutes
Cooking Time: 15 minutes

Ingredients:
- 2 pork chops, ½-inch thick
- salt and pepper, to taste
- 8 rashers bacon

Directions:
1. Preheat the Air Fryer to 350°F/180°C.
2. Season the chops with salt and pepper and wrap them with the bacon rashers.
3. Arrange them in the Air Fryer Basket and use the Air Fryer Double Layer Rack if needed.
4. Spray the chops with cooking spray and set the timer for 15 minutes.
5. Serve and enjoy!

391 - Flank Steaks and Peaches with Truffle Oil

Servings: 2
Preparation time: 5 minutes
Cooking Time: 8 minutes

Ingredients:
- 2 flank steaks
- 1 teaspoon paprika
- salt and pepper, to taste
- 4 peaches, pitted and halved
- 1 tablespoon truffle oil

Directions:
1. Preheat the Air Fryer to 350°F/180°C.
2. Season the steaks with the paprika, salt and pepper.
3. Spray the steaks with some cooking spray.
4. Arrange the steaks and peaches in the Air Fryer Basket. Use the Air Fryer Double Layer Rack if needed.
5. Set the timer for 8 minutes or until the steaks are cooked to your desired doneness.
6. Drizzle over with truffle oil before serving.

392 - Steamed Halibut with Beans and Potatoes

Servings: 2
Preparation time: 10 minutes
Cooking Time: 16 minutes

Ingredients:
- 1 cup baby potatoes, halved
- 2 cups green beans
- 2 halibut fillets
- 1 tablespoon lemon juice
- 1 tablespoon olive oil
- salt and pepper, to taste
- 1 tablespoon balsamic vinegar

Directions:
1. Preheat the Air Fryer to 350°F/180°C.
2. Place the potatoes and green beans in the Air Fryer Basket.
3. Add water in the Air Fryer as recommended by the manufacturer's instructions for steaming food.
4. Insert the Air Fryer Basket with the vegetables and set the timer for 8 minutes.
5. While the vegetables are cooking, season the halibut fillets with the lemon juice, olive oil, salt and pepper and place them on the Air Fryer Grill Pan.
6. Carefully eject the Air Fryer Basket as the steam in the Air Fryer would be very hot.
7. Attach the Air Fryer Grill Pan with the halibuts to the Air Fryer and set the timer for 8 more minutes or until the fish and vegetables are cooked through.
8. Drizzle over with balsamic vinegar before serving.

393 - Salmon Baked Broccoli and Cheese

Servings: 2
Preparation time: 5 minutes
Cooking Time: 15 minutes

Ingredients:
- 3 cups broccoli, cut into small florets
- 1 cup salmon flakes in olive oil
- ½ teaspoon pepper
- ½ cup cream
- ¼ cup cream cheese, softened
- ½ cup cheddar cheese, grated
- ½ cup mozzarella, grated
- ¼ cup fresh parsley, chopped

Directions:
1. Preheat the Air Fryer to 350°F/180°C.
2. Place the broccoli florets in the Air Fryer Baking Pan.
3. Season the salmon flakes with pepper and top them over the broccoli.
4. Whisk together the cream and cream cheese in a bowl.
5. Fold in the cheddar cheese, mozzarella cheese and fresh parsley.
6. Add the cheese/cream mixture to the Air Fryer Baking Pan.
7. Set the timer for 15 minutes or until the cheese is melted.
8. Once cheese has melted, begin to serve.

394 - Cod Fillet with Hummus

Servings: 2
Preparation time: 10 minutes
Cooking Time: 11 minutes

Ingredients:
- 2 cod fillets
- 1 tablespoon lemon juice
- salt and pepper, to taste
- 1 cup hummus
- 1 teaspoon garlic, minced
- 1 teaspoon chili flakes

Directions:
1. Attach the Air Fryer Grill Pan to the Air Fryer and preheat to 350°F/180°C.
2. Place the cod fillets on the Air Fryer Grill Pan and season with the lemon juice, salt and pepper.
3. Spray the fillets with cooking spray and set the timer for 7 minutes.
4. Mix the hummus, minced garlic and chili flakes in a bowl.
5. Season with more pepper and dollop the hummus on the cod fillets.
6. Set the timer for 4 minutes more.
7. Serve once the timer sounds!

395 - Easy Fisherman's Catch Stew

Servings: 2
Preparation time: 10 minutes
Cooking Time: 13 minutes

Ingredients:
- 1 trout fillet, cubed
- ½ cup shrimps, peeled and deveined
- ½ teaspoon paprika
- salt and pepper, to taste
- 6 ounces mussels, cleaned
- 1 tablespoon olive oil
- 1 tablespoon lemon juice
- 2 cups fish stock
- 2 tablespoons tomato paste
- 1 tablespoon olives
- 4 lemon slices
- 1 tablespoon ginger, sliced
- 1 tablespoon fresh cilantro, chopped

Directions:
1. Preheat the Air Fryer to 350°F/180°C.
2. Place the trout cubes and shrimps in the Air Fryer Baking Pan and season them with the paprika, salt and pepper.
3. Add the mussels to the Air Fryer Baking Pan and drizzle over with the olive oil and lemon juice.
4. Set the timer for 5 minutes.
5. Mix together the fish stock and tomato paste and add to the Air Fryer Baking Pan.
6. Mix in the olives, lemon slices and ginger slices and return the Air Fryer Baking Pan to the Air Fryer.
7. Set the timer for 8 minutes.
8. Serve and top with the fresh cilantro.

396 - Honey and Pineapple Beef Stew

Servings: 2
Preparation time: 10 minutes plus 30 minutes chilling time
Cooking Time: 12 minutes

Ingredients:
- 1 pound beef chunks
- 2 tablespoons olive oil
- salt and pepper, to taste
- 1 teaspoon garlic powder
- 1 cup tomato sauce
- 2 tablespoons tomato paste
- ¼ cup olives, sliced
- ¼ cup onions, chopped
- ¼ cup honey
- 1 cup pineapple chunks
- ½ cup beef stock
- 2 tablespoons fresh basil, chopped

Directions:
1. Season the beef chunks the olive oil, salt, pepper and garlic powder. Set aside to chill in the fridge for 30 minutes.
2. Preheat the Air Fryer to 350°F/180°C.
3. Place the meat in the Air Fryer Baking Pan and add in the tomato sauce, tomato paste, olives, onions, honey and pineapple chunks.
4. Pour in the beef stock and stir well to combine.
5. Set the timer for 12 minutes or until desired doneness of meat. Halfway through the cooking time, stir the beef stew to allow even cooking.
6. Serve and top with the fresh basil.

397 - Lemon Coriander Trout with Capers

Servings: 2
Preparation time: 10 minutes
Cooking Time: 8 minutes

Ingredients:
- 2 trout fillets
- salt and pepper, to taste
- 2 tablespoons olive oil
- 1 tablespoon lemon juice
- ¼ cup butter, cut into small slices
- 6 lemon slices
- 2 tablespoons capers
- ¼ cup fresh cilantro, chopped

Directions:
1. Attach the Air Fryer Grill Pan to the Air Fryer and preheat to 350°F/180°C.
2. Season the trout fillets with salt and pepper and arrange them on the Air Fryer Grill Pan.
3. Drizzle over with the olive oil and lemon juice.
4. Top the trouts with the butter slices, lemon slices, capers and fresh cilantro.
5. Set the timer for 8 minutes or until the fillets are cooked through. Halfway through the cooking time, carefully spoon the juices over the fillets for a more flavorful taste. Serve and enjoy!

398 - Pesto Air Fried Chicken with Fava Beans

Servings: 2
Preparation time: 5 minutes
Cooking Time: 9 minutes

Ingredients:
- 2 large chicken breasts
- 2 tablespoons pesto
- 1 cup fava beans
- ¼ cup parmesan cheese, shavings
- 4 lemon slices

Directions:
1. Preheat the Air Fryer to 350°F/180°C.
2. Rub the chicken breasts with the pesto and arrange them in the Air Fryer Basket.
3. Spray the chicken with cooking spray.
4. Set the timer for 7 minutes or until the chicken is cooked through. Halfway through the cooking time, flip the chicken over to allow even cooking.
5. Remove the chicken from the Air Fryer and allow to rest.
6. Place the fava beans in the Air Fryer Baking Pan.
7. Place the Air Fryer Baking Pan in the Air Fryer Basket and set the timer for 2 minutes.
8. Serve and top with the parmesan cheese shavings and lemon slices.

399 - Creamy Halibut Chowder

Servings: 1
Preparation time: 5 minutes
Cooking Time: 10 minutes

Ingredients:
- 1 halibut fillet, cut in cubes
- salt and pepper, to taste
- ½ teaspoon olive oil
- ½ teaspoon lemon juice
- 1 cup fish stock
- ¼ cup cream
- ¼ cup mushrooms, sliced
- 1 tablespoon ginger, minced
- 1 tablespoon onions, chopped
- 1 tablespoon dill, chopped

Directions:
1. Preheat the Air Fryer to 350°F/180°C.
2. Place the halibut fillets in the Air Fryer Baking Pan and season with salt and pepper.
3. Drizzle with the olive oil and lemon juice.
4. Place the Air Fryer Baking Pan in the Air Fryer Basket and set the timer for 2 minutes.
5. Pour in the fish stock and cream and add the mushrooms, ginger, and onions.
6. Stir well to combine.
7. Set the timer for 8 minutes.
8. Serve and top with the fresh dill.

400 - Snow Peas with Ginger Salmon Steaks

Servings: 1
Preparation time: 10 minutes
Cooking Time: 8 minutes

Ingredients:

- 1 tablespoon ginger, minced
- 1 salmon steak
- salt and pepper, to taste
- 1 teaspoon olive oil
- 1 tablespoon lemon juice
- ½ cup snow peas
- ½ small red bell pepper, seeds removed and sliced
- 1 tablespoon fresh cilantro, chopped

Directions:

1. Preheat the Air Fryer to 350°F/180°C.
2. Rub the ginger into the salmon steak and season with salt and pepper on both sides.
3. Drizzle over with the olive oil and lemon juice.
4. Place the fish in the Air Fryer Baking Pan with the snow peas, bell peppers, and fresh cilantro.
5. Season again with pepper.
6. Place the Air Fryer Baking Pan in the Air Fryer Basket and set the timer for 8 minutes or until the salmon is cooked through.
7. Serve and enjoy!

401 - Grilled Cumin Hanger Steak

Servings: 2
Preparation time: 5 minutes plus 10 minutes resting time
Cooking Time: 10 minutes

Ingredients:
- 2 hanger steaks
- 1 teaspoon ground cumin
- 1 teaspoon paprika
- salt and pepper, to taste
- 2 tablespoons olive oil
- 1 cup green peas
- ¼ cup mint leaves, chopped
- ¼ cup parmesan cheese, shavings

Directions:
1. Rub the steaks with cumin and paprika.
2. Season with salt and pepper and drizzle with 1 tablespoon of olive oil.
3. Rest for 10 minutes.
4. Attach the Air Fryer Grill Pan and preheat the Air Fryer to 350°F/180°C.
5. Arrange the steaks on the Air Fryer Grill Pan and set the timer for 5 minutes.
6. Remove the steaks from the Air Fryer Grill Pan and place the green peas and mint leaves on the Air Fryer Grill Pan.
7. Flip over the steaks and place them on top of the vegetables.
8. Drizzle with remaining olive oil and top with the parmesan cheese shavings.
9. Set the timer for 5 more minutes or until desired doneness of meat. Serve when ready!

402 - Grilled Chicken with Tomato and Cherry Salsa

Servings: 2
Preparation time: 10 minutes
Cooking Time: 13 minutes

Ingredients:
- ½ cup tomatoes, diced
- 2 tablespoons garlic, minced
- ½ cup avocados, diced
- ¼ cup red onions, diced
- ½ cup cherries, pitted and finely sliced
- 2 tablespoons apple cider vinegar
- 2 large chicken breasts
- salt and pepper, to taste
- 2 tablespoons fresh cilantro, chopped

Directions:
1. To make the tomato and cherry salsa: Mix the tomatoes, garlic, avocados, onions and cherries in a bowl. Add the apple cider vinegar and mix well to combine the flavors. Chill and set aside to serve with the chicken.
2. Attach the Air Fryer Grill Pan and preheat the Air Fryer to 350°F/180°C.
3. Season the chicken with salt and pepper and arrange them on the Air Fryer Grill Pan.
4. Spray with cooking spray and set the timer for 8 minutes.
5. Flip the chicken and set the timer for 5 more minutes or until the chicken is cooked through.
6. Remove the chicken from the Air Fryer and cut into slices.
7. Serve and top with the fresh cilantro.

403 - Pancetta Risotto

Servings: 2
Preparation time: 10 minutes
Cooking Time: 18 minutes

Ingredients:
- 1 small shallot, sliced
- 1 clove garlic, minced
- 1 cup arborio rice
- 2 cups chicken stock
- 1 tablespoon parmesan cheese, grated
- 4 slices of pancetta
- pepper, to taste
- ½ tablespoon chives

Directions:
1. Preheat the Air Fryer to 350°F/180°C.
2. Place the shallots and garlic in the Air Fryer Baking Pan and spray with cooking spray.
3. Stir in the rice and set the timer for 2 minutes.
4. Stir in half a cup of chicken stock and set the timer for 16 minutes.
5. Keep stirring in an extra half cup of chicken stock every 4 minutes until all the chicken stock is used.
6. Once the risotto is cooked, remove the risotto from the Air Fryer.
7. Add the cheese and pancetta.
8. Serve and season with pepper and top with chives.

404 - Tomato and Basil Short Ribs

Servings: 2
Preparation time: 5 minutes
Cooking Time: 30 minutes

Ingredients:
- 9 ounces short ribs
- salt and pepper, to taste
- ½ cup mushrooms, sliced
- 1 cup tomato sauce
- 2 tablespoons fresh basil, chopped
- 2 tablespoons garlic, minced

Directions:
1. Attach the Air Fryer Grill Pan and preheat the Air Fryer to 350°F/180°C.
2. Season the short ribs with salt and pepper and spray with cooking spray.
3. Arrange the ribs on the Air Fryer Grill Pan with the mushrooms.
4. Mix together the tomato sauce, fresh basil and garlic and pour onto the Air Fryer Grill Pan.
5. Set the timer for 30 minutes or until the ribs are cooked through. Halfway through the cooking time, flip the ribs over to allow even cooking.
6. Serve and enjoy!

405 - Teriyaki Chicken and Egg

Servings: 2
Preparation time: 10 minutes plus 10 minutes marinating time
Cooking Time: 22 minutes

Ingredients:

- 2 chicken breasts, cut into strips
- salt and pepper, to taste
- ½ cup teriyaki sauce
- 1 tablespoon olive oil
- 2 tablespoons garlic, minced
- 2 eggs
- 2 cup bean sprouts
- 2 tablespoons spring onions, chopped
- 1 teaspoon sesame seeds

Directions:

1. Preheat the Air Fryer to 350°F/180°C.
2. Season the chicken with the pepper, teriyaki sauce, olive oil and minced garlic and let it marinate for 10 minutes.
3. Spray the Air Fryer Baking Pan with cooking spray.
4. Whisk the eggs with some salt and pepper and pour into the Air Fryer Baking Pan.
5. Set the timer for 4 minutes or until the eggs are cooked through. Remove from the Air Fryer Baking Pan, cut the omelet into slices and set aside.
6. Place the chicken with the marinade sauce in the Air Fryer Baking Pan and set the timer for 15 minutes.
7. Add the bean sprouts and spring onions and set the timer for 3 more minutes.
8. To assemble: Arrange the vegetables on the serving plates and top them with the chicken and egg. Top with the sesame seeds and more fresh pepper.

406 - Creamy Mushroom Cod

Servings: 2
Preparation time: 5 minutes
Cooking Time: 11 minutes

Ingredients:
- 3 cod fillets, cut into cubes
- salt and pepper, to taste
- 1 tablespoon onion powder
- ½ cup mushrooms, sliced
- 1 cup cream
- ¼ cup parmesan cheese, grated
- ¼ cup onions, chopped
- 2 tablespoons fresh basil, chopped

Directions:
1. Preheat the Air Fryer to 350°F/180°C.
2. Place the cod fillets in the Air Fryer Baking Pan and season with some salt, pepper and the onion powder.
3. Add the mushrooms and place the Air Fryer Baking Pan in the Air Fryer Basket.
4. Set the timer for 5 minutes.
5. Mix in the cream, parmesan cheese, onions and basil and set the timer for 6 minutes.
6. Serve and top with the chopped basil.

407 - Tomato Cajun Beef Goulash

Servings: 2
Preparation time: 5 minutes plus 30 minutes chilling/marinating time
Cooking Time: 14 minutes

Ingredients:
- ½ pound beef chunks
- ½ tablespoon olive oil
- ½ tablespoon Cajun seasoning
- ½ teaspoon garlic powder
- pepper, to taste
- ½ cup tomato sauce
- ½ cup tomatoes, diced
- 1 tablespoon olives
- 1 tablespoon onions, chopped
- ½ corn on the cob, cut into 2 pieces
- 1 tablespoon fresh basil, chopped

Directions:
1. Season the beef chunks with the olive oil, Cajun seasoning, garlic powder and pepper and chill for 30 minutes.
2. Preheat the Air Fryer to 350°F/180°C.
3. Arrange the beef chunks in the Air Fryer Baking Pan and set the timer for 8 minutes.
4. Add the tomato sauce, diced tomatoes, olives, onions and corn to the Air Fryer Baking Pan.
5. Set the timer for 6 more minutes or until the beef is fork-tender.
6. Serve and top with the fresh basil.

408 - Spicy Coconut Pork Express

Servings: 2
Preparation time: 5 minutes
Cooking Time: 15 minutes

Ingredients:

- ½ pound pork belly, chopped into small cubes
- salt and pepper, to taste
- 1 cup green beans, sliced
- 5 green chilis, chopped
- 1 tablespoon onions, sliced
- ½ tablespoon garlic, minced
- 1 cup coconut milk
- ½ tablespoon shrimp paste

Directions:

1. Preheat the Air Fryer to 350°F/180°C.
2. Place the pork belly cubes in the Air Fryer Baking Pan and season them with salt and pepper.
3. Add the green beans, green chilis, onions and garlic to the Air Fryer Baking Pan and set the timer for 5 minutes.
4. Stir in the coconut milk and shrimp paste and season with more pepper.
5. Set the timer for 10 minutes or until the pork is cooked through and fork-tender.
6. Serve and enjoy!

409 - Ginger Fish Stew

Servings: 2
Preparation time: 5 minutes plus 30 minutes marinating time
Cooking Time: 12 minutes

Ingredients:

- 1 cod fillet, cut into small cubes
- 1 tablespoon sesame oil
- 1 teaspoon soy sauce
- white pepper, to taste
- ½ tablespoon fish oil
- 1 tablespoon ginger slices

- 1 tablespoon onions, sliced
- 1 tablespoon carrots, sliced
- 1 tablespoon garlic, sliced
- 1½ cups fish stock
- 1 head of bok choy, halved

Directions:

1. Marinade the fish fillets with half a tablespoon of sesame oil, the soy sauce, white pepper and fish oil for 30 minutes.
2. Preheat the Air Fryer to 350°F/180°C.
3. Place the fish fillets into the Air Fryer Baking Pan and add the ginger, onions, carrots and garlic.
4. Drizzle over with the remaining sesame oil.
5. Add water in the Air Fryer as recommended by the manufacturer's instructions for steaming food.
6. Set the timer for 7 minutes.
7. Flip the fish cubes and add in the fish stock.
8. Set the timer for 5 minutes.
9. Add the bok choy and cook for a minute more. Serve!

410 - Grilled Halibut with Sun Dried Tomatoes and Pecorino Cheese

Servings: 2
Preparation time: 5 minutes
Cooking Time: 10 minutes

Ingredients:
- 2 halibut fillets, cut into cubes
- salt and pepper, to taste
- ¼ cup butter, cut into small pieces
- ½ cup tomato sauce
- 2 teaspoons garlic, minced
- ¼ cup sun dried tomatoes, chopped
- ¼ cup pecorino cheese, shavings
- 2 tablespoons dill, chopped

Directions:
1. Attach the Air Fryer Grill Pan and preheat the Air Fryer to 350°F/180°C.
2. Season the fillets with salt and pepper and place them on the Air Fryer Grill Pan.
3. Dot the fish with the butter slices and set the timer for 5 minutes.
4. Flip the fish and add the tomato sauce, minced garlic, sun dried tomatoes, and pecorino cheese.
5. Serve and top with some dill and set the timer for 5 more minutes.

411 - Down South Spice

Servings: 2
Preparation time: 5 minutes
Cooking Time: 30 minutes

Ingredients:
- 1 cup white beans, soaked overnight
- 1 tablespoon olive oil
- salt and pepper, to taste
- ½ teaspoon Cajun seasoning
- ½ teaspoon paprika
- ¼ pound ground beef
- ½ teaspoon cumin
- ½ teaspoon nutmeg
- ½ teaspoon five spice powder
- ¼ cup onions, minced
- 1 tablespoon garlic, minced
- ½ cup tomato sauce
- 1 tablespoon olives
- ¼ cup canned tomatoes

Directions:
1. Place the beans in a large pot of salted boiling water and cook for 5 minutes.
2. Drain and season with the olive oil, salt, pepper, Cajun seasoning and paprika. Set aside.
3. Preheat the Air Fryer to 400°F/200°C.
4. Place the ground beef in the Air Fryer Baking Pan and season with the ground cumin, ground nutmeg, five spice powder, onions and garlic.
5. Mix in the tomato sauce, olives and tomatoes.
6. Place the Air Fryer Baking Pan in the Air Fryer Basket and set the timer for 25 minutes.
7. Add the beans to the Air Fryer Baking Pan and cook for 1 to 2 more minutes to warm the beans.
8. Serve and enjoy!

412 - Kimchi Stuffed Squid

Servings: 2
Preparation time: 5 minutes
Cooking Time: 12 minutes

Ingredients:
- 1 large squid, cleaned
- 1 cup kimchi

Directions:
1. Preheat the Air Fryer to 350°F/180°C.
2. Stuff the squid with the kimchi and secure it with a toothpick.
3. Place the squid in the Air Fryer Basket and spray it with some cooking spray.
4. Set the timer for 12 minutes or until the squid is cooked. Halfway through the cooking time, use kitchen tongs to rearrange the squid so that it will be cooked evenly.
5. Serve and enjoy!

413 - Garlic and Cream Cheese Rolled Pork

Servings: 2
Preparation time: 15 minutes
Cooking Time: 40 minutes

Ingredients:
- 2 tablespoons olive oil
- 3 tablespoons garlic, minced
- ½ teaspoon chili powder
- 1 teaspoon paprika
- 3 tablespoons fresh parsley, finely chopped
- salt and pepper, to taste
- ¼ cup onions, chopped
- 1 pound pork belly
- ½ cup cream cheese
- 2 tablespoons chives, chopped

Directions:
1. Preheat the Air Fryer to 350°F/180°C.
2. Combine the olive oil, 2 tablespoons of garlic, chili powder, paprika, parsley, salt and pepper. Reserve a tablespoon of garlic for step 6.
3. Add the onions and spread the mixture onto the pork belly.
4. Combine the cream cheese, the remaining minced garlic and chives and spread it over the onions on the pork.
5. Roll the meat firmly to form a log and secure with kitchen string.
6. Rub the reserved herb mixture onto the pork roll.
7. Place the pork roll seam-side down into the Air Fryer Basket and set the timer for 40 minutes or until the pork is cooked through.
8. Serve and enjoy!

414 - Tarragon and Ricotta Beef Meatballs

Servings: 4
Preparation time: 10 minutes plus 10 minutes chilling time.
Cooking Time: 10 minutes

Ingredients:
- 1 pound ground beef
- 1 tablespoon garlic, minced
- ½ cup fresh tarragon, chopped
- 1 tablespoon fresh oregano, chopped
- 1 teaspoon paprika
- ¼ cup ricotta cheese
- salt and pepper, to taste
- ½ cup breadcrumbs

Directions:
1. Mix the ground beef, garlic, tarragon, oregano, paprika, ricotta cheese, salt, pepper and breadcrumbs in a bowl and chill for 10 minutes.
2. Preheat the Air Fryer to 400°F/200°C.
3. Mold meatballs from the mixture and arrange them in the Air Fryer Basket. Use the Air Fryer Double Layer Rack if needed.
4. Set the timer for 10 minutes.
5. Serve and enjoy!

415 - Baked Salmon and Rice

Servings: 2
Preparation Time: 5 minutes
Cooking Time: 7 minutes

Ingredients:
- 1 cup cooked rice
- ½ cup cooked broccoli florets
- ½ cup cooked potatoes, diced
- ½ cup cooked carrots, diced
- ½ cup canned salmon flakes
- ½ cup parmesan cheese, grated
- salt and pepper, to taste

Directions:
1. Preheat the Air Fryer to 350°F/180°C.
2. Spray the Air Fryer Baking Pan lightly cooking spray.
3. Add the rice, vegetables and salmon.
4. Top with the parmesan cheese and season with salt and pepper.
5. Place the Air Fryer Baking Pan in the Air Fryer Basket and set the timer for 2 minutes.
6. Reduce the temperature to 325°F/170°C and set the timer for 5 more minutes.
7. Serve and enjoy.

416 - Vegetarian Chili

Servings: 2
Preparation Time: 10 minutes
Cooking Time: 40 minutes

Ingredients:

- 1 medium sweet potato, cubed
- ½ teaspoon cayenne pepper
- ½ teaspoon ground cumin
- ½ teaspoon ground cinnamon
- salt and pepper, to taste
- ½ onion, diced
- ½ red bell pepper, diced
- ½ yellow bell pepper, diced
- 1 clove garlic, minced
- ½ bunch of fresh cilantro, chopped
- ½ fresh red chili, chopped
- ½ fresh green chili, chopped
- 1 cup canned beans, drained
- 1 cup canned tomatoes, chopped
- 2 tablespoons water
- 1 tablespoon sour cream

Directions:

1. Preheat the Air Fryer to 400°F/200°C.
2. Place the sweet potatoes in the Air Fryer Baking Pan and season with the cayenne pepper, ground cumin, ground cinnamon, salt and pepper.
3. Spray with cooking spray and place the Air Fryer Baking Pan in the Air Fryer Basket.
4. Set the timer for 20 minutes.
5. Add the onions, bell peppers, garlic, fresh cilantro, chilis, beans and tomatoes to the Air Fryer Baking Pan and set the timer for 10 minutes.
6. Add the water and set the timer for another 10 minutes or until the sauce is reduced to desired consistency. Serve and top with the sour cream.

417 - Air Fried Vegan Burger

Servings: 4
Preparation Time: 10 minutes
Cooking Time: 22 minutes

Ingredients:
- 1 cup chickpeas
- 1 cup sweet corn
- ¼ cup fresh cilantro leaves, chopped
- ½ teaspoon paprika
- ½ teaspoon ground coriander
- ½ teaspoon ground cumin
- 1 teaspoon grapeseed oil
- zest of 1 lemon
- 3 teaspoons all-purpose flour, plus more for dusting
- ¼ teaspoon sea salt
- 4 burger buns, halved
- 2 tablespoons ketchup
- 2 large ripe tomatoes, sliced
- 1 small head of lettuce

Directions:
1. Preheat the Air Fryer to 350°F/180°C.
2. Blend the chickpeas, sweet corn and fresh cilantro leaves in a food processor.
3. Add the paprika, ground coriander, ground cumin, grapeseed oil, lemon zest, flour and salt.
4. Pulse until it forms a rough paste.
5. Form 4 patties and dust with flour.
6. Arrange the patties in the Air Fryer Basket and use the Air Fryer Double Layer Rack if needed.
7. Set the timer for 20 minutes or until the meat is cooked to desired doneness.
8. Remove the patties from the Air Fryer and toast the buns for 2 minutes.
9. To assemble the burgers: Spread ketchup on one bun half and top with a burger patty, some tomatoes and some lettuce. Cover with the other burger bun half.

418 - Italian Vegan Meatballs

Servings: 4
Preparation Time: 20 minutes plus 20 minutes chilling time
Cooking Time: 30 minutes

Ingredients:
- 1 cup chickpeas
- ½ cup onions, chopped
- 6 tablespoons mild salsa
- 3 tablespoons ketchup
- 2 tablespoons Italian seasoning
- 2 teaspoons regular chili powder
- ½ teaspoon black pepper
- ½ teaspoon fine sea salt
- ½ cup brown rice flour
- ½ cup spaghetti sauce

Directions:
1. Blend the chickpeas and onions until they are minced.
2. Add the salsa, ketchup, Italian seasoning, chili powder, black pepper and sea salt and blend until well combined.
3. Transfer to a bowl and chill for 20 minutes.
4. Preheat Air Fryer to 350°F/180°C.
5. Form chickpea balls and dust with the brown rice flour.
6. Arrange the balls in the Air Fryer Basket and spray with the cooking spray.
7. Set the timer for 20 minutes.
8. Remove the balls and place them in the Air Fryer Baking Pan.
9. Add the spaghetti sauce to the Air Fryer Baking Pan and return to the Air Fryer.
10. Set the timer for 10 minutes.
11. Serve and enjoy!

419 - Creamy Baked Dory

Servings: 2
Preparation Time: 15 minutes
Cooking Time: 10 minutes

Ingredients:

- 2 dory fillets
- salt and pepper, to taste
- 1 teaspoon garlic powder
- 1 teaspoon paprika
- 1 cup cream
- ½ cup cheddar cheese, grated
- 5 cloves garlic, sliced
- 2 tablespoons rosemary, chopped
- 1 tablespoon lemon juice
- 8 lemon slices
- ½ cup bacon bits

Directions:

1. Attach the Air Fryer Grill Pan and preheat the Air Fryer to 350°F/180°C.
2. Season the dory fillets with salt, pepper, garlic powder and paprika.
3. Arrange the fillets on the Air Fryer Grill Pan and set the timer for 10 minutes.
4. While the fish fillets are cooking, make the cream sauce.
5. To make the cream sauce: Mix the cream, cheese and garlic in a saucepan over medium heat. Season with the salt, pepper and chopped rosemary.
6. Remove the fish from the Air Fryer.
7. Drizzle over with the lemon juice and top with the cream sauce, lemon slices and bacon bits.

420 - Chicken Satay Rice

Servings: 2
Preparation Time: 5 minutes
Cooking Time: 15 minutes

Ingredients:

- 2 large chicken breasts, cubed
- 2 tablespoons olive oil
- 1 teaspoon turmeric
- garlic salt and pepper, to taste
- ½ cup shallots, sliced
- 1 teaspoon ginger, minced

- ¼ cup green chilis, chopped
- 1 cup coconut cream
- ¼ cup beef stock
- 2 cups cooked rice
- ¼ cup roasted peanuts, coarsely crushed

Directions:

1. Preheat the Air Fryer to 350°F/180°C.
2. Place the chicken cubes in the Air Fryer Baking Pan and season with the olive oil, turmeric, garlic salt and pepper.
3. Add the shallots, ginger and green chilis to the Air Fryer Baking Pan.
4. Place the Air Fryer Baking Pan in the Air Fryer Basket and set the timer for 10 minutes.
5. Stir in the coconut cream and beef stock and set the timer for 5 more minutes.
6. Pour over the cooked rice and top with the roasted peanuts.

421 - Mahi-Mahi with Red Onion Salsa

Servings: 2
Preparation Time: 10 minutes plus 30 minutes chilling time
Cooking Time: 10 minutes

Ingredients:

- 1 cup red onions, diced
- ¼ cup fresh cilantro, chopped
- 2 teaspoons horseradish
- 1 teaspoon garlic, minced

- 2 tablespoons tomato juice
- 2 tablespoons olive oil
- salt and pepper, to taste
- 2 mahi-mahi fillets

Directions:

1. To make the red onion salsa: Mix the red onions, fresh cilantro, horseradish, minced garlic, tomato juice, olive oil, salt and pepper in a bowl. Chill for 30 minutes.
2. Preheat the Air Fryer to 350°F/180°C.
3. Season the fillets with salt and pepper and arrange them in the Air Fryer Basket.
4. Spray with some cooking spray and set the timer for 5 minutes.
5. Flip the fish fillets and set the timer for 5 more minutes or until the fish is cooked through.
6. Serve and top with the red onion salsa.

422 - Beurre Blanc Chicken

Servings: 2
Preparation Time: 10 minutes
Cooking Time: 23 minutes

Ingredients:
- 2 chicken breasts, pounded thinly
- salt and pepper, to taste
- ¼ cup white wine
- 2 tablespoons vinegar
- ½ cup butter, melted
- 1 teaspoon lemon juice
- 2 small shallots, finely chopped
- 2 tablespoons parsley, chopped

Directions:
1. Preheat the Air Fryer to 350°F/180°C.
2. Season the chicken breasts with salt and pepper and arrange them in the Air Fryer Basket.
3. Set the timer for 8 minutes and remove from the Air Fryer.
4. Pour the white wine, vinegar, butter, lemon juice, shallots and parsley into the Air Fryer Baking Pan and stir well to combine.
5. Set the timer for 10 minutes.
6. Remove from the Air Fryer and return the chicken to the Air Fryer Basket.
7. Cook for another 5 minutes or until the chicken is cooked through.
8. Pour the white wine mixture over the chicken.
9. Serve and enjoy!

423 - Beef Tenderloin with Creamy Mushroom Gravy

Servings: 4
Preparation Time: 10 minutes
Cooking Time: 21 minutes

Ingredients:
- 1 pound beef tenderloin, cut into strips
- 2 teaspoons soy sauce
- pepper, to taste
- ½ cup button mushrooms, sliced
- 2 tablespoons garlic, minced
- 1 teaspoon Italian seasoning
- 1 cup Campbell's® cream of mushroom soup
- ½ cup vegetable stock
- 2 tablespoons chives, chopped

Directions:
1. Preheat the Air Fryer to 350°F/180°C.
2. Place the tenderloin strips in the Air Fryer Baking Pan and season them with soy sauce and pepper.
3. Spray with some cooking spray and place the Air Fryer Baking Pan in the Air Fryer Basket.
4. Set the timer for 4 minutes.
5. Remove from the Air Fryer and set aside.
6. Add the mushrooms and garlic to the Air Fryer Baking Pan and set the timer for 8 minutes.
7. Add the Italian seasoning, mushroom soup and vegetable stock to the Air Fryer Baking Pan.
8. Set the timer for 5 minutes.
9. Return the meat to the Air Fryer Baking Pan and cook for 4 more minutes or until it is cooked to your desired doneness.
10. Serve and top with the chives.

424 - Lemon Poppy Chicken Legs

Servings: 2
Preparation Time: 5 minutes
Cooking Time: 16 minutes

Ingredients:
- 2 chicken thighs, scored
- 2 teaspoons lemon juice
- salt and pepper, to taste
- 1 tablespoon rosemary, chopped
- 1 teaspoon poppy seeds
- 1 onion, cut into rings
- 4 lemon slices
- ¼ cup fresh cilantro, chopped
- ¼ cup flat-leaf parsley, chopped

Directions:
1. Preheat the Air Fryer to 350°F/180°C.
2. Season the chicken thighs with lemon juice, salt and pepper.
3. Rub the chopped rosemary and poppy seeds onto the chicken.
4. Arrange the onions in the Air Fryer Basket and lay the chicken thighs on them.
5. Spray with cooking spray and set the timer for 8 minutes.
6. Flip the chicken and arrange the lemon slices on the chicken.
7. Set the timer for another 8 minutes or until the chicken is cooked through.
8. Serve and top with the fresh cilantro and fresh parsley.

425 - Herbed Lamb Chops

Servings: 4
Preparation Time: 10 minutes
Cooking Time: 15 minutes

Ingredients:
- 1 garlic head
- 8 lamb chops, approximately 2 pounds
- 1 tablespoon fresh basil, chopped
- 3 tablespoons olive oil
- salt and pepper, to taste

Directions:
1. Preheat the Air Fryer to 400°F/200°C.
2. Spray the garlic head with cooking spray and place in the Air Fryer Basket.
3. Set the timer for 10 minutes.
4. While the garlic is roasting, marinate the lamb chops with the combined fresh basil, olive oil, salt and pepper. Set aside for 5 minutes.
5. Remove the garlic and arrange the lamb chops in the Air Fryer Basket. Use the Air Fryer Double Layer Rack if needed.
6. Set the timer for 5 minutes or until desired doneness of the meat.
7. Serve with the garlic head and enjoy!

426 - Rosemary T-Bone Steaks with Mushrooms and Potatoes

Servings: 2
Preparation time: 10 minutes
Cooking Time: 27 minutes

Ingredients:
- 4 medium potatoes, peeled and cubed
- ½ cup button mushrooms, sliced
- 1 shallot, sliced
- 2 T-bone steaks
- salt and pepper, to taste
- 2 tablespoons rosemary, chopped

Directions:
1. Preheat the Air Fryer to 400°F/200°C.
2. Place the potatoes in the Air Fryer Basket and spray with cooking spray.
3. Set the timer for 20 minutes.
4. Remove the potatoes and set aside in a warm oven until ready to serve.
5. Attach the Air Fryer Grill Pan to the Air Fryer.
6. Place the mushrooms and shallots on the Air Fryer Grill Pan.
7. Season the steaks with the salt, pepper and rosemary and place them on the mushrooms and shallots.
8. Set the timer for 5 to 7 minutes or until desired doneness of meat.
9. Serve when ready.

427 - Fully Loaded Stuffed Peppers

Servings: 2
Preparation time: 15 minutes
Cooking Time: 10 minutes

Ingredients:

- 4 medium bell peppers
- ½ cup mozzarella cheese, grated
- ½ cup feta cheese
- ¼ cup onions, chopped
- 2 tablespoons fresh cilantro, finely chopped
- freshly ground pepper, to taste
- 8 slices of deli ham
- 4 rashers bacon, roughly chopped

Directions:

1. Preheat the Air Fryer to 400°F/200°C.
2. Slice the tops off the bell peppers and remove the pith and seeds.
3. Mix the mozzarella cheese, feta cheese, onions and fresh cilantro in a bowl.
4. Season well with freshly ground black pepper.
5. Line the walls of each of the bell peppers with 2 slices of deli ham.
6. Fill the bell peppers with the cheese mixture and top with the chopped bacon.
7. Arrange the bell peppers in the Air Fryer Basket and set the timer for 10 minutes, or until the skins are slightly charred.
8. Serve and enjoy!

428 - Roasted Drumsticks in Barbecue Marinade

Servings: 4
Preparation time: 10 minutes plus 20 minutes marinating time
Cooking Time: 25 minutes

Ingredients:
- 1 tablespoon olive oil
- 1 tablespoon garlic, minced
- 2 teaspoons mustard
- 2 teaspoons brown sugar
- ½ teaspoon cayenne pepper
- 1 teaspoon chili flakes
- salt and pepper, to taste
- 4 chicken drumsticks with thighs attached, scored

Directions:
1. To make the marinade: Combine the olive oil, minced garlic, mustard, brown sugar, cayenne pepper, chili flakes, salt and pepper. Rub the chicken drumsticks with the marinade and set aside for 20 minutes.
2. Preheat the Air Fryer to 400°F/200°C.
3. Arrange the chicken drumsticks in the Air Fryer Basket and use the Air Fryer Double Layer Rack if needed.
4. Set the timer for 15 minutes.
5. Reduce the temperature to 300°F/150°C and continue roasting for another 10 minutes or until they are cooked through.
6. Serve once ready!

429 - Rosemary Rolled Pork

Servings: 2
Preparation time: 20 minutes
Cooking Time: 40 minutes

Ingredients:
- 2 tablespoons olive oil
- 2 tablespoons garlic, minced
- ½ teaspoon chili powder
- 1 teaspoon paprika
- ¼ cup fresh rosemary, chopped
- salt and pepper, to taste
- ¼ cup onions, chopped
- 3 tablespoons fresh parsley, finely chopped
- 4 pork belly slices

Directions:
1. Preheat the Air Fryer to 350°F/180°C.
2. Combine the olive oil, minced garlic, chili powder, paprika, fresh rosemary, salt and pepper in a bowl. Reserve a tablespoon for step 5.
3. Add the onions and fresh parsley to the rosemary mixture and spread onto the pork bellies.
4. Roll the meats firmly and secure with kitchen strings.
5. Rub the reserved mixture onto the pork belly rolls.
6. Arrange the pork belly rolls in the Air Fryer Basket and use the Air Fryer Double Layer Rack if needed.
7. Set the timer for 40 minutes. Halfway through the cooking time, use a pair of kitchen tongs to re-arrange the pork belly rolls to allow even cooking. Serve!

430 - Stroganoff Short Steak

Servings: 2
Preparation time: 15 minutes plus 2 hours marinating time
Cooking Time: 16 minutes

Ingredients:
- 1 pound beef steak, sliced
- 2 tablespoons soy sauce
- 4 tablespoons olive oil
- 1 tablespoon garlic, minced
- salt and pepper, to taste
- ¼ cup onions, sliced
- ½ cup button mushrooms, sliced
- ½ cup sour cream
- ¼ cup cream

Directions:
1. Marinate the steak slices with the combined soy sauce, two tablespoons of olive oil, garlic and pepper for 2 hours in the fridge.
2. Attach the Air Fryer Grill Pan and preheat to 350°F/180°C.
3. Arrange the steak slices on the Air Fryer Grill Pan and set the timer for 8 minutes or until desired doneness of meat.
4. To make the stroganoff sauce: Heat the remaining 2 tablespoons of olive oil in a non-stick frying pan and sauté the onions and mushrooms for 5 to 8 minutes or until soft. Add the sour cream and cream and season with salt and pepper. Remove from the heat and set aside before serving.

431 - Steamed Salmon with Garlic Herbed Sauce

Servings: 2
Preparation time: 10 minutes
Cooking Time: 10 minutes

Ingredients:
- 2 salmon fillets, skins removed
- salt and pepper, to taste
- ½ cup crème fraîche
- ½ tablespoon garlic, minced
- ½ tablespoon chives, chopped
- 1 tablespoon fresh dill, chopped
- 1 tablespoon olives, sliced

Directions:
1. Preheat the Air Fryer to 300°F/150°C.
2. Add water in the Air Fryer as recommended by the manufacturer's instructions for steaming food.
3. Place both salmon fillets in the Air Fryer Baking Pan and season with salt and pepper.
4. Place the Air Fryer Baking Pan in the Air Fryer Basket and set the timer for 10 minutes.
5. While the fish is cooking, combine the crème fraîche, garlic and chives in a bowl and season with pepper.
6. Remove the fish from the Air Fryer and drizzle over with the garlic herb sauce and top with the fresh dill and olives.
7. Serve once done.

432 - Cheesy Chicken Tenders

Servings: 4
Preparation time: 15 minutes
Cooking Time: 15 minutes

Ingredients:
- 1 cup breadcrumbs
- ¼ cup parmesan cheese, grated
- 1 teaspoon dried basil
- 1 egg
- salt and pepper, to taste
- 4 large chicken breasts, cut into slices
- ½ cup cheddar cheese, grated
- ¼ cup cream

Directions:
1. Combine the breadcrumbs, parmesan cheese and dried basil and set aside.
2. Lightly beat the egg with some salt and pepper.
3. Dip the chicken slices into the egg and coat evenly with the breadcrumbs. Chill for 10 minutes or until the breadcrumbs have set so that they will not fall off during cooking.
4. Preheat the Air Fryer to 350°F/180°C.
5. Arrange the chicken tenders in the Air Fryer Basket and use the Air Fryer Double Layer Rack if needed.
6. Set the timer for 15 minutes or until the chicken tenders are cooked through. Halfway through the cooking time, use a pair of kitchen tongs to flip the chicken tenders over to allow even cooking.
7. While the chicken is cooking, melt the cheddar cheese in the microwave for 1-2 minutes and add the cream and season with pepper.
8. Remove the chicken tenders from the Air Fryer and drizzle over with the cheese sauce. Serve!

433 - Mexican Chili Beans

Servings: 4
Preparation time: 10 minutes
Cooking Time: 30 minutes

Ingredients:
- 2 cups white beans, soaked overnight
- 1 tablespoon salt
- 2 tablespoons olive oil
- ½ cup onions, sliced
- ¼ cup green olives, sliced
- ½ cup canned tomatoes
- 1 teaspoon taco seasoning
- pepper, to taste
- 1 teaspoon paprika

Directions:
1. Preheat the Air Fryer to 400°F/200°C.
2. Cook the beans in a pot of salted, boiling water for 5 minutes. Drain and transfer to the Air Fryer Baking Pan.
3. Add the olive oil, onions, olives and tomatoes, and season with taco seasoning, pepper and paprika.
4. Place the Air Fryer Baking Pan in the Air Fryer Basket and set the timer for 25 minutes.
5. Serve once the timer goes off.

434 - Crispy Pork Belly

Servings: 4
Preparation time: 5 minutes
Cooking Time: 55 minutes

Ingredients:
- 4 pork belly slices, skin scored at ¼-inch intervals
- 1 teaspoon garlic powder
- 1 teaspoon onion powder
- 1 teaspoon pepper
- ½ teaspoon salt
- 2 tablespoons fresh lemon juice

Directions:
1. Preheat the Air Fryer to 325°F/170°C.
2. Rub the meat of the pork bellies with the combined garlic powder, onion powder, pepper and salt.
3. Brush the lemon juice into the scored skin of the pork bellies.
4. Arrange the pork bellies, skin sides up, in the Air Fryer Basket. Use the Air Fryer Double Layer Rack if needed.
5. Set the timer for 30 minutes.
6. Increase the temperature to 400°F/200°C and continue cooking for 25 minutes more or until the skin is crispy. Serve once done.

435 - Red Wine Braised Short Ribs

Servings: 2
Preparation time: 10 minutes
Cooking Time: 28 minutes

Ingredients:

- 9 ounces of short ribs, each cut into 3-inch segments
- salt and pepper, to taste
- 2 tablespoons onions, sliced
- 2 tablespoons celery, chopped
- 3 cloves garlic, smashed
- 1 tablespoon tomato paste
- 2 tablespoons fresh parsley, chopped
- ½ cup baby carrots
- 2 rosemary sprigs
- 1 cup red wine
- 1 cup beef stock
- ¼ cup chicken stock
- ½ tablespoon peppercorns

Directions:

1. Preheat the Air Fryer to 350°F/180°C.
2. Place the short ribs in the Air Fryer Baking Pan and season with salt and pepper.
3. Spray with cooking spray and add the onions, celery, garlic, tomato paste, fresh parsley, carrots and rosemary sprigs.
4. Place the Air Fryer Baking Pan in the Air Fryer Basket and set the timer for 8 minutes.
5. Pour in the red wine, both stocks and peppercorns.
6. Set the timer for 20 minutes.

436 - Beef Cubano

Servings: 4
Preparation time: 10 minutes
Cooking Time: 23 minutes

Ingredients:

- 1 pound ground beef
- 1 tablespoon olive oil
- 1 teaspoon paprika
- 1 teaspoon ground cumin
- 1 teaspoon dried oregano
- 1 teaspoon ground allspice

- 2 teaspoons soy sauce
- pepper, to taste
- 2 tablespoons lime juice
- ¼ cup onions, minced
- 2 tablespoons garlic, sliced
- 2 tablespoons green olives, sliced

Directions:

1. Preheat the Air Fryer to 350°F/180°C.
2. Place the ground beef in the Air Fryer Baking Pan and season with the olive oil, paprika, ground cumin, dried oregano, ground allspice, soy sauce, pepper and lime juice.
3. Place the Air Fryer Baking Pan in the Air Fryer Basket and set the timer for 5 minutes.
4. Mix in the onions, garlic and green olives and set the timer for 5 minutes.
5. Stir and set the timer for 8 minutes.
6. Stir again and set the timer for 5 more minutes.
7. Serve once done.

437 - Burger Spring Rolls

Servings: 4
Preparation time: 15 minutes
Cooking Time: 16 minutes

Ingredients:
- 1 tablespoon olive oil
- 2 cups ground beef
- ¼ cup onions, minced
- 2 teaspoons garlic powder
- 1 teaspoon paprika
- salt and pepper, to taste
- 10 spring roll wrappers
- 10 slices cheddar cheese

Directions:
1. Preheat the Air Fryer and set the temperature to 350°F/180°C.
2. Place the olive oil, ground beef and onions in the Air Fryer Baking Pan and season with the garlic powder, paprika, salt and pepper.
3. Place the Air Fryer Baking Pan in the Air Fryer Basket and set the timer for 8 minutes.
4. Remove the meat from the Air Fryer and set aside to cool slightly.
5. To assemble the spring rolls: Lay out the spring roll wrappers on a work surface. Lay a slice of cheese on each wrapper and dollop a tablespoon of meat onto an edge of the wrappers. Fold in the ends and roll tightly to encase the filling completely.
6. Arrange the spring rolls in the Air Fryer Basket and use the Air Fryer Double Layer Rack if needed.
7. Spray lightly with cooking spray.
8. Set the timer for 8 minutes or until the spring rolls are golden and crispy.
9. Serve once golden and crispy is achieved.

438 - Spicy Garlic Pork Belly

Servings: 4
Preparation Time: 10 minutes plus 10-15 minutes resting time
Cooking Time: 45 minutes

Ingredients:

- 2¼ pounds whole pork belly, skin scored
- salt and pepper, to taste
- 1 teaspoon garlic powder
- 1 teaspoon onion powder
- 2 tablespoons cayenne pepper
- 2 tablespoons five spice powder
- ¼ cup vegetable oil
- 1 handful of lemongrass
- 10 green chilis, chopped
- ½ cup garlic cloves, smashed

Directions:

1. Preheat the Air Fryer to 350°F/180°C.
2. Season the pork belly skin with salt and pepper.
3. Turn the belly skin down and season the meat with salt, pepper, garlic powder, onion powder, cayenne pepper and five spice powder.
4. Rub the oil into the meat.
5. Place the lemongrass, chilis and smashed garlic cloves along the middle of the belly lengthwise.
6. Roll the belly into a log and secure tightly with kitchen string.
7. Spray the skin with cooking spray.
8. Place the pork in the Air Fryer Basket and set the timer for 25 minutes.
9. Flip the pork belly and spray with more cooking spray. Set the timer for another 20 minutes.
10. Check the meat with a skewer to see if it is cooked through. The juices must run clear. If the juices run pink, cook a further 10 to 15 minutes.
11. Remove from the Air Fryer and allow to rest for another 10 to 15 minutes before serving.

439 - BBQ Turkey Legs

Servings: 4
Preparation Time: 10 minutes
Cooking Time: 30 minutes

Ingredients:

- 3 garlic cloves
- 2 tablespoons mustard
- ¼ cup honey
- ½ cup tomato sauce
- 2 tablespoons tomato paste
- 1 teaspoon chili powder
- 1 teaspoon soy sauce
- 4 turkey legs

Directions:

1. Preheat the Air Fryer to 400°F/200°C.
2. To make the marinade sauce: Blend the garlic cloves until they are minced. Add the mustard, honey, tomato sauce, tomato paste, chili powder and soy sauce. Blend until well combined.
3. Rub the marinade sauce onto the turkey legs.
4. Arrange the turkey legs in the Air Fryer Basket and use the Air Fryer Double Layer Rack if needed.
5. Spray the turkey legs with cooking spray and set the timer for 20 minutes. Halfway through the cooking time, rearrange them to cook evenly.
6. Reduce the temperature to 350°F/180°C and set the timer for 10 more minutes.
7. Serve once timer goes off.

440 - Crunchy Shrimp Balls

Servings: 4
Preparation Time: 20 minutes plus 30 minutes chilling time
Cooking Time: 10 minutes

Ingredients:

- 1 pound shrimps, peeled and deveined
- 2 garlic cloves, minced
- 1 teaspoon white sugar
- ½ knob of ginger, peeled and minced
- 1 teaspoon sesame oil
- 4 green onions, minced
- 2 eggs
- salt and pepper, to taste
- 1 cup breadcrumbs
- 1 teaspoon paprika

Directions:

1. Combine the shrimps, garlic, sugar, ginger, sesame oil and onions in a food processor.
2. Add an egg and season with salt and pepper.
3. Blend until smooth.
4. Transfer into a bowl and chill for 30 minutes.
5. Preheat the Air Fryer to 300°F/150°C.
6. Mix the breadcrumbs and paprika in a bowl and set aside.
7. Whisk the other egg in a bowl and set aside.
8. Scoop out balls of the shrimp mix and dip into the whisked egg.
9. Evenly coat the balls with the breadcrumbs and leave to set for a few minutes.
10. Arrange the shrimp balls in the Air Fryer Basket and use the Air Fryer Double Layer Rack if needed.
11. Spray the balls with cooking spray and set the timer for 10 minutes before serving.

441 - Tomato Seafood Casserole

Servings: 2
Preparation Time: 5 minutes
Cooking Time: 20 minutes

Ingredients:
- 1½ cups tomato sauce
- 2 tablespoons parmesan cheese, grated
- ¼ cup shredded cheddar cheese, grated
- ½ cup shredded swiss cheese, grated
- 3 teaspoons Worcestershire sauce
- ⅛ teaspoon ground nutmeg
- ⅛ teaspoon paprika
- pepper, to taste
- 1 cup shrimps, peeled and deveined
- 2 cod fillets, cut into bite-size pieces

Directions:
1. Preheat the Air Fryer to 300°F/150°C.
2. Mix the tomato sauce, cheeses, Worcestershire sauce, ground nutmeg, paprika and pepper in the Air Fryer Baking Pan.
3. Add the shrimps and cod slices to the Air Fryer Baking Pan.
4. Set the timer for 20 minutes or until cheeses have melted before serving.

442 - Roast Duck in Hoisin Sauce

Servings: 2
Preparation Time: 5 minutes
Cooking Time: 25 minutes

Ingredients:
- 1 duck, cut into quarters
- 1 star anise
- ½ cinnamon stick
- ½ tablespoon oil
- 1 dried chili, chopped
- 2 slices fresh ginger root
- 1 tablespoon soy sauce
- ½ tablespoon oyster sauce
- ½ teaspoon sesame oil
- ½ tablespoon rice wine
- 1 cup chicken stock
- 2 tablespoons spring onions, chopped

Directions:
1. Preheat the Air Fryer to 325°F/170°C.
2. Combine all the ingredients except the spring onions in the Air Fryer Baking Pan.
3. Place the Air Fryer Baking Pan in the Air Fryer Basket and set the timer for 25 minutes. Halfway through the cooking time, give the dish a stir to allow even cooking.
4. Serve and top with spring onions.

443 - Chicken Tahini with Fresh Mangoes

Servings: 4
Preparation Time: 5 minutes
Cooking Time: 40 minutes

Ingredients:
- 1 pound chicken wings
- 2 tablespoons tahini
- 2 tablespoons honey
- 1 tablespoon soy sauce
- ¼ teaspoon ground ginger
- ¼ teaspoon cayenne pepper
- 1 tablespoon ghee
- 1 cup mangoes, diced

Directions:
1. Preheat the Air Fryer to 300°F/150°C.
2. Marinate the chicken wings with the combined tahini, honey, soy sauce, ground ginger, cayenne pepper and ghee.
3. Transfer the chicken wings to the Air Fryer Basket and use the Air Fryer Double Layer Rack if needed.
4. Set the timer for 40 minutes or until the wings are cooked through and crispy.
5. Serve and top with the diced mangoes.

444 - Spicy Beef Soup with Tortillas

Servings: 2
Preparation Time: 5 minutes
Cooking Time: 16 minutes

Ingredients:
- 1 tablespoon vegetable oil
- 1 small onion, finely chopped
- 1 clove garlic, minced
- ½ teaspoon ground cumin
- ½ teaspoon chili powder
- ½ cup tomato sauce
- 1 cup ground beef
- 1 cup chicken stock
- 1 green chili, chopped
- ¾ cup whole peeled tomatoes, canned
- ½ tablespoon fresh cilantro, chopped
- 1 packet tortilla chips

Directions:
1. Preheat the Air Fryer to 400°F/200°C.
2. Place the vegetable oil, onions, minced garlic, ground cumin, chili powder, tomato sauce and ground beef into the Air Fryer Baking Pan. Mix until well combined.
3. Place the Air Fryer Baking Pan in the Air Fryer Basket and set the timer for 8 minutes.
4. Add the stock, chilis, tomatoes, and fresh cilantro to the Air Fryer Baking Pan.
5. Set the timer for another 5 to 8 minutes.
6. Transfer into soup bowls with the tortilla chips.

445 - Crunchy Chicken Katsu

Servings: 2
Preparation Time: 10 minutes
Cooking Time: 20 minutes

Ingredients:
- 2 skinless, boneless chicken breasts, halved and pounded
- salt and pepper, to taste
- 1 tablespoon all-purpose flour
- 1 egg
- ½ cup breadcrumbs

Directions:
1. Preheat the Air Fryer to 400°F/200°C.
2. Season the chicken breasts with salt and pepper and dust with flour.
3. Whisk the egg with pepper and set aside.
4. Dip the chicken pieces in the egg and coat evenly with the breadcrumbs.
5. Arrange the chicken in the Air Fryer Basket and use the Air Fryer Double Layer Rack if needed.
6. Spray with cooking spray and set the timer for 20 minutes or until the chicken is cooked through. Halfway through the cooking time, flip the chicken over with a pair of kitchen tongs.
7. Serve and enjoy!

446 - Easy Air Fried Duck

Servings: 4
Preparation Time: 10 minutes
Cooking Time: 1 hour

Ingredients:
- 2 tablespoons olive oil
- 1 tablespoon garlic powder
- 1 tablespoon onion powder
- 1 tablespoon paprika
- salt and pepper, to taste
- 1 whole duck, pierced all over with a knife

Directions:
1. Preheat the Air Fryer to 325°F/170°C.
2. Mix the olive oil, garlic powder, onion powder, paprika, salt and pepper together in a bowl.
3. Rub mixture well into duck skin, especially where pierced.
4. Place the duck in the Air Fryer Basket and set the time for 30 minutes.
5. Flip the duck over and set the timer for another 30 minutes.
6. Serve and enjoy!

447 - Rosemary Lamb Chops

Servings: 2
Preparation Time: 10 minutes
Cooking Time: 35 minutes

Ingredients:

- 1 tablespoon olive oil
- 3 teaspoons fresh rosemary, chopped
- salt and pepper, to taste
- 1 onion, chopped
- 1 large carrot, cut into ¼-inch pieces
- 5 cloves garlic, minced
- 6 lamb chops
- ½ bottle red wine
- ½ can whole peeled tomatoes with juice
- ¾ cups condensed chicken broth
- ¾ cups beef broth
- 1 teaspoon fresh thyme, chopped

Directions:

1. Preheat the Air Fryer to 300°F/150°C.
2. Combine the olive oil with 2 teaspoons of rosemary and season with salt and pepper. Set aside.
3. Place the onions, carrots, garlic and lamb chops in the Air Fryer Baking Pan and set the timer for 15 minutes.
4. Stir in the wine, tomatoes, chicken broth and beef broth to the Air Fryer Baking Pan and top with the remaining fresh rosemary and thyme.
5. Set the timer for another 20 minutes.
6. Serve and enjoy!

448 - Easy Beef Ragu

Servings: 2
Preparation Time: 5 minutes
Cooking Time: 35 minutes

Ingredients:
- ½ pound beef chunks
- salt and pepper, to taste
- 1 onion, finely chopped
- 2 sprigs fresh rosemary
- 1½ tablespoons fresh sage
- 4 cloves garlic, minced
- 1 medium carrot, peeled and diced
- 1 cup red wine
- ½ can peeled whole plum tomatoes

Directions:
1. Preheat the Air Fryer to 300°F/150°C.
2. Place the beef chunks in the Air Fryer Baking Pan and season with some salt and pepper.
3. Add the onions, fresh rosemary, sage, minced garlic and carrots.
4. Spray with cooking spray and mix well to combine.
5. Set the timer for 30 minutes. Halfway through the cooking time, flip the beef chunks over to allow even cooking.
6. Add the wine and the tomatoes to the Air Fryer Baking Pan.
7. Return the Air Fryer Baking Pan to the Air Fryer and set the timer for 5 more minutes before serving.

449 - Morning After Noodles

Servings: 2
Preparation Time: 10 minutes
Cooking Time: 16 minutes

Ingredients:

- 2 large eggs
- 3 ounces snow peas
- 1 teaspoon ginger, minced
- 1 clove garlic, minced
- 1 tablespoon low sodium soy sauce
- 1½ tablespoons rice wine vinegar
- 1½ tablespoons sesame oil
- 6 ounces egg noodles, cooked
- ½ cup broccoli, cut into small florets
- ½ cup cabbage, shredded

Directions:

1. Preheat the Air Fryer to 400°F/200°C.
2. Spray the Air Fryer Baking Pan with cooking spray and crack in the eggs. Set the timer for 5 minutes.
3. Remove the cooked eggs from the Air Fryer Baking Pan and set aside.
4. Reduce the Air Fryer temperature to 300°F/150°C.
5. Mix the snow peas with the ginger, garlic, soy sauce, vinegar and sesame oil in the Air Fryer Baking Pan and set the timer for 3 minutes.
6. Add the noodles and set the timer for 3 minutes.
7. Add the broccoli and cabbage and cook for another 5 minutes.
8. Place the eggs on the noodles and allow to warm for a minute.
9. Serve and enjoy!

450 - Crispy Noodles with Seafood Sauce

Servings: 2
Preparation Time: 15 minutes plus 20 minutes resting time
Cooking Time: 16 minutes

Ingredients:

- 6 ounces egg noodles
- 4 teaspoons cornstarch
- 2 heads bok choy, halved
- ½ cup squid rings
- 10 bay scallops
- 4 fish balls, halved
- ½ cup shrimps, peeled and deveined
- 1 cup shiitake mushrooms, sliced

- 1 tablespoon vegetable oil
- white pepper, to taste
- 2 garlic cloves, finely minced
- 1 cup chicken stock
- 2 teaspoons oyster sauce
- 1½ teaspoons soy sauce
- 1 teaspoon sesame oil

Directions:

1. Blanch the noodles in a pot of boiling water for 2 to 3 minutes until they are slightly undercooked. The noodles must not be mushy.
2. Drain the noodles and place them on a plate. Toss the noodles in 1 teaspoon of cornstarch. Loosen the noodles on the plate and sprinkle over another 1 teaspoon of cornstarch. Set aside for at least 20 minutes to remove the excess moisture.
3. Blanch the bok choy in a fresh pot of boiling water until the leaves are slightly wilted but the stems are still crunchy.
4. Blanch the squid rings in the same boiling water for 30 seconds and set aside. Repeat for the scallops, fish balls and shrimps and set aside.
5. Preheat the Air Fryer to 350°F/180°C.
6. Place the noodles in the Air Fryer Basket and spray with cooking spray.
7. Set the timer for 3 to 4 minutes or until the noodles are golden and crispy. Shake the Air Fryer Basket halfway through the cooking time to allow even cooking.
8. Remove from the Air Fryer and arrange on the serving plates with the cooked bok choy.
9. Place the mushrooms in the Air Fryer Baking Pan.
10. Place the Air Fryer Baking Pan in the Air Fryer and set the timer for 3 minutes or until the mushrooms are translucent.
11. Add the blanched seafood to the Air Fryer Baking Pan.
12. Whisk together the vegetable oil, pepper, minced garlic and chicken stock in a bowl and pour into the Air Fryer Baking Pan.
13. Set the timer for 5 minutes or until the stock is bubbling hot.
14. Combine the oyster sauce, soy sauce, sesame oil and remaining cornstarch and add to the Air Fryer Baking Pan.
15. Stir well and set the timer for 3 to 4 more minutes or until the sauce has thickened.
16. Pour over the noodles and vegetables.
17. Serve and enjoy!

451 - Shrimp and Rice Casserole

Servings: 4
Preparation Time: 10 minutes
Cooking Time: 15 minutes

Ingredients:

- ½ cup shrimps, peeled and deveined
- ¼ teaspoon ground black pepper
- 1 teaspoon Himalayan salt
- ¼ cup olive oil
- 1 teaspoon lime zests
- ¼ cup mint leaves, chopped
- ½ jalapeño pepper, seeded and diced
- 1 clove garlic, smashed
- ⅛ cup fresh lime juice
- 2 cups cooked rice
- 1 cup fresh baby spinach leaves
- lemon wedges for garnish
- ¼ cup toasted almonds, chopped

Directions:

1. Preheat the Air Fryer to 400°F/200°C.
2. Place the shrimps in the Air Fryer Baking Pan and marinate them with the pepper, salt, half of the olive oil and lime zests.
3. Blend the mint leaves, jalapeño pepper, garlic, lime juice and remaining olive oil in a blender and pour into the Air Fryer Baking Pan.
4. Stir in the cooked rice.
5. Place the Air Fryer Baking Pan in the Air Fryer Basket and set the timer for 15 minutes.
6. Serve and top with the spinach leaves, lemon wedges and chopped almonds.

452 - Easy Stuffed Lamb

Servings: 6
Preparation Time: 15 minutes
Cooking Time: 1 hour 20 minutes

Ingredients:
- 2 tablespoons olive oil
- 1 red onion, minced
- 3 garlic cloves, minced
- 2 teaspoons ground coriander
- 2 teaspoons ground cumin
- 1 teaspoon ground cinnamon
- 1 teaspoon sumac
- ½ cup breadcrumbs
- ¼ cup fresh parsley, chopped
- ¼ cup pistachios, roughly chopped
- ¼ cup feta, crumbled
- 60g pack dry sour cherries
- 2 small preserved lemons, rinds only, finely chopped
- 3 tablespoons tahini
- 2¼ pounds lamb shoulder, deboned and butterflied
- salt and pepper, to taste

Directions:
1. Preheat the Air Fryer to 300°F/150°C.
2. Heat the oil into a non-stick pan over medium heat and sauté the onions until they are translucent.
3. Remove from the pan and place in a large bowl with the garlic, ground coriander, cumin, ground cinnamon, sumac, breadcrumbs, fresh parsley, pistachios, feta cheese, sour cherries, lemon rinds and tahini.
4. Season the lamb with some salt and pepper and place it skin-side down.
5. Spoon the stuffing along the center of the lamb and roll the lamb tightly into a log. Secure with kitchen string.
6. Place the lamb into the Air Fryer Basket and set the timer for 1 hour and 20 minutes or until the lamb is cooked to desired doneness. Rearrange the lamb a few times throughout the cooking time to allow even cooking.
7. Serve and enjoy!

453 - Healthy Spinach Lasagna

Servings: 2
Preparation Time: 20 minutes
Cooking Time: 20 minutes

Ingredients:
- 1 tablespoon unsalted butter
- ¼ cup plain flour
- 1 cup milk
- 1 fresh bay leaf
- salt and pepper, to taste
- 1 cup spinach leaves, shredded
- ½ cup ricotta cheese
- 1 teaspoon ground nutmeg
- 6 ounces instant lasagna sheets, cut to fit the pan
- ¼ cup parmesan cheese, grated

Directions:
1. Preheat the Air Fryer to 400°F/200°C.
2. To make the white sauce: Melt the butter in a non-stick frying pan and whisk in the flour. Gradually add in the milk and continue whisking until the sauce has thickened. Add the bay leaf and season with salt and pepper. Simmer for five minutes and remove the bay leaf.
3. Mix the spinach, ricotta and nutmeg in a bowl and set aside.
4. To assemble the lasagna: Using the Air Fryer Baking Pan, begin with a lasagna sheet and layer with the spinach and ricotta. Add another lasagna sheet and spread with a layer of white sauce. Repeat until the Air Fryer Baking Pan is filled ending the top layer with white sauce.
5. Top with the parmesan cheese.
6. Place the Air Fryer Baking Pan in the Air Fryer Basket and set the timer for 20 minutes.
7. Serve and enjoy!

454 - Grandma Elli's Chicken Cordon Bleu with Creamy Wine Sauce

Servings: 2
Preparation Time: 25 minutes
Cooking Time: 20 minutes

Ingredients:

- 6 slices swiss cheese
- 6 slices deli ham
- 2 small chicken breasts
- 3 tablespoons all-purpose flour
- 1 teaspoon paprika
- 1 egg
- salt and pepper, to taste
- 1 cup breadcrumbs
- 6 tablespoons butter
- ½ cup dry white wine
- 1 teaspoon chicken stock cube
- 1 tablespoon cornstarch
- 1 cup heavy whipping cream

Directions:

1. Turn the chicken breasts up on their sides and slice into the side of breast to create 3 even slices pure chicken breast (total 6 slices). Each slice should have the same perimeter as the original chicken breast before you sliced it (creating 3 flat sliced chicken breasts). Thus, making it easy to roll the chicken breast slices up in the next steps.
2. Place a slice each of the cheese and ham on each chicken breast slice.
3. Roll the chicken breasts up and secure them with toothpicks.
4. Mix the flour and paprika in a bowl and set aside
5. Whisk the egg with the salt and pepper and set aside.
6. Dust the chicken rolls in the flour and dip them in the egg.
7. Drip off any excess egg and coat the chicken rolls evenly with the breadcrumbs.
8. Set aside and preheat the Air Fryer to 400°F/200°C.
9. Arrange the chicken rolls in the Air Fryer Basket and use the Air Fryer Double Layer Rack if needed.
10. Set the timer for 20 minutes. Halfway through the cooking time, flip the chicken rolls over to allow even cooking.
11. While the chicken cordon bleus are cooking, make the creamy wine sauce.
12. To make the creamy wine sauce: Melt the butter in a non-stick saucepan and pour in the wine. Dissolve the chicken stock cube and bring to a boil. Reduce the heat and simmer for 10 minutes. Dissolve the cornstarch in the whipped cream and gradually stir into the pan. Continue simmering until the sauce has thickened.
13. Serve by removing the chicken from the Air Fryer and top over with the wine sauce.

455 - Baked Tomato, Beans and Rice

Servings: 2
Preparation Time: 10 minutes
Cooking Time: 21 minutes

Ingredients:

- 2 turkey sausages, casings removed
- 1 cup dried red beans, cooked
- 1 stalk celery, finely chopped
- ½ green bell pepper, finely chopped
- ½ red bell pepper, finely chopped
- ½ sweet onion, finely chopped
- 1 clove garlic, minced
- ½ tablespoon Italian seasoning
- ½ cup tomato sauce
- ¼ cup water
- salt and pepper, to taste
- ½ cup cooked long-grain rice
- 1 tablespoon green onions, chopped
- 1 tablespoon red onions, chopped

Directions:

1. Preheat the Air Fryer to 300°F/150°C.
2. Place the turkey sausages in the Air Fryer Baking Pan and set the timer for 15 minutes.
3. Add the beans, celery, bell peppers, onions, garlic, Italian seasoning, tomato sauce, water, salt and pepper.
4. Mix in the cooked rice.
5. Place the Air Fryer Baking Pan in the Air Fryer Basket and set the timer for 6 minutes or until the vegetables are cooked. Halfway through the cooking time, fluff the rice and mix well with the sauce.
6. Serve and top with the green onions and red onions.

456 - Easy Cheesy Herbed Rice Casserole

Servings: 2
Preparation Time: 5 minutes
Cooking Time: 20 minutes

Ingredients:
- ½ onion, diced
- ⅛ teaspoon cayenne pepper
- 4 ounces frozen spinach, thawed, drained and chopped
- ½ cup milk
- 1 egg, whisked
- 1 cup sharp cheddar cheese, grated plus extra for topping
- 2 cups cooked rice
- ½ teaspoon fresh parsley, chopped
- ½ teaspoon fresh thyme, chopped
- ½ teaspoon fresh basil, chopped
- salt and pepper, to taste

Directions:
1. Preheat the Air Fryer to 300°F/150°C.
2. Spray the Air Fryer Baking Pan with cooking spray, add all the ingredients into the Air Fryer Baking Pan and give a light stir.
3. Top with the extra cheddar cheese and place the Air Fryer Baking Pan in the Air Fryer Basket.
4. Set the timer for 20 minutes. Halfway through the cooking time, fluff the rice with a fork and mix well with the spinach and cheese.
5. Serve and enjoy!

457 - One Pan Cauliflower Quinoa

Servings: 2
Preparation Time: 10 minutes
Cooking Time: 15 minutes

Ingredients:
- 1 cup cooked quinoa
- ½ cup parmesan cheese, grated
- 2 eggs, whisked
- 1 cup cauliflower, cut into small florets
- salt and pepper, to taste
- 1 cup sour cream
- 2 tablespoons garlic, minced
- 1 tablespoon chives, chopped

Directions:
1. Preheat the Air Fryer to 350°F/180°C.
2. Place the cooked quinoa, parmesan cheese and whisked eggs into the Air Fryer Baking Pan.
3. Add the cauliflower florets and season with salt and pepper. Mix well to combine.
4. Place the Air Fryer Baking Pan into the Air Fryer Basket and set the timer for 10 minutes.
5. Flip the cauliflower quinoa to cook the other side for another 5 minutes.
6. While the quinoa is cooking, combine the sour cream, minced garlic and chives in a bowl and chill until the cauliflower quinoa is ready. Serve when done!

458 - Spicy Tuna Sushi Crisp

Servings: 1
Preparation Time: 10 minutes
Cooking Time: 13 minutes

Ingredients:

- 1 cup of cooked sushi rice
- 1 tablespoon rice vinegar
- ½ teaspoon of sugar

- 2 ounces sashimi grade tuna, cut into small cubes
- 1 stalk green onion, thinly sliced
- ½ teaspoon sriracha sauce

Directions:

1. Preheat Air Fryer to 400°F/200°C.
2. Combine the rice, vinegar and sugar and set aside.
3. Place rice on a flat surface. Mold and roll into a long strip. Cut into bite sizes.
4. Carefully place rice bites into the Air Fryer and set the timer for 13 minutes.
5. Mix together the tuna and onions.
6. Serve and top each rice bite with some tuna and sriracha sauce.

459 - Baked Chicken and Mushroom Rice

Servings: 2
Preparation Time: 10 minutes
Cooking Time: 28 minutes

Ingredients:

- 1 cup long-grain rice
- ½ cup sour cream
- ½ cup cream of mushroom soup
- ½ steamed chicken, shredded
- ¼ cup butter, melted
- ½ cup dry sherry
- 1 celery stalk, chopped
- ½ onion, quartered
- ¼ teaspoon curry powder
- ⅛ teaspoon garlic powder
- ⅛ teaspoon paprika
- salt and pepper, to taste
- ½ cup mushrooms, sliced
- ½ cup green onions, chopped

Directions:

1. Preheat the Air Fryer to 300°F/150°C.
2. Place the rice in the Air Fryer Baking Pan.
3. Mix together the sour cream and cream of mushroom soup and pour over the rice. Mix well to ensure the rice is well coated with the cream.
4. Place the Air Fryer Baking Pan in the Air Fryer Basket and set the timer for 20 minutes.
5. Mix together the chicken, butter, sherry, celery, onions, curry powder, garlic powder, paprika, salt and pepper and set aside.
6. Add the chicken mixture, mushrooms and green onions to the rice and set the timer for another 8 minutes.
7. Serve and enjoy!

460 - All Season Dumpling Casserole

Servings: 2
Preparation Time: 15 minutes
Cooking Time: 35 minutes

Ingredients:

- 1 tablespoon light olive oil
- 3 shallots, peeled and halved
- ½ cup small new potatoes, halved
- 1 clove garlic, halved
- ¼ cup baby carrots,
- 1 fennel bulb, cut into wedges
- 1½ cups vegetable stock
- ½ cup fruity white wine
- ½ teaspoon raw sugar
- ¼ teaspoon light soy sauce
- ¼ cup snow peas
- ½ cup chestnut mushrooms, halved
- ¼ cup baby zucchini, cut into chunks
- ¼ tablespoon fresh red chili, seeded and finely chopped
- ½ tablespoon chives, minced
- 1 teaspoon cornstarch
- ½ tablespoon water
- 8 store bought frozen dumplings, thawed
- ½ tablespoon fresh parsley, chopped

Directions:

1. Preheat the Air Fryer to 275°F/140°C.
2. Place all the ingredients into the Air Fryer Baking Pan except the cornstarch, water, frozen dumplings and fresh parsley.
3. Place the Air Fryer Baking Pan in the Air Fryer Basket and set the timer for 10 minutes.
4. Dissolve the cornstarch with the water until it becomes a paste.
5. Stir the cornstarch paste into the Air Fryer Baking Pan and set the timer again for five minutes.
6. Stir again and arrange the dumplings on the vegetables.
7. Set the timer for 20 minutes or until the dumplings are cooked through.
8. Remove from the Air Fryer and allow to cool for 5 minutes.
9. Serve and top with the fresh parsley.

461 - Seafood Jambalaya

Servings: 4
Preparation time: 10 minutes
Cooking Time: 20 minutes

Ingredients:

- 1 tablespoon extra-virgin olive oil
- ½ cup red onions, sliced
- 1 cup tomatoes, diced
- ½ cup bell peppers, chopped
- 1 cup long grain white rice
- ¾ teaspoon cayenne pepper
- ½ teaspoon paprika
- 2½ teaspoons Cajun seasoning
- 1¼ cups chicken stock
- 1 cup shrimps, peeled and deveined with tails intact
- ½ cup squid rings
- 1 pound mussels, cleaned

Directions:

1. To cook the rice: Heat the olive oil in a large deep non-stick frying pan over medium heat and sauté the onions, tomatoes and bell peppers for a few minutes. Add the rice, a quarter teaspoon of cayenne pepper, a quarter teaspoon of paprika, a half teaspoon of Cajun seasoning and the chicken stock to the vegetables and bring to a boil. Reduce the heat and simmer for 15 minutes or until the rice is cooked.
2. While the rice is cooking, preheat the Air Fryer to 350°F/180°C.
3. Add the shrimps, squids and mussels to the Air Fryer Baking Pan.
4. Season with the remaining amounts of cayenne pepper, Cajun seasoning and paprika.
5. Spray the seafood with cooking spray and place the Air Fryer Baking Pan in the Air Fryer Basket.
6. Set the timer for 6 minutes or until the seafood is cooked through.
7. Serve by topping the seafood over the rice.

462 - Guilt-Free Sweet and Sour Pork

Servings: 4
Preparation Time: 10 minutes
Cooking Time: 20 minutes

Ingredients:

- ½ cup cornstarch plus 2 tablespoons for the sauce
- salt and pepper, to taste
- 1 egg white
- 1 pound pork belly, cut into cubes
- 1 can pineapple chunks in syrup
- ½ medium red bell pepper, cut into 1-inch pieces
- ½ medium yellow bell pepper, cut into 1-inch pieces
- 1 medium onion, cut into wedges
- 1 cup water, plus a little more to dissolve the cornstarch for the sauce
- ¼ cup white sugar
- ¼ cup ketchup
- ⅓ cup apple cider vinegar
- ½ teaspoon soy sauce

Directions:

1. Preheat the Air Fryer to 350°F/180°C.
2. Season the cornstarch with some salt and pepper.
3. Whisk the egg white and season with pepper.
4. Dip the pork cubes into the egg and then coat them lightly with the cornstarch.
5. Arrange the pork cubes in the Air Fryer Basket and spray with cooking spray.
6. Set the timer for 20 minutes.
7. When the meat is cooking, make the sweet and sour sauce.
8. To make the sweet and sour sauce: Combine the pineapple chunks with their syrup, red bell peppers, yellow bell peppers, onions, water, sugar, ketchup, apple cider vinegar and soy sauce in a non-stick sauce pan over medium heat. When the sauce has come to a boil, reduce the heat. Dissolve the remaining 2 tablespoons of cornstarch in a little water, and gradually stir into the sauce. Continue simmering until the sauce has thickened.
9. Remove the meat from the Air Fryer and serve by coating the meat evenly with the sweet and sour sauce.

463 - Beef Katsu

Servings: 2
Preparation Time: 10 minutes
Cooking Time: 20 minutes

Ingredients:
- 500 grams beef, cut into ¾ inch thick strips
- Salt and pepper, to taste
- 1 tablespoon all-purpose flour
- 1 egg
- ½ cup breadcrumbs

Directions:
1. Preheat the Air Fryer to 400°F/200°C.
2. Season the beef strips with salt and pepper and dust with flour.
3. Whisk the egg with pepper and set aside.
4. Dip the beef strips in the egg and coat evenly with the breadcrumbs.
5. Arrange the beef strips in the Air Fryer Basket and use the Air Fryer Double Layer Rack if needed.
6. Spray with cooking spray and set the timer for 20 minutes or until the beef strips are cooked through. Halfway through the cooking time, flip the beef strips over with a pair of kitchen tongs.
7. Serve and enjoy!

464 - Lamb Stew

Servings: 2
Preparation Time: 5 minutes
Cooking Time: 30 minutes

Ingredients:
- 500 grams lamb, cut into chunks
- Salt and pepper, to taste
- 1 teaspoon garlic powder
- 3 cups lamb stock
- 1 cup potatoes, cut into cubes
- 1 cup baby carrots

Directions:
1. Preheat the Air Fryer to 350°F/180°C.
2. Place the lamb in the Air Fryer Baking Pan and season with salt, pepper and garlic powder.
3. Spray the lamb with cooking spray and set the timer for 5 minutes.
4. Add lamb stock, potatoes and baby carrots.
5. Set the timer for 25 minutes.
6. Serve and enjoy!

465 - Rosemary Lamb and Potato Air Fried

Servings: 2
Preparation Time: 5 minutes
Cooking Time: 18 minutes

Ingredients:
- ¼ cup white onions, chopped
- 500 grams lamb, cut into chunks
- 1 cup potatoes, cut into cubes
- 2 cloves garlic, minced
- 3 rosemary stalks
- Salt and pepper, to taste

Directions:
1. Preheat the Air Fryer to 350°F/180°C.
2. Place the white onions and lamb in the Air Fryer Baking Pan and spray with some cooking spray.
3. Set the timer for 3 minutes.
4. Add the potatoes and garlic to the Air Fryer Baking Pan.
5. Crumble the stalks of rosemary over the lamb.
6. Set the timer for 15 minutes or until lamb is cooked through.
7. Serve and season with salt and pepper.

---

466 - Beef Enchilada

Servings: 2
Preparation Time: 5 minutes
Cooking Time: 18 minutes

Ingredients:
- 500 grams tender beef chunks, cut to ideal size
- 1 teaspoon taco seasoning
- Salt and pepper, to taste
- 2 teaspoons garlic, minced
- ½ cup onions, chopped
- ½ cup tomatoes, diced
- 1 tablespoon jalapeños
- 1 teaspoon olive oil
- 1 cup tomato sauce
- 2 tablespoons fresh basil, chopped

Directions:
1. Preheat the Air Fryer to 350°F/180°C.
2. Place the beef chunks in the Air Fryer Baking Pan and season with the taco seasoning, salt and pepper.
3. Add the garlic, onions, tomatoes, jalapeños and olive oil.
4. Place the Air Fryer Baking Pan in the Air Fryer Basket and set the timer for 10 minutes.
5. Pour in the tomato sauce and fresh basil and stir well.
6. Return to the Air Fryer and set the timer for 8 more minutes or until the beef is cooked through.
7. Serve and enjoy!

Dessert Recipes

467 - Coffee & Date Cake

Servings: 2
Preparation Time: 10 minutes
Cooking Time: 12 minutes

Ingredients:

- 1½ cups almond flour
- ¾ tablespoon baking powder
- ¼ teaspoon salt
- ⅛ cup stevia
- ½ large egg
- ½ teaspoon vanilla extract
- ½ teaspoon ground cinnamon
- ½ teaspoon espresso shot
- ¾ cups water
- ½ tablespoon canola oil
- ¼ cup dates, chopped

Directions:

1. Preheat the Air Fryer to 350°F/180°C.
2. Mix together the almond flour, baking powder, salt and stevia and set aside.
3. Whisk the egg, vanilla extract and ground cinnamon in a stand mixer.
4. Pour in the espresso shot and let it mix for 30 seconds.
5. Gradually add in the flour mixture.
6. Add in the water.
7. Pour in the canola oil slowly.
8. Mix the batter until smooth.
9. Fold in the dates.
10. Pour the mixture into the Air Fryer Baking Pan.
11. Place the Air Fryer Baking Pan into the Air Fryer Basket and set the timer for 12 minutes or until the cake is cooked through.
12. Remove the Air Fryer Baking Pan from the Air Fryer.
13. Allow the cake to cool before removing it from the Air Fryer Baking Pan.
14. Serve and enjoy!

468 - Blueberry and Peach Crumble a la Mode

Servings: 4
Preparation Time: 10 minutes
Cooking Time: 20 minutes

Ingredients:
- ½ cup fresh blueberries
- ½ cup peaches, sliced
- 1 cup plain flour
- ½ teaspoon ground cinnamon
- ¼ cup butter, cubed
- 2 tablespoons caster sugar
- 4 scoops vanilla ice cream

Directions:

1. Preheat the Air Fryer to 400°F/200°C.
2. Divide the blueberries and peaches between 4 ramekins and set aside.
3. Sift the flour and ground cinnamon into a bowl.
4. Add the butter and sugar and rub together with your fingertips until large clumps form.
5. Top the ramekins with the crumbs.
6. Arrange 2 ramekins into the Air Fryer Basket. Place the Air Fryer Double Layer Rack into the Air Fryer Basket and arrange the remaining 2 ramekins on the rack.
7. Set the timer for 20 minutes and cook until the crumb topping turn golden brown.
8. Serve and top with the vanilla ice cream.

469 - Mango and Peach Crumble

Servings: 2
Preparation Time: 10 minutes
Cooking Time: 25 minutes

Ingredients:
- ¼ cup caster sugar
- 2 tablespoons butter
- ½ cup plain flour
- 1 cup peaches, sliced
- ½ cup mangoes, sliced
- 1 teaspoon lemon juice
- 1 teaspoon ground cinnamon

Directions:
1. Preheat the Air Fryer to 400°F/200°C.
2. Rub together the caster sugar, butter and flour in a bowl until large clumps form and set aside.
3. Arrange the peaches and mangoes in layers in the Air Fryer Baking Pan.
4. Drizzle over the lemon juice.
5. Top the fruits with the crumb topping and press down lightly to ensure that there are no gaps between the fruits and the crumb topping.
6. Sprinkle over the ground cinnamon.
7. Place the Air Fryer Baking Pan into the Air Fryer Basket and set the timer for 25 minutes.
8. Serve and enjoy!

470 - Sweet Cinnamon Doughnut Holes

Servings: Makes 12 doughnut balls
Preparation time: 15 minutes
Cooking Time: 8 minutes

Ingredients:
- 2¼ cups all-purpose flour
- 1½ teaspoons baking powder
- 1 teaspoon salt
- 2 tablespoons butter, softened
- ½ cup caster sugar
- 2 large egg yolks
- ½ cup buttermilk

- 3½ tablespoons melted butter, for brushing

For the cinnamon sugar:

- ⅓ cup caster sugar
- 1 teaspoon ground cinnamon

Directions:
1. Preheat the Air Fryer to 350°F/180°C.
2. Sift the flour, baking powder and salt in a bowl and set aside.
3. Mix the butter and sugar in a bowl until large clumps form.
4. Mix in the egg yolks until well combined.
5. Gradually add the flour mixture.
6. Add the buttermilk and mix well until a dough forms.
7. Lightly dust a work surface with flour and roll the dough to ½-inch thick.
8. Use a 2-inch round cookie cutter to cut out balls from the dough.
9. Brush the balls with the melted butter.
10. Place them in the Air Fryer Basket and set the timer for 8 minutes. Use the Air Fryer Double Layer Rack if the balls will not fit on a single layer.
11. While the balls are cooking, prepare the cinnamon sugar by mixing the sugar and cinnamon in a bowl and set aside.
12. Remove the balls from the Air Fryer and brush again with the melted butter.
13. Serve and coat the balls in the cinnamon sugar.

471 - Cinnamon Apple and Cranberry Bites

Servings: 2
Preparation time: 10 minutes
Cooking Time: 25 minutes

Ingredients:

- 4 granny smith apples, peeled, cored and sliced
- 2 tablespoons raisins
- 1 teaspoon dried cranberries
- 1 tablespoon brown sugar
- 1 teaspoon ground cinnamon
- 2 sheets puff pastry
- 2 tablespoons melted butter

Directions:

1. Preheat the Air Fryer to 350°F/180°C.
2. Mix the apples, raisins, cranberries, brown sugar and ground cinnamon.
3. Cut the puff pastry into 3x3-inch squares.
4. Put some apple mixture in the center of a square sheet of puff pastry and top with another square sheet of puff pastry.
5. Fold in the sides of the pastry so that the apple filling is completely encased in the pastry.
6. Brush the squares with the melted butter.
7. Arrange the squares in the Air Fryer Basket and use the Air Fryer Double Layer Rack if needed.
8. Set the timer for 25 minutes or until the squares are golden and crisp.
9. Serve and enjoy!

472 - Lemon Poppy Banana Cake

Servings: 4
Preparation time: 10 minutes
Cooking Time: 30 minutes

Ingredients:
- 1 banana, thinly sliced
- 1 teaspoon lemon juice
- 1 cup all-purpose flour
- ⅛ teaspoon salt
- ½ cup butter
- ¼ cup caster sugar
- 1 egg
- 1 teaspoon lemon extract
- 1 teaspoon poppy seeds
- 1 teaspoon lemon rinds
- ¼ cup almond flakes

Directions:
1. Preheat the Air Fryer to 350°F/180°C.
2. Mix the sliced bananas and the lemon juice and arrange in the Air Fryer Baking Pan.
3. Sift together the flour and salt in a bowl and set aside.
4. Cream the butter, caster sugar, egg and lemon extract in a bowl until it becomes light and fluffy.
5. Gradually add the flour mixture to the batter.
6. Fold in the poppy seeds and lemon rinds.
7. Pour the batter into the Air Fryer Baking Pan and top with the almond flakes.
8. Place the Air Fryer Baking Pan into the Air Fryer Basket and set the timer for 30 minutes.
9. Remove from the Air Fryer and allow to cool.
10. Serve and enjoy!

473 - Cappuccino Cake

Servings: 2
Preparation time: 10 minutes
Cooking Time: 15 minutes

Ingredients:

- 1 cup all-purpose flour
- 1 teaspoon espresso powder
- ½ cup butter
- ¼ cup caster sugar
- 1 egg
- 2 tablespoons milk
- ¼ cup walnuts, chopped

Directions:

1. Preheat the Air Fryer to 350°F/180°C.
2. Sift together the flour and espresso powder in a bowl and set aside.
3. Cream the butter, caster sugar and egg in a bowl until the mixture becomes light and fluffy.
4. Sift in the flour mixture.
5. Pour in the milk and mix well to combine.
6. Pour the batter into the Air Fryer Baking Pan.
7. Top with the chopped walnuts.
8. Place the Air Fryer Baking Pan in the Air Fryer Basket and set the timer for 15 minutes.
9. Remove from the Air Fryer and allow to cool before serving.

474 - Apricot and Coconut Pound Cake

Servings: 2
Preparation time: 10 minutes
Cooking Time: 15 minutes

Ingredients:
- 3 tablespoons plain flour
- ⅛ teaspoon salt
- 3 tablespoons butter, softened
- 3 tablespoons caster sugar
- 1 egg
- 1 tablespoon apricot jam
- 1 tablespoon coconut cream
- 1 tablespoon icing sugar

Directions:
1. Preheat the Air Fryer to 325°F/170°C.
2. Sift together the flour and the salt in a bowl and set aside.
3. Cream the butter and sugar in a bowl until it becomes light and fluffy.
4. Mix in the egg and apricot jam.
5. Add the flour mixture.
6. Add the coconut cream and mix until the batter is well combined.
7. Pour the batter into the Air Fryer Baking Pan.
8. Place the Air Fryer Baking Pan into the Air Fryer Basket and set the timer for 15 minutes or until the cake is cooked through.
9. Remove from the Air Fryer and allow to cool.
10. Dust with icing sugar before serving.

475 - Cinnamon Crispy Bread

Servings: 2
Preparation time: 5 minutes
Cooking Time: 6 minutes

Ingredients:
- 2 eggs
- ⅛ teaspoon salt
- ½ teaspoon ground cinnamon
- 2 tablespoons butter, softened
- 4 slices white bread
- 2 tablespoons sugar

Directions:
1. Preheat the Air Fryer to 350°F/180°C.
2. Whisk the eggs with the salt and ground cinnamon in a bowl and set aside.
3. Butter both sides of the bread slices and cut them into strips.
4. Sprinkle the bread strips with the sugar and coat them with the egg mixture.
5. Spray the Air Fryer Baking Pan with cooking spray and arrange the bread strips in a single layer. You may need to cook in two batches if the strips do not fit.
6. Place the Air Fryer Baking Pan into the Air Fryer Basket and set the timer for 2 minutes.
7. Remove the Air Fryer Basket and using a pair of tongs, flip over the bread strips.
8. Spray with cooking spray and return to cook for 4 more minutes or until they turn golden brown.
9. Serve and enjoy!

476 - Hazelnut and Blueberry Muffins

Servings: Makes 12 muffins
Preparation time: 10 minutes
Cooking Time: 20 minutes

Ingredients:

- 1¼ cups all-purpose flour
- ½ teaspoon baking powder
- ⅓ cup butter
- ½ cup granulated sugar
- 1 egg
- ½ teaspoon hazelnut extract
- 1 cup milk
- ¼ cup blueberries
- ¼ cup hazelnuts, chopped

Directions:

1. Preheat the Air Fryer to 325°F/170°C.
2. Sift together the flour and the baking powder and set aside.
3. Cream the butter and sugar with a hand mixer until light and fluffy.
4. Add the egg, hazelnut extract and milk and mix well.
5. Gradually add in the flour mixture and continue mixing for about 3 minutes until the batter is well combined.
6. Use a rubber spatula to scrape the sides of the mixing bowl and fold in the blueberries and hazelnuts.
7. Pour the batter into individual muffin cups until each cup reaches three-quarters full.
8. Arrange the muffin cups into the Air Fryer Basket of the Air Fryer and use the Air Fryer Double Layer Rack if needed to fit in all the cups.
9. Set the timer for 20 minutes.
10. Remove the muffin cups from the Air Fryer and allow to cool before serving.

477 - Macadamia Butter Scones

Servings: Makes 10 scones
Preparation time: 15 minutes
Cooking Time: 15 minutes

Ingredients:
- 2 cups all-purpose flour
- ¼ teaspoon salt
- ½ teaspoon baking soda
- 1 teaspoon baking powder
- ¼ cup granulated white sugar
- ½ cup unsalted butter, chilled and cut into pieces
- ⅔ cup milk, plus more for brushing
- ¼ cup macadamia nuts, crushed

Directions:
1. Preheat the Air Fryer to 350°F/180°C.
2. Sift together the flour, salt, baking soda and baking powder in a large bowl.
3. Mix in the sugar.
4. Rub in the butter using your fingertips until it resembles breadcrumbs.
5. Add the milk, a little at a time, and continue mixing with your fingers until a dough forms.
6. Mix in the macadamia nuts.
7. Lightly dust a work surface with flour and roll out the dough to 1-inch thick.
8. Use a round cookie cutter to cut out scones from the dough and brush the tops with milk.
9. Arrange the scones in the Air Fryer Basket, using the Air Fryer Double Layer Rack if needed, and set the timer for 15 minutes.
10. Remove the scones from the Air Fryer and allow to cool on a cooling rack before serving.

478 - Spiced Buttermilk Cookies

Servings: 2
Preparation time: 10 minutes
Cooking Time: 8 minutes

Ingredients:
- 1¼ cups all-purpose flour
- ½ cup cake flour
- ½ teaspoon baking powder
- ¼ teaspoon baking soda
- 1 teaspoon granulated sugar
- 1 teaspoon ground nutmeg
- 1 teaspoon ground cinnamon
- ¾ teaspoon salt
- 4 tablespoons unsalted butter, melted
- ¾ cup buttermilk, chilled

Directions:
1. Preheat the Air Fryer to 400°F/200°C.
2. Sift together the all-purpose flour, cake flour, baking powder, baking soda, granulated sugar, ground nutmeg, ground cinnamon and salt in a bowl.
3. Add the butter and buttermilk to the flour mixture and stir with a spatula until well combined.
4. Lightly dust the work surface with a little flour and roll the dough to ½-inch thick.
5. Cut out cookies using cookie cutters.
6. Arrange the cookies inside the Air Fryer Basket, using the Air Fryer Double Layer Rack if needed.
7. Set the timer to 8 minutes and cook until the biscuits turn golden brown.
8. Serve and enjoy!

480 - Peanut Butter Pecan Pie

Servings: 2
Preparation time: 15 minutes
Cooking Time: 25 minutes

Note: You will need a Non-Stick Pie Pan that is small enough to fit inside the Air Fryer Basket.

Ingredients:
- 9" inch store-bought piecrust
- 1 tablespoon unsalted butter, softened
- ½ cup pecans, chopped
- 2 eggs
- ¾ cup maple syrup
- 2 tablespoons sugar
- ¼ cup creamy peanut butter
- ¾ teaspoon vanilla extract
- ½ teaspoon salt
- ½ teaspoon ground cinnamon

Directions:
1. Lightly dust your work surface with flour.
2. Place the piecrust on the work surface and cut out the size required for your pie pan.
3. Grease the pie pan with the butter and line it with the piecrust.
4. Fold the edges of the pie crust so that they sit on the rim of the pie pan.
5. Add the pecans into the pie pan and place the pie pan into the Air Fryer Basket and set aside.
6. Whisk together the eggs, maple syrup, sugar, peanut butter, vanilla extract, salt and ground cinnamon in a bowl until well combined.
7. Pour the batter carefully into the pie pan.
8. Set the temperature at 350°F/180°C and the timer for 25 minutes.
9. Remove the pie from the Air Fryer and allow to cool a little before serving.

481 - Chocolate Tea Scones

Servings: 4
Preparation time: 15 minutes
Cooking Time: 10 minutes

Ingredients:
- 2 cups flour
- 2½ teaspoon baking powder
- 2 tablespoons cocoa powder
- ½ teaspoon salt
- 1 teaspoon sugar
- 1 tablespoon butter, chilled
- 1 egg
- ¾ cup milk, plus more for brushing
- ¼ cup dark chocolate, melted

Directions:
1. Sift together the flour, baking powder, cocoa powder, salt and sugar in a bowl.
2. Rub in the butter using your fingertips until it resembles breadcrumbs.
3. Whisk together the egg and the milk.
4. Make a hole in the center of the flour mixture and pour in the egg mixture.
5. Combine to form a dough and transfer the dough to a lightly-floured work surface.
6. Knead the dough lightly and flatten to ¼-inch thick.
7. Use a lightly-floured round cookie cutter and cut out as many scones as you can. Brush their tops with milk.
8. Arrange the scones in the Air Fryer Basket and use the Air Fryer Double Layer Rack if necessary.
9. Set the Air Fryer to 190°C/375°F and the timer for 10 minutes.
10. Remove the scones from the Air Fryer and allow to cool.
11. Drizzle over with melted chocolate before serving.

482 - Nutella Filled Slices

Servings: 2
Preparation time: 5 minutes
Cooking Time: 8 minutes

Ingredients:
- 1 packet of rolled puff pastry
- 1 cup Nutella
- whipped cream, optional

Directions:
1. Preheat the Air Fryer to 350°F/180°C.
2. Unroll the puff pastry and spread evenly with the Nutella.
3. Roll the pastry to form a log and cut into ½-inch thick slices.
4. Place the slices in the Air Fryer Basket and use the Air Fryer Double Layer Rack if needed.
5. Set the timer for 8 minutes or until the slices are golden brown.

6. Serve and top with whipped cream if desired.

---

483 - Caramel Chocolate Fudge

Servings: 4
Preparation: 5 minutes
Cooking Time: 20 minutes

Ingredients:
- 1 cup plain flour
- ½ cup caster sugar
- 1 cup desiccated coconut
- 2 tablespoons cocoa powder
- ¾ cup butter, melted
- ½ teaspoon vanilla extract
- ¼ cup caramel discs, melted

Directions:
1. Preheat the Air Fryer to 350°F/180°C.
2. Mix together the flour, caster sugar, desiccated coconut and cocoa powder in a bowl.
3. Add the melted butter and vanilla extract and mix well to combine.
4. Pour the batter into the Air Fryer Baking Pan and press down, using your hands, to ensure it is firm and compact.
5. Place the Air Fryer Baking Pan into the Air Fryer Basket and set the timer for 20 minutes.
6. Remove from the Air Fryer and allow to cool.
7. Serve and drizzle over the melted caramel.

---

484 - Peppermint Green Tea Cookies

Servings: 4
Preparation time: 10 minutes plus 30 minutes chilling time
Cooking Time: 12 minutes

Ingredients:
- ¼ cup butter
- ¼ cup caster sugar
- 1 cup all-purpose flour
- 2 teaspoons green tea powder
- ¼ teaspoon salt
- 1 teaspoon peppermint oil
- ¼ cup almonds, chopped

Directions:
1. Cream together the butter and caster sugar with a hand mixer until it becomes light and fluffy.
2. Sift together the flour, green tea powder and salt and add to the butter mixture.
3. Add in the peppermint oil and mix well to combine.
4. Fold in the chopped almonds.
5. Knead the dough into a ball and wrap with a plastic wrap.
6. Chill in the refrigerator for 30 minutes.
7. Preheat the Air Fryer to 300°F/150°C.
8. Roll out the dough to ¼-inch thick. Use cookie cutters to cut out cookies of your desired shapes.
9. Place the cookies into the Air Fryer Basket and use the Air Fryer Double Layer Rack if needed.
10. Set the timer for 12 minutes.
11. Remove the cookies from the Air Fryer and allow to cool before serving.

485 - Granola Cookies

Servings: 4
Preparation time: 10 minutes
Cooking Time: 10 minutes

Ingredients:
- 2 cups flour
- 1 cup icing sugar
- 1 teaspoon salt
- 1½ cups granola
- ¼ cup dried cranberries
- 1 cup vegetable oil

Directions:
1. Preheat the Air Fryer to 300°F/150°C.
2. Sift together the flour and icing sugar in a bowl.
3. Add in the salt, granola and dried cranberries.
4. Add the vegetable oil and mix evenly until a soft but firm dough forms. Adjust with more flour or oil if needed.
5. Scoop out dollops of dough and roll into balls.
6. Arrange the balls in the Air Fryer Basket and use the Air Fryer Double Layer Rack if needed.
7. Set the timer for 10 minutes.
8. Remove the Air Fryer Basket from the Air Fryer and allow to cool for a few minutes before transferring the balls to a serving plate.

486 - Almond and Oatmeal Cookies

Servings: Makes 30 cookies
Preparation time: 10 minutes
Cooking Time: 15 minutes

Ingredients:
- 1 cup almond flour
- 1¼ cups plain flour
- 1 teaspoon baking powder
- 1 teaspoon baking soda
- ½ cup castor sugar
- ½ cup cooking oil
- ¼ cup instant oatmeal

Directions:
1. Preheat the Air Fryer to 275°F/140°C.
2. Line the Air Fryer Basket with parchment paper. If using the Air Fryer Double Layer Rack, line also with parchment paper.
3. Mix together the almond flour, plain flour, baking powder and baking soda in a bowl and set aside.
4. Whisk together the castor sugar and cooking oil.
5. Gradually add the flour mixture and mix until well combined.
6. Fold in the instant oatmeal.
7. Drop teaspoonfuls of the batter in the Air Fryer Basket and rack.
8. Set the timer for 15 minutes.
9. When done, allow the almond cookies to cool inside the Air Fryer for a few minutes before transferring to a serving plate.

487 - Easy Almond and Jam Cookies

Servings: Makes 12 cookies
Preparation time: 10 minutes plus 30 minutes chilling time
Cooking Time: 15 minutes

Ingredients:
- 1 cup unsalted butter
- 1 cup caster sugar
- 1 cup almond flour
- ¼ cup strawberry jam

Directions:
1. Preheat the Air Fryer to 275°F/140°C.
2. Cream the butter and sugar using a hand mixer.
3. Add the flour to form a soft dough.
4. Wrap the dough in plastic wrap and chill in the refrigerator for 30 minutes until it is firm.
5. Divide the dough into 12 balls and indent the middle of each ball with your thumb.
6. Arrange the balls in the Air Fryer Basket and use the Air Fryer Double Layer Rack if needed.
7. Set the timer for 15 minutes or until the cookies become golden brown.
8. Remove the cookies from the Air Fryer and fill each dent with a dollop of strawberry jam.
9. Serve and enjoy!

488 - Strawberry Lemon Cake

Servings: 4
Preparation time: 10 minutes
Cooking Time: 15 minutes

Ingredients:
- ¼ cup strawberries, stems removed and chopped
- ½ cup butter
- 5 tablespoons sugar
- 1 cup flour
- 2 tablespoons milk
- 1 teaspoon lemon juice
- icing sugar, for dusting

Directions:
1. Preheat the Air Fryer to 350°F/180°C.
2. Puree the strawberries in a food processor until smooth and set aside.
3. Cream the butter and sugar in the food processor.
4. Add the flour and milk gradually.
5. Add the lemon juice and the strawberry puree and blend everything the batter is smooth.
6. Pour into the Air Fryer Baking Pan and place the Air Fryer Baking Pan in the Air Fryer Basket.
7. Set the timer for 15 minutes.
8. Serve and dust with icing sugar if desired.

489 - Cinnamon Banana Walnut Cake

Servings: 2
Preparation time: 10 minutes
Cooking Time: 30 minutes

Ingredients:
- ¼ cup butter, softened
- 1 egg
- ⅓ cup brown sugar
- 1 banana, mashed
- ½ teaspoon ground cinnamon
- 1 cup flour
- ⅛ teaspoon salt
- ¼ cup walnuts, chopped

Directions:
1. Preheat the Air Fryer to 325°F/170°C.
2. Cream the butter with the egg and brown sugar using a hand mixer.
3. Mix in the mashed bananas and ground cinnamon.
4. Mix together the flour and salt and add to the mixture.
5. Fold in the walnuts.
6. Pour the batter into the Air Fryer Baking Pan and place in the Air Fryer Basket.
7. Set the timer for 30 minutes.
8. Serve once the timer strikes!

490 - Strawberry and Banana Puff Pastry

Servings: 2
Preparation time: 10 minutes
Cooking Time: 5 minutes

Ingredients:
- 2 sheets puff pastry
- 4 tablespoons Nutella®
- 1 large banana, sliced
- 1 cup strawberries, stems removed and sliced
- 1 egg, beaten
- 2 tablespoons powdered sugar

Directions:
1. Preheat the Air Fryer to 350°F/180°C.
2. Cut each pastry sheet into 2.
3. Spread the Nutella evenly on each half of the pastry sheets.
4. Place the sliced bananas and strawberries on the Nutella® sheet and cover with the other half of pastry sheet. Fold the edges so that the fruits are enclosed in the pastry.
5. Brush each pastry with the egg
6. Arrange the pastries in the Air Fryer Basket and set the timer for 5 minutes.
7. Allow to cool slightly and slice each pastry in half.
8. Serve and dust with the powdered sugar.

491 - Pineapple and Peach Chocolate Cake

Servings: 2
Preparation time: 10 minutes
Cooking Time: 15 minutes

Ingredients:
- ¼ cup butter
- 3 tablespoons sugar
- 1 egg
- 1 teaspoon pineapple jam
- ½ cup peaches, diced
- ¼ cup flour
- 1 teaspoon cocoa powder
- ¼ teaspoon salt

Directions:
1. Preheat the Air Fryer to 325°F/170°C.
2. Cream the butter and sugar in a bowl.
3. Mix in the egg and pineapple jam.
4. Fold in the peaches.
5. Mix together the flour and cocoa powder and gradually add to the mixture.
6. Add the salt and mix until well combined.
7. Pour the batter into the Air Fryer Baking Pan and place the Air Fryer Baking Pan in the Air Fryer Basket.
8. Set the timer for 15 minutes.
9. Serve and enjoy!

492 - Banana Puffs a la Mode

Servings: 4
Preparation Time: 10 minutes
Cooking Time: 8 minutes

Ingredients:
- 3 bananas, peeled
- 2 sheets puff pastry
- 1 egg white, lightly whisked
- 1 cup brown sugar
- 4 scoops vanilla ice cream

Directions:
1. Preheat the Air Fryer to 350°F/180°C.
2. Cut the puff pastry so that it can wrap around each banana.
3. Wrap the bananas with the puff pastry.
4. Brush the pastry with the egg white and top with the brown sugar.
5. Place the puffs in the Air Fryer Basket and set the timer for 8 minutes until the pastry is golden brown.
6. Allow to cool a little and cut each pastry in half.
7. Serve with vanilla ice cream and enjoy.

493 - Simple Moist Chocolate Cake

Servings: 4
Preparation Time: 10 minutes
Cooking Time: 35 minutes

Ingredients:
- 1 cup flour
- 2 tablespoons unsweetened cocoa powder
- ½ teaspoon baking soda
- ¼ teaspoon salt
- ½ cup brown sugar
- ½ teaspoon vanilla extract
- ½ tablespoon white vinegar
- 3 tablespoons vegetable oil
- ½ cup water

Directions:
1. Preheat the Air Fryer to 325°F/170°C.
2. Sift together the flour, cocoa powder, baking soda and salt in a large bowl.
3. Mix in the brown sugar and make a well in the middle of the flour mixture.
4. In another bowl, mix together the vanilla extract, white vinegar, vegetable oil and water and pour into the well of the flour mixture.
5. Mix well to combine.
6. Pour the batter into the Air Fryer Baking Pan.
7. Cut a piece of foil that is large enough to cover the Air Fryer Baking Pan. Poke it with holes and cover the Air Fryer Baking Pan with it.
8. Place the Air Fryer Baking Pan in the Air Fryer Basket and set the timer for 30 minutes.
9. Remove the foil and cook for 5 to 8 minutes more.
10. Remove the Air Fryer Baking Pan from the Air Fryer and allow to cool before serving.

494 - Easy Victoria Sponge Cake

Servings: 4
Preparation Time: 15 minutes
Cooking Time: 25 minutes

Ingredients:

- ½ cup butter
- ½ cup caster sugar
- 2 medium eggs
- 1 cup plain flour
- 4 tablespoons strawberry jam
- 1 tablespoon whipped cream
- 1 cup icing sugar

Directions:

1. Preheat the Air Fryer to 350°F/180°C.
2. Cream the butter with the sugar until it becomes light and fluffy.
3. Beat in the eggs and mix well.
4. Gradually add in the flour and mix well to combine.
5. Pour the batter into the Air Fryer Baking Pan.
6. Place the Air Fryer Baking Pan in the Air Fryer Basket and set the timer for 15 minutes.
7. Reduce the temperature to 325°F/170°C and set the timer for 10 more minutes.
8. Remove the Air Fryer Baking Pan from the Air Fryer and allow to cool.
9. Slice the cake in half to make 2 layers.
10. Spread the strawberry jam on the bottom layer of the cake and top with the whipped cream.
11. Press the top layer of the cake gently on the cream and jam filling and dust with icing sugar.
12. Serve and enjoy!

495 - Mango Mambo Cuppies

Servings: 4
Preparation Time: 10 minutes
Cooking Time: 8 minutes

Ingredients:

- ½ cup butter
- ½ cup caster sugar
- ½ teaspoon vanilla extract
- 2 medium eggs
- 1 cup self-rising flour
- 1 cup icing sugar
- ¼ cup butter, melted
- 1 cup mango puree
- 1 tablespoon whipped cream
- ¼ cup fresh mangoes

Directions:

1. Preheat the Air Fryer to 325°F/170°C.
2. Cream the butter with the sugar until it becomes light and fluffy.
3. Add the vanilla extract and beat in the eggs one at a time.
4. Gradually add in the flour and mix well to combine.
5. Pour the batter into cupcake molds and arrange the molds in the Air Fryer Basket. Use the Air Fryer Double Layer Rack if needed.
6. Set the timer for 8 minutes.
7. Remove the cupcake molds from the Air Fryer and allow to cool.
8. Dissolve the icing sugar in the melted butter. Add the mango puree and whipped cream and mix well. Transfer into a piping bag.
9. Pipe some mango icing onto each cupcake and top with the fresh mangoes.
10. Serve and enjoy!

496 - Air Fryer Doughnuts

Servings: Makes 12 doughnuts
Preparation Time: 15 minutes plus 1 hour resting time
Cooking Time: 25 minutes

Ingredients:

- 1 cup full cream or low fat milk, as desired
- 1 cup unsalted butter, melted
- 3 cups plain flour
- 1½ teaspoons instant dried yeast
- ¼ cup caster sugar
- ½ teaspoon ground cinnamon
- ½ cup chocolate glaze
- ¼ cup sprinkles

Directions:

1. Preheat the Air Fryer to 300°F/150°C.
2. Microwave the milk in a microwave-proof bowl at medium-high for 30 seconds.
3. Remove the bowl from the microwave and stir in the melted butter. Set aside.
4. Sift the flour into a bowl and add the yeast, sugar and ground cinnamon. Mix well and create a well in the middle of the flour mixture.
5. Pour the milk and butter mixture into the well and knead for about 10 minutes until a soft dough is formed.
6. Place the dough in a greased bowl and let it rest in a warm spot for an hour.
7. Knead the dough until smooth and roll out the dough to ¾-inch thick.
8. Cut 12 rounds with a 2-inch round cookie cutter.
9. Cut out the centers of each round with a 1-inch round cookie cutter so that it now becomes a doughnut.
10. Arrange the doughnuts in the Air Fryer Basket and use the Air Fryer Double Layer Rack if needed.
11. Set the timer for 5 minutes.
12. Allow to cool slightly. Glaze with doughnuts with the chocolate glaze and top with sprinkles before serving.

497 - Strawberry Lime 'Flambe'

Servings: 4
Cooking Time: 6 minutes

Ingredients:
- ¼ cup butter, melted
- ½ cup brown sugar
- 1 cup fresh strawberries, stems removed and sliced
- 1 teaspoon vanilla extract
- ¼ cup rum
- 1 teaspoon lime juice
- 4 scoops vanilla ice cream

Directions:
1. Preheat the Air Fryer to 350°F/180°C.
2. Place the Air Fryer Baking Pan in the Air Fryer Basket and toss in the butter, brown sugar, strawberries, vanilla extract.
3. Set the timer for 3 minutes.
4. Stir in the rum and lime juice.
5. Set the timer for 3 more minutes to reduce the liquids.
6. Pour over the vanilla ice cream before serving.

498 - Cookies and Cream Cake

Servings: 2
Preparation time: 5 minutes
Cooking Time: 15 minutes

Ingredients:
- ¼ cup butter
- 3 tablespoons sugar
- 1 egg
- 2 tablespoons Oreos, crushed
- ¼ cup flour
- ¼ teaspoon salt

Directions:
1. Preheat the Air Fryer to 325°F/170°C.
2. Cream the butter with the sugar in a bowl.
3. Add the egg and mix well.
4. Fold in the crushed Oreos.
5. Mix together the flour and salt and gradually add to the butter mixture. Mix until well combined.
6. Pour the batter into the Air Fryer Baking Pan and place it in the Air Fryer Basket.
7. Set the timer for 15 minutes.
8. Serve and enjoy!

499 - Carrot Walnut Cake

Servings: 2
Preparation time: 10 minutes
Cooking Time: 30 minutes

Ingredients:
- 1 egg
- ⅓ cup brown sugar
- 1 cup carrots, grated
- 1 teaspoon ground nutmeg
- ½ teaspoon ground cinnamon
- 1 cup flour
- ⅛ teaspoon salt
- 2 tablespoons orange juice
- ¼ cup walnuts, chopped

Directions:
1. Preheat the Air Fryer to 325°F/170°C.
2. Whisk the egg and sugar with a hand mixer.
3. Add the carrots, ground nutmeg and ground cinnamon.
4. Mix together the flour and salt and add to the mixture.
5. Add the orange juice and mix well to combine.
6. Fold in the walnuts.
7. Pour the batter into the Air Fryer Baking Pan and place in the Air Fryer Basket.
8. Set the timer for 30 minutes.
9. Serve and enjoy!

500 - Mint Blueberry Lime Cake

Servings: 4
Preparation time: 10 minutes
Cooking Time: 15 minutes

Ingredients:
- ¼ cup blueberries, mashed with a fork
- 1 teaspoon peppermint oil
- 1 teaspoon lime juice
- ½ cup butter
- 5 tablespoons sugar
- 1 cup flour
- 2 tablespoons milk
- icing sugar, according to taste

Directions:
1. Preheat the Air Fryer to 350°F/180°C.
2. Mix together the blueberries, peppermint oil and lime juice and set aside.
3. Cream the butter and sugar in a food processor.
4. Gradually add in the flour and milk and mix until well combined.
5. Fold in the blueberries.
6. Pour the batter into the Air Fryer Baking Pan and place the Air Fryer Baking Pan in the Air Fryer Basket.
7. Set the timer for 15 minutes.
8. Remove from the Air Fryer and dust with the icing sugar before serving.

501 - Blueberry Cookies

Servings: 4
Preparation time: 15 minutes
Cooking Time: 8 minutes

Ingredients:

- 1¼ cups all-purpose flour
- ½ cup cake flour
- ½ teaspoon baking powder
- ¼ teaspoon baking soda
- ¾ teaspoon salt
- 1 teaspoon granulated sugar
- 4 tablespoons unsalted butter, melted
- ¾ cup cold milk
- ¼ cup blueberries, mashed with a fork

Directions:

1. Preheat the Air Fryer to 400°F/200°C.
2. Sift the all-purpose flour, cake flour, baking powder, baking soda and salt in a bowl.
3. Mix in the sugar.
4. Add the butter into the flour mixture.
5. Add the milk and blueberries and mix well until a dough is formed.
6. Dust a work surface with a little flour and roll out the dough to ½-inch thick.
7. Cut out cookies using a cookie cutter.
8. Arrange the cookies in the Air Fryer Basket and use the Air Fryer Double Layer Rack if needed.
9. Set the timer for 8 minutes or until the biscuits turn golden brown.
10. Serve once biscuits/cookies are golden brown.

502 - Coffee Cookies

Servings: 4
Preparation time: 15 minutes
Cooking Time: 8 minutes

Ingredients:
- 1¼ cups all-purpose flour
- ½ cup cake flour
- ½ teaspoon baking powder
- ¼ teaspoon baking soda
- ¾ teaspoon salt
- 1 teaspoon granulated sugar
- 4 tablespoons unsalted butter, melted
- 1 shot espresso
- ½ cup cold milk
- ¼ cup white chocolate, melted

Directions:
1. Preheat the Air Fryer to 400°F/200°C.
2. Sift the all-purpose flour, cake flour, baking powder, baking soda and salt in a mixing bowl.
3. Mix in the sugar.
4. Add the butter to the flour mixture.
5. Mix together the espresso and milk and pour into the flour mixture.
6. Mix well until a dough forms.
7. Dust the work surface with a little flour and roll the dough to ½-inch thick.
8. Cut out cookies from the dough with cookie cutters.
9. Arrange the cookies in the Air Fryer Basket and use the Air Fryer Double Layer Rack if needed.
10. Set the timer to 8 minutes or until the cookies become golden brown.
11. Remove the cookies from the Air Fryer and allow to cool.
12. Serve and drizzle over with the melted white chocolate.

503 - Lemon Poppy Muffins

Servings: Makes 12 muffins
Preparation time: 10 minutes
Cooking Time: 15 minutes

Ingredients:
- ⅓ cup butter
- ½ cup granulated sugar
- 1 egg
- 2 tablespoons lemon juice
- 1 cup milk
- 1¼ cups all-purpose flour
- ½ teaspoon baking powder
- 1 tablespoon lemon rinds
- 1 teaspoon poppy seeds

Directions:
1. Preheat the Air Fryer to 350°F/180°C.
2. Cream the butter and sugar with a hand mixer until it becomes light and fluffy.
3. Whisk in the egg.
4. Add the lemon juice and milk and continue beating for 3 minutes until the mixture is well combined.
5. Sift together the flour and baking powder and gradually add to the mixture.
6. Scrap down the sides of the mixing bowl and fold in the lemon rinds and the poppy seeds.
7. Pour the batter into the muffin cups until they reach three-quarters full.
8. Arrange the muffin cups in the Air Fryer and use the Air Fryer Double Layer Rack if needed.
9. Set the timer for 15 minutes.
10. Remove the muffins from the Air Fryer and allow to cool before serving.

504 - Blackberry and Granola Muffins

Servings: Makes 12 muffins
Preparation time: 15 minutes
Cooking Time: 20 minutes

Ingredients:

- ⅓ cup butter, softened
- ½ cup granulated sugar
- 1 egg
- 1 cup milk
- 1¼ cups all-purpose flour
- ½ teaspoon baking powder
- ¼ cup blackberries
- ¼ cup granola

Directions:

1. Preheat the Air Fryer to 325°F/170°C.
2. Cream the butter and sugar with a hand mixer until the mixture becomes light and fluffy.
3. Whisk in the egg.
4. Add the milk and continue mixing for 3 minutes until the mixture is well combined.
5. Sift together the flour and baking powder and gradually add to the butter mixture.
6. Use a rubber spatula to scrape the sides of the mixing bowl.
7. Fold in the blackberries and granola.
8. Pour the batter into muffin cups until each cup is three-quarters full.
9. Arrange the muffin cups in the Air Fryer Basket and use the Air Fryer Double Layer Rack if needed.
10. Set the timer for 20 minutes.
11. Remove the muffins from the Air Fryer and allow to cool before serving.

505 - Mango and Butterscotch Cupcakes

Servings: Makes 12 cupcakes
Preparation time: 15 minutes
Cooking Time: 15 minutes

Ingredients:

- ⅓ cup butter
- ½ cup granulated sugar
- 1 egg
- 1 teaspoon butterscotch extract
- 1 cup milk
- ¼ cup butterscotch, melted
- 1¼ cups all-purpose flour, sifted
- ½ teaspoon baking powder
- ¼ cup dried mangoes, chopped

Directions:

1. Preheat the Air Fryer to 325°F/170°C.
2. Cream the butter and sugar with a hand mixer until the mixture becomes light and fluffy.
3. Whisk in the egg.
4. Mix in the butterscotch extract, milk and melted butterscotch.
5. Sift together the flour and baking powder and gradually add to the mixture. Mix until well combined.
6. Use a rubber spatula to scrape the sides of the mixing bowl.
7. Fold in the dried mangoes.
8. Pour the batter into cupcake molds until each cup reaches three-quarters full.
9. Arrange the cupcakes in the Air Fryer Basket and use the Air Fryer Double Layer Rack if needed.
10. Set the timer for 15 minutes.
11. Remove the cupcakes from the Air Fryer and allow to cool before serving.

506 - Red Velvet Cake

Servings: 2
Preparation time: 15 minutes
Cooking Time: 15 minutes

Ingredients:

- ½ cup butter
- 1 egg
- ¼ cup caster sugar
- 1 cup all-purpose flour
- 1 tablespoon cocoa powder
- ⅛ teaspoon salt
- 4 tablespoons sour cream
- 2 tablespoons red food coloring

Directions:

1. Preheat the Air Fryer to 350°F/180°C.
2. Cream the butter, egg and sugar until it becomes light and fluffy.
3. Sift in the flour, cocoa powder and salt.
4. Add in the sour cream and red food coloring and mix until well combined.
5. Pour the batter into the Air Fryer Baking Pan and place in the Air Fryer Basket.
6. Set the timer for 15 minutes.
7. Remove the Air Fryer Baking Pan from the Air Fryer Basket and allow to cool before serving.

507 - Chocolate Chip Cookie Cups

Servings: 2
Preparation time: 15 minutes
Cooking Time: 15 minutes

Ingredients:
- ½ cup butter
- 1 egg
- ¼ cup caster sugar
- 1 cup all-purpose flour
- 1 tablespoon cocoa powder
- ⅛ teaspoon salt
- 4 tablespoons milk
- ¼ cup Chips Ahoy! cookies, crushed
- ¼ cup chocolate chips

Directions:
1. Preheat the Air Fryer to 350°F/180°C.
2. Grease 4 ramekins with cooking spray.
3. Cream the butter, egg and sugar until the mixture is light and fluffy.
4. Sift in the flour, cocoa powder and salt.
5. Pour in the milk and mix until well combined.
6. Fold in the crushed cookies and chocolate chips.
7. Pour the batter into the ramekins until each ramekin reaches three-quarters full.
8. Arrange the ramekins in the Air Fryer Basket and use the Air Fryer Double Layer Rack if needed.
9. Set the timer for 15 minutes.
10. Remove the ramekins from the Air Fryer and allow to cool before serving.

508 - Peach and Walnut Cake

Servings: 2
Preparation Time: 10 minutes
Cooking Time: 15 minutes

Ingredients:
- ½ large egg
- ½ teaspoon vanilla extract
- ½ teaspoon ground cinnamon
- 1½ cups almond flour
- ¾ tablespoons baking powder
- ¼ teaspoon salt
- ⅛ cup sugar
- ¾ cups water
- ½ cup peaches, mashed with a fork
- ½ tablespoon vegetable oil
- ¼ cup walnuts, chopped

Directions:
1. Preheat the Air Fryer to 350°F/180°C.
2. Whisk together the egg, vanilla extract and ground cinnamon in a stand mixer.
3. Mix together the flour, baking powder, salt and sugar and gradually add to the mixture.
4. Add in the water, mashed peaches and oil and continue mixing until well combined.
5. Fold in the chopped walnuts.
6. Pour the batter into the Air Fryer Baking Pan and place the Air Fryer Baking Pan in the Air Fryer Basket.
7. Set the timer for 12 minutes or until the cake is cooked through.
8. Remove the cake from the Air Fryer and allow to cool completely in the Air Fryer Baking Pan.
9. Serve and enjoy!

509 - Vanilla and Almond Cake

Servings: 2
Preparation Time: 10 minutes
Cooking Time: 15 minutes

Ingredients:
- ½ large egg
- 1 teaspoon vanilla extract
- ½ teaspoon ground cinnamon
- 1½ cups almond flour
- ¾ tablespoons baking powder
- ¼ teaspoon salt
- ⅛ cup sugar
- ¾ cups water
- ½ tablespoon vegetable oil

Directions:
1. Preheat the Air Fryer to 350°F/180°C.
2. Whisk the egg, vanilla extract and ground cinnamon in a stand mixer.
3. Mix together the flour, baking powder, salt and sugar and gradually add to the mixture.
4. Add in the water and oil and mix well to combine.
5. Pour the batter into the Air Fryer Baking Pan and place the Air Fryer Baking Pan in the Air Fryer Basket.
6. Set the timer for 15 minutes.
7. Remove the Air Fryer Baking Pan from the Air Fryer Basket and allow the cake to cool completely before removing it from the Air Fryer Baking Pan.

510 - Matcha Cuppies

Servings: 4
Preparation Time: 10 minutes
Cooking Time: 15 minutes

Ingredients:
- 1 large egg
- 2 teaspoons vanilla extract
- 1 teaspoon ground cinnamon
- 3 cups almond flour
- 1½ tablespoons baking powder
- 2 tablespoons matcha powder
- ½ teaspoon salt
- ¼ cup sugar
- 1½ cups water
- 1 tablespoon vegetable oil

Directions:
1. Preheat the Air Fryer to 350°F/180°C.
2. Whisk together the egg, vanilla extract and ground cinnamon.
3. Mix together the flour, baking powder, matcha powder, salt and sugar and gradually add to the egg mixture.
4. Pour in the water and the oil and mix well to combine.
5. Pour the batter into cupcake molds and arrange them in the Air Fryer Basket. Use the Air Fryer Double Layer Rack if needed.
6. Set the timer for 15 minutes.
7. Remove the cupcakes from the Air Fryer and place them on a serving plate.

511 - Hazelnut and Strawberry Squares a la Mode

Servings: 4
Preparation Time: 10 minutes
Cooking Time: 8 minutes

Ingredients:

- 4 sheets puff pastry
- ½ cup hazelnut spread (or Nutella®)
- 1 cup strawberries, stems removed and sliced
- 1 egg
- 1 cup brown sugar

Directions:

1. Preheat the Air Fryer to 350°F/180°C.
2. Cut the puff pastry sheets into squares.
3. Spread a puff pastry square with the hazelnut spread.
4. Top with some strawberries and cover with another square of puff pastry.
5. Press in the edges so that the filling is completely encased.
6. Brush the pastry with the egg and sprinkle with brown sugar.
7. Place the squares in the Air Fryer and use the Air Fryer Double Layer Rack if needed.
8. Set the timer for 8 minutes or until the pastry becomes golden brown.
9. Serve with vanilla ice cream.

512 - Death by Chocolate Cake

Servings: 2
Preparation Time: 15 minutes plus 30 minutes chilling time
Cooking Time: 23 minutes

Ingredients:
- ½ cup flour
- 1 tablespoon unsweetened cocoa powder
- ¼ teaspoon baking soda
- ¼ teaspoon salt
- ¼ cup brown sugar
- ¼ teaspoon vanilla extract
- ¼ tablespoon white vinegar
- 1½ tablespoons vegetable oil
- ¼ cup water
- ¼ cup Nutella®
- 12 wafers KitKat®, chopped

Directions:
1. Preheat the Air Fryer to 325°F/170°C.
2. Sift together the flour, cocoa powder, baking soda and salt in a bowl.
3. Stir in the sugar.
4. Make a well in the middle of the flour mixture.
5. Mix together the vanilla extract, white vinegar, vegetable oil and water and pour into the well.
6. Mix until the ingredients are well combined.
7. Pour the batter into the Air Fryer Baking Pan and cut a piece of foil large enough to cover the Air Fryer Baking Pan.
8. Poke random holes in the foil and cover the Air Fryer Baking Pan with the foil.
9. Set the timer for 20 minutes or until the cake is cooked through.
10. Remove the foil and set the timer for 3 more minutes.
11. Remove from the Air Fryer and allow to cool completely in the Air Fryer Baking Pan.
12. Slice the cake in half to make 2 layers.
13. Spread the bottom layer with Nutella® and top with the chopped KitKats®.
14. Cover with the top layer of the cake and spread the entire cake with Nutella®
15. Chill for 30 minutes before serving.

513 - Blueberries and Cream Cake

Servings: 2
Preparation time: 10 minutes
Cooking Time: 15 minutes

Ingredients:
- ¼ cup butter
- 3 tablespoons sugar
- 1 egg
- ¼ cup flour
- ¼ teaspoon salt
- ½ cup blueberries, mashed with a fork
- 1 cup whipped cream
- fresh blueberries, for topping

Directions:
1. Preheat the Air Fryer to 325°F/170°C.
2. Cream the butter and sugar in a bowl.
3. Mix in the egg.
4. Mix together the flour and salt and gradually add to the mixture.
5. Fold in the blueberries.
6. Pour the batter into the Air Fryer Baking Pan and place the Air Fryer Baking Pan in the Air Fryer Basket.
7. Set the timer for 15 minutes.
8. Remove from the Air Fryer and allow to cool.
9. Serve and top with the whipped cream and fresh blueberries.

514 - Lemon Cake

Servings: 2
Preparation time: 10 minutes
Cooking Time: 15 minutes

Ingredients:
- ¼ cup butter
- 3 tablespoons sugar
- 1 egg
- 1 tablespoon lemon juice
- ¼ cup flour
- ¼ teaspoon salt
- 1 tablespoon lemon rind

Directions:
1. Preheat the Air Fryer to 325°F/170°C.
2. Cream the butter and sugar in a bowl.
3. Mix in the egg and lemon juice.
4. Mix together the flour and salt and gradually add to the mixture.
5. Fold in the lemon rind.
6. Pour the batter into the Air Fryer Baking Pan and place the Air Fryer Baking Pan in the Air Fryer Basket.
7. Set the timer for 15 minutes.
8. Remove from the Air Fryer and allow to cool before serving.

515 - Pomegranate and Kiwi Cake

Servings: 2
Preparation time: 10 minutes
Cooking Time: 15 minutes

Ingredients:
- ¼ cup butter
- 3 tablespoons sugar
- 1 egg
- 1 tablespoon pomegranate extract
- ¼ cup flour
- ¼ teaspoon salt
- ¼ cup pomegranate puree
- 1 cup whipped cream
- 1 cup kiwis, sliced

Directions:
1. Preheat the Air Fryer to 325°F/170°C.
2. Cream the butter and sugar in a bowl.
3. Mix in the egg and pomegranate extract.
4. Mix together the flour and salt and gradually add to the mixture.
5. Fold in the pomegranate puree and mix well to combine.
6. Pour the batter into the Air Fryer Baking Pan and place the Air Fryer Baking Pan in the Air Fryer Basket.
7. Set the timer for 15 minutes.
8. Remove from the Air Fryer and allow to cool.
9. Serve and top with the whipped cream and kiwi slices.

516 - Granola Cookies

Servings: Makes 30 cookies
Preparation time: 10 minutes
Cooking Time: 15 minutes

Ingredients:
- ½ cup caster sugar
- ½ cup cooking oil
- ½ cup ground almonds
- 2 cups plain flour
- 1 teaspoon baking powder
- 1 teaspoon baking soda
- ¼ cup granola

Directions:
1. Preheat the Air Fryer to 275°F/140°C.
2. Mix together the caster sugar, cooking oil and ground almonds in a stand mixer.
3. Mix together flour, baking powder and baking soda and gradually add to the ground almond mixture.
4. Fold in the granola.
5. Line the Air Fryer Basket and Air Fryer Double Layer Rack with parchment paper. Drop teaspoonfuls of batter onto the parchment papers.
6. Set the timer for 15 minutes.
7. Allow the cookies to cool in the Air Fryer for a few minutes before transferring to a serving plate.

517 - Chocolate Chip Mint Tea Scones

Servings: 4
Preparation time: 15 minutes
Cooking Time: 10 minutes

Ingredients:
- 2 cups flour
- 2½ teaspoons baking powder
- 2 tablespoons cocoa powder
- ½ teaspoon salt
- 1 teaspoon sugar
- 1 teaspoon peppermint oil
- 1 tablespoon butter, melted
- 1 egg
- ¾ cup milk, plus more for brushing
- ¼ cup chocolate chips
- ¼ cup dark chocolate, melted

Directions:
1. Preheat the Air Fryer to 375°F/190°C.
2. In a mixing bowl, combine flour, baking powder, cocoa powder, salt, sugar and peppermint oil.
3. Add the butter and mix until the consistency of the mixture resembles breadcrumbs. Make a well in the center of the mixture.
4. Mix together the egg and the milk and pour into the well.
5. Mix until a dough forms.
6. Transfer the dough to a floured work surface and knead lightly.
7. Add the chocolate chips.
8. Make scones using round cookie cutters.
9. Arrange the scones in the Air Fryer Basket and use the Air Fryer Double Layer Rack if needed.
10. Brush the scones with a little milk.
11. Set the timer for 10 minutes.
12. Remove the scones from the Air Fryer and allow to cool.
13. Serve and drizzle over the melted chocolate.

519 - Nutella Crunch Pie

Servings: 2
Preparation time: 10 minutes plus 1 hour chilling time
Cooking Time: 5 minutes

Note: You will need a Non-Stick Pie Pan that is small enough to fit inside the Air Fryer Basket.

Ingredients:
- 8-inch pie dough
- ½ cup Nutella®
- ½ cup cocoa puffs
- whipped cream, to top

Directions:
1. Preheat the Air Fryer to 325°F/190°C.
2. Place the pie dough on a work surface lightly dusted with flour.
3. Grease the pie pan with cooking spray.
4. Cut out an 8-inch pie dough and line the pie pan.
5. Fold the edges of the pie dough so that they sit on the rim of the pie pan.
6. Place the pan in the Air Fryer Basket and set the timer for 5 minutes.
7. Remove the pan from the Air Fryer and allow to cool completely.
8. Spread the Nutella® on the crust.
9. Add the cocoa puffs into the crust.
10. Top with the whipped cream
11. Chill the pie for an hour before serving.

520- Strawberry and Lime Cookies

Servings: 2
Preparation time: 10 minutes
Cooking Time: 8 minutes

Ingredients:
- 1¼ cups all-purpose flour
- ½ cup cake flour
- ½ teaspoon baking powder
- ¼ teaspoon baking soda
- ¾ teaspoon salt
- 1 teaspoon granulated sugar
- 1 teaspoon lime juice
- 1 teaspoon strawberry extract
- 4 tablespoons unsalted butter, melted
- ¾ cup cold buttermilk

Directions:
1. Preheat the Air Fryer to 400°F/200°C.
2. Sift the all-purpose flour, cake flour, baking powder, baking soda and salt in a bowl.
3. Mix in the sugar, lime juice and strawberry extract.
4. Mix in the butter and buttermilk and mix until a dough forms
5. Roll the dough on a lightly-floured work surface to ½-inch thick.
6. Use cookie cutters to cut out cookies from the dough.
7. Arrange the cookies in the Air Fryer Basket and use the Air Fryer Double Layer Rack if needed.
8. Set the timer to 8 minutes and cook the cookies until they are golden brown.
9. Serve once the cookies are golden brown.

521 - Mango Jam Cookies

Servings: 2
Preparation time: 15 minutes plus 30 minutes chilling time
Cooking Time: 6 minutes

Ingredients:
- 1 cup plain flour
- 2 tablespoons cornstarch
- 2 tablespoons icing sugar
- 3 tablespoons custard powder
- ⅛ teaspoon salt
- ½ cup unsalted butter, chilled
- 1 egg yolk
- cold water, if needed
- 1 cup ready-made mango jam
- 1 teaspoon lemon juice

Directions:
1. Sift together the plain flour, cornstarch, icing sugar, custard powder and salt in a bowl.
2. Rub in the butter until the mixture resembles breadcrumbs.
3. Mix in the egg yolk and knead to form a dough. Add some cold water if the dough is too dry.
4. Divide the dough into 2 equal portions and wrap each portion with plastic wrap.
5. Chill in the refrigerator for at least 30 minutes.
6. While the dough is chilling, make the mango filling by mixing the mango jam with the lemon juice with a fork until the jam becomes a smoother consistency.
7. Preheat the Air Fryer to 300°F/150°C.
8. Roll out the dough onto a lightly-floured work surface until ¼-inch thick.
9. Cut out cookies using cookies cutters.
10. Arrange the cookies in the Air Fryer Basket and use the Air Fryer Double Layer Rack if needed.
11. Set the timer for 6 minutes or until the cookies are golden brown.
12. Remove the cookies from the Air Fryer and allow to cool.
13. Spread each cookie with the mango jam.
14. Serve and enjoy!

522 - Valentine Sweetheart Pie

Servings: 2
Preparation Time: 20 minutes
Cooking Time: 30 minutes

Note: You will need a Non-Stick Pie Pan that is small enough to fit inside the Air Fryer Basket.

Ingredients:
- 2 ready-made pie pastry dough
- 1 cup strawberries
- ¼ cup sugar
- ¼ cup cornstarch
- 1 tablespoon fresh lemon juice
- ½ tablespoon grated lemon zest
- ½ teaspoon vanilla extract
- ½ egg
- ½ tablespoon water

Directions:
1. Preheat the Air Fryer to 350°F/180°C.
2. Mix together the strawberries, sugar, cornstarch, lemon juice, lemon zest and vanilla extract and set aside.
3. Roll out a portion of dough onto a lightly-floured work surface until it is large enough to line the pie pan. Pierce the bottom of the pastry with a fork.
4. Fold the edges of the pie dough so that they sit on the rim of the pie pan
5. Fill with the strawberry filling.
6. Roll out the second portion of dough large enough to cover the pie pan. Cut out a heart shape in the middle of the dough with a cookie cutter. Cover the top of the pie in the pie pan.
7. Whisk the egg with the water for the egg wash.
8. Seal the edges of the pastry with the egg wash and pinch with your fingers to seal the dough together.
9. Place the pie pan in the Air Fryer Basket and set the timer for 30 minutes or until the pie turns golden brown.
10. Remove from the Air Fryer Basket and allow to cool before serving.

523 - Peach and Mango Tartlets

Servings: Makes about 20 tartlets
Preparation time: 15 minutes plus 30 minutes chilling time
Cooking Time: 30 minutes

Ingredients:

- 1 cup plain flour
- 2 tablespoons cornstarch
- 2 tablespoons icing sugar
- 3 tablespoons custard powder
- ½ cup unsalted butter, chilled

- 1 egg yolk, beaten
- 1 cup mangoes, diced
- 1 cup peaches, sliced
- 1 teaspoon lemon juice

Directions:

1. Sift together the flour, cornstarch, icing sugar and custard powder.
2. Rub in the butter until it resembles breadcrumbs.
3. Mix in the egg yolk and knead to form a dough.
4. Wrap the dough in plastic wrap and chill for at least 30 minutes.
5. Mix the mangoes, peaches and lemon juice and set aside.
6. Preheat the Air Fryer to 300°F/150°C.
7. Roll out the dough on a lightly-floured surface to ¼-inch thick.
8. Cut out circles using a cookie cutter to the size that fits the mini tart molds.
9. Arrange the mini tartlets in the Air Fryer Basket and use the Air Fryer Double Layer Rack if needed.
10. Set the timer for 6 minutes or until they are golden brown.
11. Remove from the Air Fryer and fill with the fruits.
12. Serve and enjoy!

Conclusion

I hope you enjoyed all the delicious "Air Fryer" recipes in this cookbook! For more simple and delicious cookbooks, be sure to check out my author page on Amazon at "Gloria Lee," as I'm constantly creating more cookbooks to accommodate those who wish to eat towards a healthier lifestyle.

If you enjoyed this cookbook and found it helpful, please take the time to leave me a review on Amazon. I appreciate your honest feedback, and it really helps me to continue producing high-quality cookbooks/books in the future.

CPSIA information can be obtained
at www.ICGtesting.com
Printed in the USA
LVHW061618131118
596984LV00017B/137/P